Philosophical Studies in Contemporary Culture

Volume 29

This series explores the philosophical issues, concerns, and controversies framing our contemporary culture. The volumes address studies of the perennial philosophical questions and major thinkers whose works have shaped current intellectual debates. The series draws on the intellectual heritage of the past in order to illuminate current concerns. The goal is to offer volumes whose perspective and focus can contribute through philosophical studies to a better appreciation of the contemporary human condition.

Kevin Wm Wildes, S.J.

Organizational Ethics and Moral Integrity in Secular Societies

The Ethics of Bureaucracies

Springer

Kevin Wm Wildes, S.J.
Saint Joseph's University
Philadelphia, PA, USA

ISSN 0928-9518 ISSN 2215-1753 (electronic)
Philosophical Studies in Contemporary Culture
ISBN 978-3-031-39096-8 ISBN 978-3-031-39097-5 (eBook)
https://doi.org/10.1007/978-3-031-39097-5

This Springer imprint is published by the registered company Springer Nature Switzerland AG
The registered company address is: Gewerbestrasse 11, 6330 Cham, Switzerland

This book is dedicated to Ms. Gail Howard who was my Executive Assistant at Loyola University New Orleans when I served as president. Gail was an essential part of my civic work in New Orleans post-Katrina. She patiently assisted me in my work with the New Orleans Ethics Review Board, the Inspector General's Office, the Public Belt Railroad, and the New Orleans Civil Service Commission. And, she did all this while assisting me in my work with leading and renewing Loyola University. Each endeavor helped shape the content of this book and nurtured my reflections on organizations and ethics. Her patience helped me in my work and public service and she helped me to see each task through, and "fight the good fight and finish the race" (2 Timothy 4:7).

Do what you can, with what you've got, where you are.

Bill Widener quoted by Theodore Roosevelt

Foreword

I first met Rev. Kevin Wildes, S.J., in 2007 when he was Chair of the then newly created Ethics Review Board for the City of New Orleans and I was hired as the City's first Inspector General. The New Orleans Inspector General reports to the Ethics Review Board of the City.

Before I began my work in New Orleans, I had served as a member of the Massachusetts House of Representatives and I was the former Inspector General of the Commonwealth of Massachusetts. As Inspector General for the Commonwealth, I was involved in a number of oversight projects including those raising questions about the "Big Dig." In 1997, I helped to found the Association of Inspectors General nationally which currently has over 200 members working on the oversight of state and federal government agencies.

As Inspector General for New Orleans, I worked with Rev. Wildes, and other City leaders, to establish the office of Inspector General for the city and to help the city address issues of efficiency and waste, as well as potential issues of corruption, in post-Katrina New Orleans. The first offices for the Inspector General were located at Loyola University since, while it had established the Office the City had not developed a plan to house the Office. The early days of establishing the office were challenging, and we had to deal with people that did not understand or welcome change to the way the City operated. In those days, I often referred to Father Wildes as "Pope Leo" since Pope Leo the Great was the bishop of Rome who is best known for having met Attila the Hun in 452 and persuading Attila to turn back from his invasion of Italy and the destruction of Rome. In the early days of establishing the Office of Inspector General and the Ethics Review Board, Father Wildes had to meet with and persuade those who wanted to thwart the development of the office and the ERB.

This book, which is a philosophical investigation of Organizational Ethics, began with work in post-Katrina New Orleans. Rev. Wildes, S.J., applied his background and expertise in ethics to questions of public ethics and the way the City was organized. In this book, he has developed that experience to think about ethical issues for organizations in education and health care.

Robert A. Cerasoli is a former member of the Massachusetts House of Representatives, the former Inspector General of the Commonwealth of Massachusetts, and the first Inspector General of the City of New Orleans. He also founded the Association of Inspectors General in 1996.

Preface

> Do what you can, with what you've got, where you are.[1]

I have always liked this quote, attributed to Theodore Roosevelt, for many reasons. One reason that I am fond of this Roosevelt quote is that I have found it to be an appropriate guide for my work in fields of applied ethics as well as for my work in academic administration and in leading organizations. Areas of applied ethics and administration are areas where one has imperfect knowledge and yet they are areas where decisions must be made with imperfect knowledge.

Decisions need to be made with what one knows at the moment and with one's best judgment. On this point, Teddy Roosevelt was a good mentor both for administration and for ethics.

This book about organizations and ethics is an investigation into areas of imperfect knowledge and decision making. I think it may be helpful for readers of this book to understand at least two things as they explore the ideas in this book. First it is important to remember that this is a book about practical ethics or what has often been referred to as "applied" ethics. Fields like bioethics, or other areas of professional ethics, are often considered areas of applied ethics. The quote above, borrowed from Theodore Roosevelt, makes an important point about applied ethics and the work of this book. In applied ethics, decisions must be made with imperfect knowledge about the situation and possible outcomes.

This book follows an insight and line of thought developed from Aristotle. Aristotle made an important distinction between theoretical and practical reason and he treated ethics as part of practical reason. Practical wisdom is deciding what is good, right, or best, in the particular set of circumstances at the moment one is making a decision. The particular set of circumstances helps to define decisions of practical wisdom. Fields like bioethics, and other areas of applied ethics, may often

[1] This quote is attributed to Theodore Roosevelt. However, Roosevelt credits it, in his *Autobiography* Chapter IX, to Squire Bill Widener of Widener's Valley, Virginia. See *An Autobiography* by Theodore Roosevelt: Complete and Unabridged with Appendices and Notes (New York: Charles Scribner and Sons, 2018).

raise theoretical and speculative questions about ethics; however, the fields of applied ethics are primarily concerned with resolving practical ethical problems. The first thinkers in the field of bioethics, who helped to establish the field, sought to develop ways to address common ethical issues in health care without getting caught up in the quagmires of theoretical ethics.

A second point, which will be important for the reader to understand, is that this book is a philosophical investigation and it explores how we can think and talk about ethical issues philosophically in a secular society (Chap. 3). This book is not an investigation guided by theological methods, language, or resources. As a philosophical investigation, this book is guided by reason and experience. This philosophical approach to organizations and ethics is important for thinking about organizations in a secular society (Chap. 3) as philosophy, potentially, opens the door for ethical conversation outside of the particularism of different faith traditions. Philosophy provides a way to move beyond the particularism of different religious traditions, and it provides a way to ask ethical questions as we grapple with the openness of secular societies. It is also important to understand the limits of philosophical methods to develop content-full moral discourse.[2]

This book examines organizations in education and health care as moral actors in applied ethics and it tries to address how organizations in these areas can maintain their moral identity and integrity while they operate in secular, morally pluralistic societies. Many of the ethical issues in health care and education cannot be classified simply as issues of individual choice or government policy. Ethical controversies like end-of-life care or curriculum development are broader than any particular case. Organizations in health care and education play key roles in developing a range of choices that are available to individuals. Because education and health care have developed as social enterprises, rather than simply individual choices, we need to find ways to address the ethical issues in education and health care which involve organizations. Organizations in health care and education fill a middle space in the discussion of ethics and social policy. Organizations in education and health care fall between individual agents and society as a whole. Organizations occupy a middle space in these areas where organizations become the principle actors and decision-makers.

By focusing on organizations in education and health care, this book examines ways to identify how we can think about organizations, as moral actors in secular societies, by identifying procedures to resolve some of these moral issues without resolving deeper theoretical issues in moral philosophy. The book also recognizes that, while individual agents and government agencies are moral actors in education and health care, they do not exhaust the cast of moral actors in these areas. We need to include organizations such as schools, universities, hospitals, and healthcare

[2] K. Wildes, S.J., "Solidarity in Secular Societies: Engelhardt and the Post-Modern Dilemma", in *Solidarity*, ed. Kurt Bayertz (Dordrecht: Kluwer Academic Publishers, 1999) 309–315. See also, K. Wildes, *Moral Acquaintances: Methodology in Bioethics,* (Notre Dame, IN: University of Notre Dame Press, 2000).

systems, which make decisions and set policies, as moral actors in education and health care.

It is also important to be clear that this book is a philosophical work about ethics which is grounded in the author's experience of working for, and leading, both public and private organizations. While the author is a Roman Catholic priest, this book is not a theological investigation of practical ethics grounded in one's religious faith. Hopefully, this exploration of organizations as moral actors can help to develop further our understanding both of social organizations and their roles as moral agents in morally diverse, secular societies and can also help to understand how important it is for these organizations to maintain a clear sense of their identity so they can function as moral agents, with integrity, in morally diverse, secular societies. This exploration can help further to develop a comprehensive account of ethics in post-modern, secular societies.

Some of the basic ideas in this book initially began to develop for me as a result of my work in the field of bioethics while I was a faculty member of the Philosophy Department and the Kennedy Institute of Ethics at Georgetown University. At that time, health care was first dealing with the evolution of managed healthcare and addressing impact on the practice of health care. The development of managed care as a payment system for Medicine raised different types of ethical questions for physicians, healthcare professionals, clinics, hospitals, patients, and employers in the everyday practice of Medicine nationally. Changes in the way health care is financed meant that it was no longer adequate to think about medical ethics only in terms of physicians and patients making decisions in the clinic. Managed care, indeed every insurance payment structure, meant that we are using the resources of others to finance our health care. Health insurance is not like a person's savings account. Health insurance, whether it is public or private, is based on a model of pooled, collective resources. To adequately address ethical issues in health care, one had to include all of the unseen figures who shaped clinical decisions in the clinic. The cast of decision-makers include employers, human resource managers, insurance companies, and administrators of healthcare systems, and government regulators, among others, along with patients and families. Each of them are actors in making ethical decisions in the clinic and each has some voice, and authority, in decision-making about patient care, and this means that we should think about ethics in health care in a new way.

The ideas in this book continued to develop after I left Georgetown and when I served as president of Loyola University New Orleans. In my second year at Loyola, New Orleans experienced Hurricane Katrina, and in the years after Katrina, my work was focused on the renewal of the university and the city. As part of that work, I also became involved in the renewal of the city whose name the university bore. My post-Katrina experiences, as a citizen, a university president, and as a civic leader, led me to think even more deeply about some of the fundamental questions about the relationships of organizations to society, to other organizations, to consumers as well as other payers, as well as to individuals. And it taught me about the need to ask about the impact of particular choices within an organization, to all its partners, and to society.

In post-Katrina New Orleans, I was involved in several experiences that led me to think about important ethical questions that are embedded in discussions of how a society is organized and structured. The questions about social organization led me to think about organizations, within a society, as moral actors and to think carefully about the ethical implications of organizations and their structures. The way institutions are put together is often more than an expression of efficiency. How organizations are built and function reflect assumptions about moral values, race, economics, class, and gender which are embedded in an organization. These reflections led me to think about many of the issues addressed in this book, and how we, in a postmodern, secular, morally diverse society, can think about organizations and how they operate as moral actors.

In post-Katrina New Orleans, I was also privileged to be part of the efforts to establish the first Ethics Review Board (ERB) for the city. The ERB oversees the Inspector General's Office for the City of New Orleans. In post-Katrina New Orleans, I later served on the Civil Service Commission for the City and helped to lead efforts to reform, update, and modernize the City's Civil Service system. After completing service on the Civil Service Commission, I was asked to serve on the board of the city owned and operated by Public Belt Railroad and, in doing so, assisted efforts to reform the organization and structure of the Railroad. Each of these different experiences led me to think more carefully about organizations as moral actors and helped me to develop my questions and thoughts about organizations, which have shaped this book. Practical ethics are, at some level, about choices and the choices people do make in their lives. However, in many cases, the range of choices that individuals make are shaped by the prior choices and decisions that have been made by organizations that create the range of choices for individuals. Yet, we rarely examine the moral assumptions and decisions of organizations, which shape the decisions individuals can make. This book was developed, in part, to help ask ethical questions about how organizations are put together and how organizations can represent moral commitments in a secular society.

These observations about organizations is not only relevant to organizations in education and health care, which are freighted with moral values and which are delivered by organizations, but they are relevant to any organization with moral commitments in a morally diverse, secular society. Many people tend to think of moral issues and choices being made by individual persons or, at times, by government agencies. The American imagination is rooted in the experience of the individual and the questions about government regulation and power. While these foci are important, morally, they miss the reality that often the range of moral choices are shaped by the decisions and policies created by organizations rather than other individual agents or government agencies.

Health care and education are particularly interesting subjects to consider in post-modern, morally diverse, secular societies for several reasons. First, both areas have some type of moral values embedded in their framework whether or not they are explicitly expressed. Both health care and education make underlying assumptions about what it is to be a good, functioning person who is healthy and well-educated. Second, in secular societies, both health care and education are considered goods that should be available to members of society. Both make, often unarticulated, assumptions about what it is to be a healthy, fully functioning human being as part of the necessary conditions for a good society. However, secular societies rarely think about the challenges of supporting social organizations which have moral commitments, like those in health care and education, in a morally diverse society.

To borrow a phrase from the *Wizard of Oz*, these experiences have helped me to "look behind the curtain" and pay more attention to organizations as moral actors. This book examines how the structures of organizations, along with the development and execution of organizational policies, should be included in the ethical analysis of social organizations. This book should help to explore how organizations can choose to maintain a particular moral identity in a diverse secular society and help to explore the question of why the moral identity of organizations can be enriching for post-modern, secular societies. How an organization is put together can be just as important to ethical analysis as what an organization actually does in a secular, morally diverse, society. Decisions by organizations to pursue certain policies, for example, often reflect the moral values and choices of the organization or the society in which it finds itself. For example, many decisions made by governments and organizations under the aegis of the Jim Crow laws and practices were choices influenced by social and moral assumptions of the broader society, which influenced the values and moral commitments of organizations.

The field of business ethics has examined organizations as moral actors for some time.

This book, however, takes a further step in exploring non-profit organizations in the social realms of education and health care as moral actors. The areas of education and health care are both areas which are freighted with moral values, and they are both areas where organizations are moral actors, both in their fields as well as in the broader, secular, post-modern society. And, even if privately held, organizations in health care and education are held accountable by the processes of certification for the broader secular society which will be open to moral pluralism and diversity. The exploration of this book, it is hoped, can help us to better understand and assess organizations with a moral identity as they function as moral actors in post-modern, secular societies. This exploration can also provide an opportunity to understand better the moral complexities of post-modern, secular societies.

Philadelphia, PA, USA
31 July 2022

Kevin Wm Wildes, S.J.

Acknowledgments

The reflections in this book about ethics and organizations have grown from different experiences I have had over the years, and they have developed from those experiences and the people who accompanied and challenged me along the way. They began with my work at the Kennedy Institute at Georgetown University when I first began to think about the role of organizations in making clinical decisions about patient care. My reflections about organizations continued in post-Katrina New Orleans through my work at Loyola University and as a citizen involved with the renewal of the city after Hurricane Katrina.

There are many people who should be acknowledged for their contributions to the work which led to this book. I am grateful to Mitchell Landrieu, then Mayor of New Orleans, who asked me to help establish and serve on the first Ethics Review Board of the City. I am particularly grateful to Mr. Robert Cerasoli, who was the first Inspector General for the City of New Orleans, and David Marcello, who helped envision the IGs office for the City and whose work was so important in the creation of the New Orleans Ethics Review Board and the Office of Inspector General Ed Quatraveaux. I am grateful to Dr. Michael Cowan for his civic engagement with the Common Good organization and his support for civic reforms. Of course I am grateful to all of the first members of the Ethics Review Board, Winston Brown, Beverly Favre, Betsy Nalty, the wonderful Ms. Leah Chase, and Kathy Lorio, for their wisdom, leadership, and service. I am grateful to Ms. Ruthie Frierson and *Citizens for One Greater New Orleans* as well as to Ms. Ann Milling and *Women of the Storm* for their support for reform initiatives. I am also grateful to the Business Council of New Orleans and the River Region for their support in the work of establishing the Ethics Review Board and the work of Civil Service reform. I am grateful to Archbishop Gregory Aymond for his support and friendship as well as his leadership of the Archdiocese and in the City. I am grateful to the Jesuit Community of Loyola University for their support and friendship through these challenges and to the Association of Jesuit Colleges and Universities, particularly Rev. Michael Sheeran, S.J., and Rev. Michael Garanzi, S.J., for their leadership during and after Katrina and their help in the writing of this book. I am forever grateful to Mr. Tommy Screen, who served as Director of Government Affairs and Legal

Counsel for Loyola University New Orleans through all this. He guided me through the challenges of government reform as well as the challenges of rebuilding a university and counselled me to patience; a virtue I do not possess. I am indebted to the Faculty, and the Staff of Loyola University for their work in renewing a university and their work in rebuilding their homes, as well as the city and their support for my endeavors on behalf of the university and the city. I am most grateful to Loyola's Board of Trustees who counselled and supported me through my work both for the University and in the City. Each of the Board members were helpful to me and supportive. But, I am particularly grateful to Paul Pastorek, Edgar Chase, John Finan, Suzanne Mestayer, and Joe Mahoney for their wisdom. I am most grateful to Kristine David-Leong, Martha Alguera, Tammy Dearie, and Colleen Wildes, all of whom worked in my office and supported my work for the university and the city. I am also very grateful to Deanna Howes Spiro, Vice President for Communications for the AJCU, and to Desiree Rodriguez, Executive Assistant to the President and Secretary for the Board of Trustees at Loyola University, who helped me navigate the mechanics of bringing this manuscript together. I am grateful to Andrea Campana who helped edit this manuscript. Of course, I am most grateful to Ms. Gail Howard, my Executive Assistant, to whom this book is dedicated. Gail supported not only my work at the university but also supported all of my endeavors in public service which shaped my thoughts in this book!

> Consult not your fears but your hopes and dreams. Think not about your frustrations, but about your unfulfilled potential. Concern yourself not with what you tried and failed in, but with what is still possible for you to do (St. Pope John XXIII).

University Professor
Saint Joseph's University
Philadelphia, PA, USA
17 January 2022

Kevin Wm Wildes, S.J.

Contents

About the Author

Kevin Wm Wildes, S.J., Ph.D., is a University Professor at St. Joseph's University, Philadelphia, PA. He holds advanced degrees in Theology and in Philosophy. He received his Ph.D. from Rice University in 1993 after studies at Rice and Baylor College of Medicine. His professional work is in the field of bioethics and health policy.

He has authored *Moral Acquaintances: Methodology in Bioethics* published by the University of Notre Dame Press (2000). Wildes is also the editor or co-editor of four other books on ethics. He has published 70 referred articles and book chapters as well as a number of invited articles and book chapters.

In addition to his writing, Wildes has lectured widely delivering over 90 invited lectures nationally and internationally. Wildes has also written a number of invited articles and book chapters on bioethics and public policy as well as testifying before the U.S. Congress on matters of bioethics and healthcare policy.

Wildes served as the 16th President of Loyola University New Orleans from 2004 to 2018.

Active in the New Orleans community during the post-Katrina recovery, Wildes was involved civically in New Orleans. Wildes was also a founding member of the Ethics Review Board for the City of New Orleans, which oversees the New Orleans Office of the Inspector General, and he served as the first Chair of the ERB from its creation in 2007 until 2010. He then served as a Commissioner of the New Orleans Public Belt Railroad for two years leading reforms in the organization. He was then elected as a member of the New Orleans Civil Service Commission, which he chaired, and oversaw a reform of the New Orleans Civil Service system.

Wildes has been a member of several professional associations, and he has served as a Trustee of several colleges and universities as well as a trustee of two Jesuit high schools. He has also served on the Advisory Board for Independence Blue Cross of Pennsylvania.

Abbreviations

ACCU	Association of Catholic Colleges and Universities
AIG	Association of Inspectors General
AJCU	Association of Jesuit Colleges and Universities
CHA	Catholic Health Association
ERB	Ethics Review Board
IG	Inspector General
JC	Jesuit Conference
NCCB	National Conference of Catholic Bishops
S.J.	Society of Jesus
USCC	United States Catholic Conference

The original version of the book has been revised. A correction to this book can be found at https://doi.org/10.1007/978-3-031-39097-5_15

Chapter 1
Introduction: Expanding the Horizon of Post-modern Ethics: Ethical Questions in Education and Health Care

> *It takes a very unusual mind to undertake the analysis of the obvious (This is why philosophy is also known as the 'discovery of the obvious' – which is really just a polite way of saying that we humans are blind to the obvious most of the time (and easily misled by our imaginations when it comes to thinking about truth and reality). Alfred North Whitehead, Science and the Modern World.).*
>
> Alfred North Whitehead, *Science in the Modern World*

It is important at the beginning of any investigation to be clear about the object of the investigation. If we can be clear about the object and purpose of an investigation that clarity can help people assess what has been found. The investigation in this book really has two objects. Primarily it is an investigation of *organizations as moral actors* in health care and education in a secular society. Most organizations in society are commercial enterprises regulated by law and the rules of commerce and the markets.

However, organizations in education and health care different from other types of organizations in secular societies for several reasons. First, organizations in education and health care offer services to patients and students and they are, generally, not considered as normal consumers. Because of age and personal development or, because they are dealing with illness, students and patients do not fit well under the normal model of consumers. Because patients and students are different from normal consumers, organizations in education and health care have moral or fiduciary duties toward those who use their services, which differentiates them from normal commercial enterprises.

Organizations in education and health care are also different from most commercial enterprises because the object of their work in education and health care is the development of the human person and not an object outside the person. Furthermore, the object of organizations in education and health care is the person using the services of the organization. This should mean that these organizations bear some type

K. W. Wildes, S.J., *Organizational Ethics and Moral Integrity in Secular Societies*, Philosophical Studies in Contemporary Culture 29,
https://doi.org/10.1007/978-3-031-39097-5_1

of moral commitments toward the person using their services and these moral commitments shape the work of the organization. Furthermore, organizations in education and health care are seen, not only contributing to the good of the particular person, but they are also seen as contributing to the good of society as a whole. The assumption that these organizations contribute to the good of society reflects another level of moral commitments that are a part of the work of these organizations.

Because the human person is at the center of the work of organizations in health care and education there are often moral assumptions intrinsic to the work of these organizations. While we often acknowledge moral diversity among individuals, we rarely think about moral diversity in terms of organizations. The investigation of this book will expand the scope of how we think about ethics in morally pluralistic secular societies and it will examine organizations as moral agents in secular, morally pluralistic societies. This book will explore the groundwork for how organizations, with moral identities, can participate in the life of morally diverse, secular societies.

The investigation of this book will examine how, and to what extent, we can think of organizations as moral agents in post-modern, secular societies. It should be clear from the start of this investigation that many organizations do *not* have a sense of themselves as moral agents. These would be organizations of commerce and their moral commitments are limited to the promises they make, the goods and services they sell, their honesty in commerce, and their fidelity in fulfilling their promises. However, there are organizations that are classified often as non-profit organizations in health care and education. One might describe them as selling services in health care and education. However, these organizations are more than simply the providers of services. In the services they provide, they care for the weak and vulnerable in a society. This investigation will argue that the missions, identities, and moral commitments of these organizations should both shape the organizations and the services they offer.

The first chapters of this book examine how we can speak of organizations in health care and education as mora actors. Then the investigation will turn to try to understand how organizations, with moral identities, can function as they face the challenges of moral pluralism in post-modern, secular societies. The first two parts of this book explore how an organization can have a moral identity and how an organization with a moral identity can exists in a morally pluralistic, secular society. In a secular society, these organizations, in part, should be understood and evaluated by how they articulate and live out their identities and moral commitments.

The challenges of thinking about collaboration between agents in morally diverse, secular societies is relevant for endeavors in education and health care for two reasons. First, both education and health care are endeavors imbued with moral values. Implicitly, both education and health care each have some type of underlying ideal of what it is to be a flourishing human being. Second, individuals rarely accomplish undertakings in education and health care by themselves. Instead, what is achieved is accomplished by cooperative endeavors and organizations that represent a social interest. This means that people, perhaps with different moral views about health care and education, will need to work together in enterprises, which have a framework of moral values embedded within the enterprise. Since both education and health care are freighted with moral values, and since both areas rely on organizations as important actors, we need to investigate how organizations can be moral actors in education and health care in a secular society. How can organizations, in education and health care act, with moral integrity, as part of a secular, morally pluralistic society? By reflecting on the role of organizations as ethical actors in education and health care, we can further clarify the role, and limits, of the moral authority of secular governments in enforcing any particular moral points of view in law or policy in secular societies.

This investigation will focus on organizations like schools, hospitals, universities, clinics, and colleges, which exist in the social space between students or patients, on the one hand, and the rest of a secular society on the other hand. While society regulates health care and education generally, organizations such as schools, hospitals, and clinics are intermediate actors, which exist between the individual patient or student and society in general.

How do we understand the term organization as a moral agent and what does it mean for an organization to be a moral agent? These are important questions for our ethical analysis. An organization is an entity—such as a company, an institution, or an association—comprising one or more people and having a common or particular purpose. If we think of the term "organization" as identifying a genus of actors then one can argue that there are many different species of organizations. We often use the term organization to classify business organizations, or church groups, or volunteer civic associations. However, this book will argue that organizations in education and health care are a class of moral actors in secular societies (Part II). In addition, we can achieve a better and more complete understanding of moral controversies in secular, post-modern societies, if we consider organizations as moral actors in the moral controversies of secular societies.

Most organizations, particularly business organization, are moral actors to the extent that they make and keep promises to consumers and follow the rules of a particular society about commerce. This is a minimal, procedural model of businesses as moral actors. However, this book will argue that we should consider organizations, in education and health care, as significant moral actors, in post- modern, secular societies. Organizations in health care and education both set policies and procedures, which direct the actions of the organization and the choices that can be made by individual actors who are members of the organization. They must also comply with the regulations of a given society Part I of this book will argue that we need to consider organizations, with moral commitments, as moral actors in secular, post-modern secular societies and it will argue that we need to have a clear understanding of the relationship of post-modern, secular societies to moral pluralism.

This investigation will argue that while the government and individuals are important moral actors they do not exhaust the set of moral actors. We often forget that organizations play important roles as moral actors in these secular societies. Organizations are actors that mediate between individuals and society as a whole. Often, individual persons do not simply act on their own; instead, they act as part of an organization. Many people, in the USA, for example, get their health insurance through their employers and the employers and insurers set policies that govern the particular decisions that individuals can make. These organizations are moral actors that affect the particular decisions that individuals can make.

Because both the areas of health care and education are areas freighted with moral values and commitments, they provide a distinct opportunity to think about how we can examine organizations, as moral agents. The questions about how these organizations function, in morally pluralistic, secular societies, provide another way to explore and better understand ethical questions in post-modern, secular societies. To understand organizations as moral actors in secular societies it is important to understand the challenges for addressing ethical issues in secular, post-modern societies (Chaps 3 and 4). Moral discourse in secular, post-modern societies is more than simply a collection of diverse opinions about ethical matters. The argument of this book builds on the work of H.T. Engelhardt, Jr. who explored how we can talk about ethics in secular, morally pluralistic societies.

Engelhardt focused primarily on the field of bioethics[1] and he used bioethics a heuristic to investigate the challenges for addressing ethical issues in secular, post-modern societies.[2] His work identified challenges of how ethical issues can be discussed and addressed in secular, morally pluralistic societies (Chap. 3). However, this book will seek to expand the ethical analysis beyond a focus on individual actors and acts, and beyond a focus on the role of the government in regulating actions. This investigation will ask how we can understand and consider, organizations, which have moral identities (Chap. 4) as moral actors in secular, post-modern societies.

The first important challenge of this book is to develop a framework for how we can understand ethics in secular, postmodern society.[3] Chapter 3 will explore the various possible meanings and uses for the notion of "secular" and argue that secular societies are, in principle, open to moral pluralism. People often do not understand the variety of implications for moral pluralism, beyond the idea that there are differing opinions on moral issues, in secular societies. They often fail to grasp that different moral views can also reflect deeper, more profound differences about moral thinking in secular societies.[4]

Alasdair MacIntyre, who argues that the phrase "moral pluralism" can signify far more than a variety of different moral views about issues, has highlighted the conceptual issues surrounding moral pluralism in secular societies, which often go unnoticed.[5] One of the key challenges that moral pluralism presents in a secular

---

[1] H.T. Engelhardt, Jr., *The Foundations of Bioethics*, 2nd Edition, (New York: Oxford University Press, 1966).

[2] See H.T. Engelhardt, Jr. *Bioethics and Secular Humanism: The Search for Common Morality*, (Eugene, OR: Stock Publishers, 1991).

[3] H.T. Engelhardt, *After God: Morality and Bioethics in a Secular Age*, (Yonkers, NY: St. Vladimir's Seminary Press, 2017).

[4] K. Wildes, S.J. *Moral Acquaintances: Methodology in Bioethics*, (Notre Dame: University of Notre Dame Press, 2000).

[5] A. MacIntyre, *Whose Justice? Which Rationality?* (London: Duckworth, 1988).

society is not whether or not there is a variety of moral truth, but the challenge is how we can know (epistemology) what moral reality is. Moral pluralism, in a secular society, can also mean a variety of different views and assumptions about the nature of moral rationality as well as different views for how moral values and judgements and be justified. In secular societies with diverse moral languages and diverse ways of thinking about morality, people can often wind up speaking different moral languages at one another while using the same words and phrases.

When that happens public, moral analysis can become an exercise that resembles the tower of Babel more than it does coherent ethical analysis and argument. Alasdair MacIntyre writes about "rootless cosmopolitans" as one way to describe the chaos of morally diverse, secular societies, with diverse moral languages and conceptual frameworks.[6] In secular, morally diverse societies, there is a risk for social organizations that seek to maintain moral identities. It is the risk that, by participating in a morally diverse, secular society, they can lose their own sense of their identity and mission and, consequently, they can add to the confusion of moral language and babel in secular societies.

Indeed, a fundamental challenge for an organization that thinks of itself as having a moral identity will be how to maintain its own moral identity in a changing, morally pluralistic, secular world. One approach to the challenge of maintaining an organization's identity in a changing world is to maintain a strict internal code of identity and conduct which never changes for the organization.

The risk, of course, is that in time a social organization will be disconnected from the society it was created to serve. Another way to approach changes in society is to allow the organization to keep changing and stay up with the times. The risk to this approach is that the organization may lose any sense of its mission and identity. A third approach is one that seeks to balance the tension between the organization's identity and mission with the changing needs of the society it serves.

A further challenge in addressing ethical issues in morally diverse secular societies is to explore what are the appropriate ethical roles, and limits, for governmental moral authority in secular societies in resolving ethical disputes and controversies. A secular society that is, in principle, open to cultural and moral pluralism, should also consider limits to the appropriate use of government authority to enforce any particular moral view. Unfortunately, people often do not distinguish these questions about moral pluralism and the moral authority of limited government and they often take the position that a particular moral view is the correct view and, therefore, it should be enforced by the law or by regulatory authority. When a moral position is imposed on a diverse, secular society, it does not represent the triumph of the best moral argument but rather it is an example of Thrasymachus' position in *The Republic* that might makes right.[7] Often the use of might or power is not restricted to brute force but it can be the might of having enough votes to pass a law or enact a regulation to enforce a particular moral position.

---

[6] A. MacIntyre, *Whose Justice? Which Rationality?* (London: Duckworth, 1988), p. 388.

[7] Plato, *The Republic*, 338c.

A reader may well ask, at the beginning of this book, "why bother?" to investigate these questions about organizations and ethics in light of the challenges of moral pluralism in secular societies. One reason to pursue these questions is that some organizations, in health care and education, claim to have their own moral identity. However, in a secular, morally pluralistic society we need to ask if and how such claims can be assessed. Organizations that claim to have a moral identity run the risk, in diverse secular societies, of becoming corporate versions of Alasdair MacIntyre's category of rootless cosmopolitans.[8] One hope, for this investigation of organizations, is that those organizations with moral identities can develop ways to maintain their moral commitments and, by doing so, enrich the morally diversity of a secular society.

Another reason to pursue this investigation of social organizations is that it may help to develop a more complete, comprehensive understanding of secular ethics in post-modern societies where ethical questions often involve more than individual actors or government agencies, regulators, laws, or government policies. To develop a more comprehensive understanding of ethics in post-modern, secular societies it is important to consider the possibility of organizations as moral actors in education and health care.

There are numerous challenges when exploring ethics in contemporary, secular societies. To understand these challenges, it is important that we understand how we use terms like "post-modern" and that is explored, in relationship to ethical discourse in Part I. Chapter 3 develops a more complete overview of how ethics can be understood in a secular world and the possibilities for ethical language in a post-modern world. One can argue that in the western world ethical questions have often been addressed in terms of people's religious faith. However, after the Reformation and Wars of Religion, public discourse about ethical issues sought a grounding outside of any particular religious faith or tradition. One can describe post-modern, secular societies as, in principle, open to moral pluralism because there is no comprehensive ethical narrative for secular societies. Either one can argue that most of the time we investigate particular ethical issues of a particular type of action or we focus on the freedom of individuals to commit the particular action in question. Of course, these debates inevitably raise the question about the moral authority of the government to regulate the actions of individual moral agents.

Organizations make decisions, articulated and implemented in policies and procedures, which shape the terrain for future decisions made in the clinic, the bedside, hospital, or the classroom.

However, if our focus is limited only to what happens only in the clinic or the classroom, our ethical analysis will be too narrow and limited. We will miss the complex reality that education and health care organizations are important moral actors in post-modern, secular societies.

---

[8] A. MacIntyre, *Whose Justice? Which Rationality*? (London: Duckworth, 1988), Chapter Nineteen. "Tradition and Translation".

Often, in terms of ethical analysis, we do not have a conceptual scheme that allows us to account for these organizational actors, often unseen, in either education or health care. The first step is to recognize how an organization can be a moral actor. The second step is to think about how moral agency can be structured in the life of an organization with a moral identity so that the organization's acts align with its moral commitments. The third step is to think about how organizations, with moral identities, can function in a morally pluralistic, secular society.

To investigate organizations as moral actors in a secular society, we also need to consider how they can be moral actors in the context of postmodern, morally pluralistic, secular societies, which are, in principle, open to moral and cultural diversity (Chaps. 3 and 4 focus on these questions). In doing so, this book will explore, how moral language and concepts can be used for organizations (Chap. 5) and how the organization can operate, with moral integrity (Chap. 6), in morally diverse, secular societies. Indeed, we will need to clarify the concept of integrity as it is, by definition, dependent on the moral values that are held by each agent (Chap. 6). We also know from examples of moral failure by organizations, like those which occurred in Boy Scouts USA or the clergy abuse scandals in the Roman Catholic Church, that organizations can not only fail to live out their moral commitments. Moreover, we know from past examples that they can also fail to act with integrity when, they do things that are contrary to the moral values to which they say they are committed. This book will argue that we can learn from the moral failures of organizations to develop tools to analyze how to examine how organizations might be judged ethically successful, or judged as moral failures, in post-modern, secular societies.

This book will argue that organizations in the non-profit sector have relied, traditionally, on an assumption of public trust (Chap. 4). Exploring these questions can help us to think more deeply about how secular societies should hold organizations accountable for their identity and their work in society.

Health care is not the only social institution where one finds moral controversies. One also finds similar moral controversies in education. Reading the daily news one finds moral controversies about curriculum, science, and student discipline. Often moral controversies in education emerge in debates about curriculum. They emerge in controversies about what should be taught, or what should not be taught, as part of a curriculum. For many years, there have been local debates about educational programs in sex education with questions about how appropriate they are ethically. More recently, there have been disputes about whether or not critical race theory should be part of an educational curriculum. Other issues in education also make moral assumptions, such as the teaching of creationism and evolution, or global warming, or social debates about restitution for slavery, or even debates about what constitutes science! Contemporary issues like these highlight that educational curricula can be morally controversial depending on the views and goals that people hold about what constitutes education and what they hope that educational programs will achieve. Contemporary debates about the goals for education, the skills students should learn, history curriculums and critical race theory are each examples, in the final analysis, of the value assumptions, which underlie educational policy decisions. There are unarticulated questions, such as what the purpose of education is, or what the goals of an educational system are, or who should set the goals for the system. These questions pinpoint basic questions about the assumptions that should underlie an educational system or organization and they are questions that need to be asked when we inquire about the purpose of an educational system or organization.

This book has been shaped by my own experiences of organizations in education and health care, which have also provided me opportunities to wrestle with questions about ethics and organizations, their identities as organizations and their moral values, and to think about ethics in the life of organizations. Some of these experiences will serve as examples for the important questions in this book. In this book, I do use examples from the Roman Catholic tradition for several reasons. First, they are examples with which I have had the most direct experience and know well. Second, this tradition in the Christian faith is a tradition, which has emphasized the importance of the good works of institutions in health care, and education as part of the Church's understanding of Christianity.

There are, no doubt, other religious traditions that have wrestled with the questions of organizational identity and action. However, this is a tradition that has developed and maintained significant institutional presence in education and health care. Third, I also use this tradition, because it is a tradition, which has supported organizations in, health care and education and which engage the broader secular societies in their work. Perhaps because of the tradition's commitment to organizations in health care and education the Roman Catholic tradition has developed both content-full statements on the identity of colleges, universities, and health care institutions, and it is a tradition that has also developed procedures to assess the Catholic identity of these organizations. It is because of this background that this book often uses examples from the Roman Catholic tradition for exploring organizations with particular identities and moral commitments in postmodern, secular societies. The appendices in this book are included, *as examples,* of how one moral tradition has sought to address the challenging issues of organizational identity in secular societies.

Some of the essential ideas in this book began to develop initially because of my work in the field of bioethics while I was a faculty member of the Philosophy Department and the Kennedy Institute of Ethics at Georgetown University. The evolution of managed health care was such that it was becoming a presence in Medicine. This raised numerous ethical questions and issues in the practice of health care. The ideas in this book continued to develop after I left Georgetown and when I served as university president at Loyola University New Orleans. In my second year at Loyola, New Orleans experienced Hurricane Katrina. In the years after Katrina, I became involved not only in the renewal of the university but also in the renewal of the city in a number of different roles and capacities. Those post-Katrina experiences, as a citizen, a university president, and civic leader, led me to think even more deeply about some of the fundamental questions about organizations and ethics and the types of questions I had already considered while working in bioethics.

I was involved in several experiences in New Orleans, both working for Loyola University and the City, which led me to think about ethical questions that are embedded in discussions of how a society is organized. In addition, it became clear that the decisions made, with regard to how a society is organized, are choices laden with value assumptions. The way organizations are put together can be more than an expression of efficiency how organizations are put together is also an expression of moral commitments and values. These reflections led me to think about many of the issues addressed in this book and how we, in a postmodern, secular society, can think about organizations and how they operate as moral actors.

In post-Katrina New Orleans, I was privileged to be part of the efforts to establish the first Ethics Review Board (ERB) for the city. The ERB oversees the Inspector General's Office for the City of New Orleans. In post-Katrina New Orleans, I later served on the Civil Service Commission for the City and helped to lead efforts to reform, update, and modernize the City's Civil Service system. After completing service on the Civil Service Commission, I was asked to serve on the board of the city's Public Belt Railroad and, in doing so, assisted efforts to reform the organization and structure of the Railroad. Each of these different experiences led me to think more carefully about organizations as moral actors and helped me to develop my thoughts on organizations as moral actors. People do make choices in their lives. However, in many cases, the range of choices that individuals can make is shaped by the choices and decisions that have been made by organizations.

These experiences have helped me, to borrow a phrase from the *Wizard of Oz*, to "look behind the curtain" and pay more attention to organizations as moral actors. These experiences have caused me to think about their structures and the creation and execution of policies, to think that organizations should be included in ethical analysis of social questions.

The investigation of organizational ethics allows us to connect the dots and think about how an organization is put together can be just as important for an ethical evaluation as the evaluation of what an organization actually does. Decisions by organizations to pursue certain policies, for example, often reflects the moral values and choices of an organization and the society in which it finds itself. For example, many decisions made by governments and organizations under the aegis of the *Jim Crow* laws and practices were choices influenced by social and moral assumptions of the broader society, which, in turn, influenced the values and moral commitments of organizations.

This book focuses on organizations in health care and education because both areas are laced with at least some minimal level of moral assumptions about the goals of the work that these organizations do. These two areas are imbued with at least some level of moral values, as both health care and education operate with underlying assumptions about what it is to be human. As will be argued in Chapter 4 organizations in education and health care often make moral assumptions, about what it is to be a flourishing human being. With these assumptions, organizations, like hospitals, clinics, schools, colleges, universities, and volunteer associations, become actors in a morally pluralistic world.

It is a goal of this book to develop a framework and set of tools by which we can explore organizations in health care and education as moral agents in a morally diverse, secular society.

Most of the time, when we examine ethical issues in postmodern, secular societies, we do not think of organizations as moral actors and we lack the tools to understand organizations in health care and education as moral actors in a secular, morally pluralistic world.

Chapter 2 of this book will examine examples of moral failures by organizations, such as Boy Scouts, USA and the Roman Catholic Church. These examples are used for two reasons. First, they are well-known examples of moral failure by organizations. The mistakes that were made were mistakes of individual people; however, the organizations took steps to cover up these mistakes and failed to take steps to correct the problems.

The book begins with failure because, if we can identify failure in an area, then there is reason to think that we can identify the conditions needed for moral success. From the examples of moral failure, the book will examine what are the possible necessary conditions for organizations to act as moral agents in secular, postmodern societies and achieve moral success.

Chapter 3 will develop a more complete exploration of how we can talk about ethics in postmodern, secular societies. That chapter outlines the important groundwork for considering organizations as moral actors in secular postmodern societies.

Chapters 4 and 5 examine the roles filled by organizations as moral agents in secular, post-modern societies and the possibilities for developing a moral language and grammar that can speak of organizations, as moral agents, in secular, postmodern societies. The fifth chapter develops one way to think about how moral language can be applied to organizations in secular, postmodern societies and how one might think about the idea of moral responsibility when an organization is the moral agent.

The Second Section of this book (Chaps. 6 and 7) explores some of the conditions that are needed for organizations to operate, with integrity as moral agents in secular, morally diverse societies. Now, in morally diverse, post-modern, secular societies one cannot assume to know the moral commitments of any organization. However, every organization will have the responsibility to articulate its moral commitments and act with integrity. Integrity, for an organization, will be built on the moral identity of an organization (Chap. 5). Moreover, the identity of an organization should be the cornerstone for how an organization lives and works in a morally diverse secular society. The identity of an organization should also be important for any cooperative relationship an organization has with other organizations, as explored in the third part of this book in Chaps. 8 through 11. The identity of an organization should allow those who choose to work with an organization to have informed consent about the organization with which they engage. However, it will be important for any organization with a distinct moral identity to be attentive to its identity. There is a risk that, in working with others, individuals and organizations, in a morally pluralistic, secular society, an organization may compromise or gradually give away its own distinctive identity.

However, it is quite possible for an organization to lose its identity and mission in the midst of profound challenges or change. The loss of an organization's mission and identity can mean that an organization can also loses its ability to act as a moral agent since it will have lost its moral compass. When an organization loses sight of its mission, identity, and moral commitments then the character of the organization simply becomes the output of the will of the leadership of the organization. The character of the organization would no longer be grounded in the mission and identity of the organizations but simply in the will of the leadership of the organization and its voluntarist moods and whims. It is hoped that this book will help develop methods to evaluate organizations as moral actors in postmodern, secular societies and will help to expand discussion of ethics in secular, postmodern societies to include organizations and not only individual agents or governments.

This investigation of the ethical challenges for organizations in secular societies may help to contribute to a more comprehensive understanding of how we can talk about ethics in postmodern, secular societies. Organizations in both health care and education offer services that will have at least some level of ethical commitments, even if these commitments are minimal. In addition, we know that moral commitments in health care and educational organizations can be controversial. Recall, for example, the continuing public controversies that often surround educational curriculum, from the teaching of evolution to sex education, to controversies over the content of history curricula, as well as the controversies over critical race theory. Issues like these frequently bedevil local school boards and politics. Alternatively, consider controversies surrounding the questions about what kind of services should be offered under the rubric of "health care" services. Should services such as reproductive medical services or family planning be a part of health care services? Educational and health care organizations routinely make these types of decisions about the content of the services they offer. Organizations, at least in education and health care, operate in a middle space, socially, between individual persons and society as a whole, and they should be considered as moral agents in that can operate with moral commitments and structure.

This investigation will resist insofar as possible, any serious discussion of national health care or national standards for educational systems. They are very important policy issues, but they require a different type of investigation than the focus of this investigation. The focus of the investigation of this book is to examine the middle ground of organizations in education and health care, which lies between the choices of individual agents and national social policy, and which is an area that is often neglected.

The Third Section of this book explores some of the challenges that social organizations with identities and missions need to consider when they work with other organizations in postmodern secular societies. Organizations rarely work in isolation. Working with other organizations, in education and health care, can be particularly challenging if the organizations involved have different moral commitments and ways of proceeding. The fundamental question for an organization considering a working relationship with another organization should be the question of whether or not an organization can maintain its moral integrity if it is working with another organization that has its own identity, moral commitments, and way of proceeding. The obvious risks, for either organization in shared ventures, is that one or both of the organizations can lose its moral identity, or have its moral identity and commitments significantly compromised in the eyes of society by establishing a working relationship with other organizations with different moral commitments.

It should be made clear for the reader that this book is a *philosophical* exploration. By this, I mean that philosophy is a form of rational inquiry that hopes to achieve conclusions that are systematic, coherent, and consistent. This investigation is not a theological exploration, which would begin from certain commitments of faith. Nevertheless, while this book is a philosophical exploration of these questions, this book does use examples of organizations in education and health care from the Roman Catholic community. These examples are used for three reasons. First, the Roman Catholic community, as a community, has a well-developed tradition that has a systematic commitment to serve its members and the wider community through health care and education. Second, because of these organizations in health care and education, the Roman Catholic community also has a tradition of reflection on the issues and questions concerning the identity of organizations that are engaged with the world around them. In diverse, secular societies, the Roman Catholic community has consciously worked to maintain its own identity, as a community, and developed both guidelines and structures to assist organizations in education and health care maintain their identity as part of the Roman Catholic community while they are engaged in service the world around them. Third, the Roman Catholic Church has developed juridical structures and processes to evaluate the identity of organizations in health care and education that claim affiliation with the Catholic Church. Finally, they are offered as examples, in this book, because they illustrate a community, with a particular identity, which also has developed methods that can be used to assess the identity of organizations in health care and education and because the community has structures to assess these organizations in relationship to the larger Roman Catholic community.

It should also be noted that the Roman Catholic community could also be an example of organizational moral failures as well. Moreover, these moral failures have been both the failures of individual members as well as organizational failures where the organization overlooked and, in some cases, covered up individual failures. However, the Roman Catholic community can also be an example of change and correction, as the community has taken clear, public steps to implement measures by which to address and avoid these types of moral failings now and in the future. In addition, because of this book, it should be noted that the changes that have been made from annual clergy education to reporting to rehabilitation have been organizational changes.[9]

Health care and education in contemporary secular societies are important areas for the ethical analysis of organizations. One reason is that both education and health care organizations are enterprises, each of which have at least some level of moral commitments underlying the work of these organizations. Cultural and ethical diversity creates, potentially, challenges for social organizations, especially for those in health care and education, because organizations can have their own identities and moral commitments as organizations. To draw a contrast, if one goes to a

[9] Paul Dokecki, *The Clergy Sexual Abuse Crisis: Reform and Renewal in the Catholic Community*, (Washington, DC: Georgetown University Press, 2004).

fast-food restaurant, like a McDonald's, it will be just like any other McDonald's franchise. However, one cannot make the same assumption about either education or health care organizations. Because of their different missions, identities, and histories, organizations in health care and education vary from other types of organizations in health care and education. While these organizations may share a family resemblance,[10] one should not assume that they are all the same. The variations between organizations, which can enrich the larger society, can also present a challenge for people searching for services in education and health care, because organizations can vary in what they do, how they function, and how they deliver their services because of their identity, mission, moral commitments and history.

If the scope of our ethical inquiries in secular societies is too narrow, we run the risk that our ethical analysis of secular societies as a whole will be deficient and incomplete of secular societies as a whole. We will miss the reality, for example, that when physicians and patients make decisions, they are *not* alone in the examination room and in their decision-making. Even though they may be together in an exam room, other actors are also present and part of the decision-making process. The decisions that they can make about treatment for the patient have already been shaped by decisions that many others, like insurers, employers, and health care facilities, about the range of treatments that will be available to the patient. The voices that form a chorus in the patient-physician exchange include the voices of the clinic or hospital that defines the menu of treatment options for the patient, as well as the benefits manager of the patient's present employer who made insurance purchases for the patient and had a voice in defining the range of benefits for the patient. State and federal regulators, who oversee treatments and standards of care, also have a voice in the decision-making. What happens in the clinical setting is not an isolated exchange between the patient and physician rather it is an exchange that involves the patient, the physician, the employer, the insurance company, the benefits manager, the insurance company, and government regulators.

As with health care, we need to expand the framework we understand the moral actors are in education. While the student and teacher may be together in the classroom, many other actors influence and shape what transpires in the educational experience. Local boards of education, state and federal agencies, and other certifying authorities all have voices in what transpires in the exchange between students and teachers. All participate in determining what it is to be "educated." Historically, education in the United States has gone through a different though analogous development in its structure and organization. Following World War II, in the United States there was a significant federal investment in education though the GI Bill. The federal investment in higher education reshaped higher education in the United States and expanded the stakeholders in higher education. Then in the 1950s and 1960s, Russian advances in the sciences and into outer space became an impetus for the United States to invest in education. The federal investment in education gives the federal government a voice on what transpires in the educational enterprise.

[10] L. Wittgenstein, *Philosophical Investigations* 65ff: (New York: Wiley-Blackwell, 1998).

Depending on location, each state makes investments in education as well, and these investments give the state a voice in the goals and outcomes in education.

Policy decisions are choices that are morally important, as they shape what actually happens in the practices of health care and in education, but these decisions and choices are often unseen or unnoticed. They are examined rarely in terms of ethics and policy. In addition, if we are to do a thorough ethical analysis of an immediate ethical controversy, we need to bring these decisions under the microscope. From this experience, there are two key insights that I have garnered. One is that we need to take account of bureaucracies as actors in our postmodern society. Americans often focus on the individual person for understandable reasons. However, in many areas of human life people deal with bureaucracies as much as they do individual persons and agents. This can be clearly seen in health care, whether it is the bureaucracy of the government, the insurance company, or the hospital. It can also be seen in commerce, civil society, and often in private organizations such as churches. This complexity leads one to ask how a bureaucracy, in any kind of organization, can be held accountable for its actions.

The exploration of organizations in this book can help to develop a more complete understanding of the complexities of what it is to address ethical issues in a secular, morally diverse society. Thinking about the role of moral organizations in morally diverse secular societies is important for thinking about ethics and public policy. A society that is secular will be open, in principle, to be morally pluralistic and will need to develop frameworks for how people can live together, peacefully, with moral disagreements and still live with moral integrity. Part of that framework should include organizations. An organization may have a clear moral identity, or it may be ambiguous about its identity and moral commitments. Alternatively, it may be that, over time, an organization may lose its identity and moral commitments. Whatever the case may be, it is important for an organization to be clear about its identity and moral commitments whatever they may be if any!

The fourth section of the book brings together both the internal and external foci of this investigation. The fourth section goes back to the fundamental relationship of an organization to its environment and the society that surrounds it. Health care and educational organizations emerge in response to needs in the society in which they live. The final question of this book, in part four, explores the questions of what happens to an organization if a society changes in ways that the particular mission of an organization is no longer needed in a society. What happens to an organization if society changes so that that the social needs, which helped shape the organization, are no longer present? This type of question is rarely, if ever, asked by organizations or associations. Yet, it is an obvious question to ask if we assume that societies are not static and that they can change.

Depending on the degree of social change, an organization in education and health care will be challenged to reevaluate its historic mission and identity. It may be that the mission of the organization is no longer relevant or necessary for a society because of changes that have taken place in a society. The organization needs to recognize social change and either redefine its mission or, perhaps, end the work of the organization. A society may change in such a way that the mission of the organization is no longer necessary or relevant to a society.

The final part of this book raises important questions about the relationship of social organizations in education and health care to the society in which they exist. However, throughout this book, it will be assumed that organizations in health care and education are social organizations, which exist in a dialogical relationship with the wider society in which they exist. The questions about this relationship go beyond the scope of the book. However, it is important to identify these questions because of their importance for understanding the ethical commitments of social organizations in education and health care. Social organizations are situated within a particular society and the relationship between social organizations and the society in which they live. The book is focused on questions about how health care and educational organizations can be structured so they can function with moral integrity in postmodern, secular societies. The relationship between organizations and the wider secular society is developed in Part I of the book. However, it is important to keep in mind that changes in the surrounding society cam affect the work of social organizations. If a society changes how it is organized and delivers education or health care, it will affect how organizations in these fields can function. If a society changes significantly then social organizations will need to reflect on their mission and identity and how decide how and if they can respond to changes in a society.

In recent years, in the United States for example, the passage and implementation of Federal legislation like *The Affordable Care Act* or *No Child Left Behind* have reshaped the social environment for organizations in health care and education. The investigation of this book is focused on organizations themselves. Nevertheless, this investigation, which centers on the intermediary structures of health care and education, will implicitly raise broader social questions about how a society creates and delivers the social goods of education and health care. These larger social questions should be the focus of another investigation. The questions about how a society is structured are beyond the focus of this book as this book, which is focused on the intermediate organizations that exist between individuals and society as a whole. If the needs for which an organization was created no longer exist in society, organizations should reevaluate its mission and ask the very challenging question of whether or not society has changed in ways that the mission of the organization has ended as it is no longer needed in a society. These are important questions and they point to the need for social organizations to have a dialogical relationship with the society in which they are situated and created to serve.

The investigation of this book, however, naturally leads to another set of questions that are beyond the investigation of this book. These are the questions which ask how *a society* should organize and structure itself so that there can be access to goods, like health care and education, that are part of secular societies but which do not always fit neatly into the framework of a free market model. What are the obligations of a secular, postmodern society, if any, to see that these goods are available to the members of society? This is an important set of questions, which leads to a more in-depth exploration of how a culturally and morally diverse postmodern society should be structured. This book, however, is focused on organizations in health care and education, and it deliberately avoids excursions into the questions of public health and education policy. There is no doubt that questions about public health and public education are important questions for a society, and these questions merit ethical investigation. However, they are topics and questions for another inquiry, at another time, and, perhaps, another book. This investigation is focused on ethical questions on the role of organizations within any system of education or health care.

A fundamental goal of this book is to expand the tools for the analysis of ethical questions in postmodern, secular societies by moving beyond the actions and choices of individual agents or the role of government in moral discourse and regulation. The book will expand the tools for analysis of ethical issues in postmodern, sectarian societies by exploring how we can include organizations as moral actors. Organizations can be for-profit businesses; they can be volunteer groups and non-profit organizations. Organizations fill important roles in secular societies, and they often shape how individual agents can respond to ethical questions. Organizations can also provide another dimension for understanding what it is to live in a morally and culturally diverse secular society. The exploration of organizations as moral actors can also be an important step in achieving a more comprehensive understanding of ethics in postmodern, secular societies. Some of the social structures in post-modern, secular societies, like religion, political, or economic affiliations, play important roles in modern social life through organizations.

This book, which focuses on organizations, may leave the reader with further questions about how diverse secular societies should be organized, how societies should allocate resources, and how they should support and regulate the areas of health care and education. These important social, ethical, and philosophical questions, which should be explored, as they address the social environment for organizations in health care and education. However, these social, ethical questions are better explored in a different investigation about social policy. This book is focused on organizations in health care and education and it does not engage in a systemic analysis of how the social systems of health or public education are organized in a post-modern, secular society. However, while systems of public health and education are important systems in secular societies, they warrant their own investigation, which is beyond the focus of this book.

The focus of this book is exploring how organizations in education and health care can act as moral agents in secular, post-modern societies. However, these organizations do not exist in isolation. Organizations in education and health care are social organizations and they exist in a "middle" role. By that, I mean that they clearly work with individual students, patients, and their families and loved ones, in giving direct care and attention. However, these organizations also exist in a dialectical relationship with the society around them. Organizations are situated in societies and almost all organizations, whether for-profit businesses or non-profit organizations, have some relationship with the society around them. Organizations in education and health care not only have general relationships with the society abound them but they also have reporting responsibilities to the wider society, particularly to government agencies, for the work they do. Most societies develop some method or mechanism to evaluate the work of social organizations and often use processes like accreditation and licensure to certify the social standing of these organizations.

One role of society, in somehow certifying organizations in the work they do, not only points to how the organizations bare verified but the processes of verification also raises other questions about how the society, as a whole, is structured and what its role should be in moral discourse and exchanges. How does the society understand and regulate the social goods of health care and education as good for its members? Each organization, depending on its mission and identity, will need to determine if, and how, it should act as a social critic toward the society in which it exists. For example, when a society practices racial or sexual discrimination social organizations may become critics of a society. Alternatively, organizations may raise questions about how health care and education services are organized in a particular society. These are public policy questions that go beyond an investigation of organizations. These questions examine the way a society organizes the social goods of health care and education. These are broader questions about a society organizes itself and how it allocates resources for social goods are questions for another investigation and they go beyond the scope of this book!

It will be important to remember, throughout this investigation, that social organizations in education and health care are created with a particular identity and mission in a society. Nevertheless, it is also important to remember that they exist in a relationship to the society in which they exist. In most cases, these social organizations are created to serve a particular need in a society. They are situated in morally diverse, secular societies and their own mission and identity and they can be affected by changes in a society. Therefore, these organizations will need to be attentive to changes in the societies they serve. Social organizations, which ignore changes in a society, may find themselves unable to serve the societies they were created to serve. Think of examples of change that have happened in secular society through programs like the New Deal, the Great Society, Welfare Reform, or the Affordable Care Act. In the midst of great social change, it will be important for social organizations to assess changes in a society, the needs of the society they serve, and the mission of the organization. It may be that a society may change to such an extent that the mission of a social organization may be no longer needed or seen as being complete.

However, the broader questions about how a society is organized and how a society addresses social issues in health care and education are matters for another investigation. The focus of this investigation is about how to understand and integrate the moral identity of social organizations in post-modern, secular societies and this is important if one is to understand the depths of moral diversity of such societies and the challenges of social cooperation. This investigation does lead one to the broader questions of how post-modern, secular societies should develop and distribute social goods, such as those in education and health care, and how these societies should address questions of social and distributive justice. These are important questions. However, these are questions for another investigation best left for another time!

Part I
The Ethical Terrain for Organizations in the Post-modern World

Chapter 2
Organizations and Moral Failure

This book has grown out of my experiences of working for organizations in health care and education, as well as organizations in public service. It focuses on how we can think about organizations in health care and education as moral actors and how they can confront ethical challenges in secular, morally diverse societies. One reason to focus on organizations in health care and education is that both industries are, at some level, tied to moral values, and, for that reason, they present a fruitful area of exploration to understand postmodern, secular societies.

This book argues that, in moral controversies, we often focus on the actions, roles, and decisions of individuals, or we focus on the role of governments or governmental agencies in regulating the choices of individuals. But we rarely examine the role of organizations in regulating what individuals can or cannot do or the role of organizations in responding to government law and regulations. This book argues that organizations, particularly in health care and education, are forgotten actors in the moral landscape.

This chapter lays the foundation for a new way of looking at organizations, particularly in education and health care: as moral agents. Notably, the moral agency of organizations in health care and education is a particular challenge in secular, morally pluralistic societies. This book brings together the author's different experiences as a bioethicist, faculty member, trustee of several universities, and academic administrator, as well as his experience of working in public ethics. Both health care and education are complex fields; the organizations in these fields have evolved, in their respective areas, in complexity as well. Faced with the complexity of these fields and their organizations, it is challenging to identify a starting point for an exploration into organizations and ethics.

Failure probably seems like an odd place to start an investigation or exploration into *any* topic, but for this probe of organizational ethics, failure is a good place to begin. This investigation is focused primarily on non-profit organizations in education and health care. Non- profits rely on the trust of the individuals who engage them, as well as the trust of the societies in which they are situated and operate. We

K. W. Wildes, S.J., *Organizational Ethics and Moral Integrity in Secular Societies*, Philosophical Studies in Contemporary Culture 29,
https://doi.org/10.1007/978-3-031-39097-5_2

cannot assume that organizations in health care and education deal with clients who can be understood according to the normal consumer model that we use for businesses in secular societies. People who use services in health care and education often have some level of vulnerability, either because of illness or lack of knowledge. This book argues that it is important to understand organizations in education and health care as moral agents in secular, morally pluralistic societies. This investigation begins with organizational failure on the belief that, if we can recognize failure, hopefully, we can recognize success.

While there have been important explorations of ethics across the entire realm of "business ethics", this book explores a topic that is often overlooked: organizational ethics for non-profit organizations. What is the distinction? Traditionally, non-profit organizations operate to serve some public good and with some level of public trust. The organizations examined in this book serve the goods of education and health care. From the start these organizations operate with at least a minimal level of moral commitment in secular, morally pluralistic societies because of the moral nature of both health care and education. Their very mission statements announce that these organizations operate in service of some particular good, which is seen to have a moral component, while relying on the moral element of public trust in what they do.

The two areas of health care and education are distinct and important examples for thinking about organizational ethics. Although they are often seen as industries that are objective and scientific, both areas are influenced by some level of moral assumption. While often unarticulated, views about good health and health care or what it is to be an educated human being are rooted in a moral vision of what it is to be a human being. This means that health care and educational organizations are multidimensional entities in contemporary, secular societies.

One the one hand both health care and educational organizations deliver services that are often understood as objective or scientific. However, at the same time, both health care and education are imbued with moral commitments. One has only to recall the controversies that often surround health care services provided to individuals, such as reproductive health services. Or, one may call to mind the controversies that arise from curriculum offerings, such as sex education. The ethical commitments in health care and education, which are commitments about the ideals and goals of educating a person or healing a person, are often unspoken, and yet they are suffused in the ideals and goals of the organization and its culture. Both health care and education are imbued, at least at a minimal level, with moral values and commitments. Both have at least a minimal view of what it is to be a healthy, educated human being, and these views are infused with at least a minimal level of moral commitment. And, in secular, morally diverse societies, these commitments can become points of tension in how the organization operates.

The moral failures of other non-profit organizations, like the Boy Scouts USA or organizations of the Roman Catholic Church, provide a place to start. The moral cost of the failure of organizations like these is the erosion of public trust. Hopefully, if we identify organizational failures we can think through issues for the moral successes of organizations.

Every organization makes decisions that affect how they operate with clients and customers, other organizations, society in general, and, of course, the people who are part of the organization, such as employees or volunteers. But there are several reasons to focus specifically on organizations in education and health care, as this book does, in contemporary, secular societies. First, it is good to remember that most often, when questions of ethics are explored, they are explored in terms of individual persons or particular actions, or they are explored in terms of the role of government and law. A particular action by a person was wrong or right. The government should outlaw or promote certain actions. These are the most common ways that ethical questions are investigated in contemporary, secular societies. In the debate around abortion, for example, the major question, indeed, sometimes the *only* question, is if there should be a law prohibiting or limiting the practice of abortion.

While we focus on individuals and their actions, or we focus on the role of government and law in regulating individuals, we rarely think about organizations as moral actors. An important exception is the area of business ethics and business law, which dictates codes of conduct, and enforces laws, for businesses and how they operate. However, in many parts of human life organizations are active moral participants that shape the decisions people face.

In examining organizations in health care and education, this book also takes a further step in developing a more complete understanding of postmodern, secular societies. Discussions of postmodern, secular societies most often focus on the appropriate role and limits of government authority in terms of ethics. However, ethical issues in secular societies are not restricted to questions of government authority and individual action. Often, when we discuss ethical issues in secular societies the conversation is limited to the morally legitimate role of government. However, part of the argument of this book is that such conversations are limited in their views of a secular society, because secular societies also include organizations as moral actors, in addition to individual persons and government.

This book focuses on ethical issues for organizations in health care and education as *moral* actors in contemporary, postmodern, secular societies. The reason for this focus is that because both education and health care are areas which are embedded with moral values and assumptions, even if they are not articulated. While health care organizations may look similar, and educational organizations may have common resemblances, they may have very different models of education and health care that underlie the mission of the organization. While organizations in these two fields may share a family resemblance to other organizations in the field, they also can be very different from one another because of the mission and identity of the organization (See Chap. 6). There are different ways to be educated and to judge education. And there are different models for how health can be assessed and measured. So, it is important to know the mission and identity of an organization, as these elements should influence the way the organization operates. Presumably the mission, vision, and moral commitments of an organization will influence the services offered, how the organization operates itself, and the relationship of the organization to other organizations and to the morally diverse, secular society in which it exists.

One can argue that all organizations rely on public trust regarding who they are and what they do. This reliance is particularly important for organizations in health care and education.

Since we often do not ask these deeper questions about the identity of an organization and its relationship to the larger society, one way to start this investigation is with the recognition of moral failures by organizations. And, in recent years, from the Boy Scouts USA to the Roman Catholic Church, headlines in the news have relayed many stories of moral failure by organizations. Organizational failures serve as a starting point for this exploration for two reasons. First, when we can identify something as a failure it is reasonable to think that we can also recognize the criteria for success. And in reflecting on the examples of moral failures in organizations we can then move to establish a range between success and failure and what might be needed to prevent moral failure. Second, by looking at examples of moral failure, not just by individual agents but organizations, we can begin to think about organizations as moral actors, allowing one to develop a language for moral success within organizations and a language that will help understand how moral success might be achieved.

In recent years, several examples of moral failure by organizations have become well- known. Too many! In scandals surrounding the Boy Scouts USA[1] or the sex abuse scandals that have plagued the Roman Catholic Church,[2] we find examples not only of individual moral failure but also organizational moral failure. The moral failures in the Boy Scouts or the Catholic Church were more than the failures of individual agents. They were also failures of the organizations. These two examples of moral failure can only be understood fully if we look beyond the particular cases to the organizational structures and cultures that contributed to or enabled the moral failures. A full exploration, along with the development of possible remedies, must go beyond individual agents. The moral failures in these cases are not merely about the failings of particular individual Scout leaders or clerics. The moral failures in these cases cannot be fully attributed to the individuals who failed but can only be fully explained if one includes an account of the organizations themselves in terms of the failure to act, the cover-up, and, to some degree, the facilitation of the moral failures of individuals. Moral failure can often happen within any organization because of the failures of individuals involved. However, these examples are not merely about individuals working within the organization who made egregious moral errors; rather they are examples of how the organizations themselves failed in keeping the trust that society had invested in them. Our judgments in these cases tell us, at least implicitly, that we think we should hold organizations, and not just individuals, ethically accountable.

[1] "These Men Say the Boy Scouts' Sex Abuse Problem Is Worse Than Anyone Knew", *Time* , Eliana Dockterman, June 1, 2019 7 https://time.com/longform/boy-scouts-sex-abuse

[2] https://www.nytimes.com/topic/organization/roman-catholic-church-sex-abuse-cases

There has been a great deal of thought about ethics and organizations in the area of business ethics for many years.[3] However, less attention has been given to ethical issues that confront charitable, non-profit organizations such as churches and the Boy Scouts. There have been some very thoughtful works that address particular ethical issues, which organizations, like universities, encounter. James Keenan, S.J., for example, has developed a careful, thoughtful analysis of many of the important ethical issues confronting universities today, such as cheating and diversity.[4]

In addition to thinking about basic ethical issues that confront any type of organization, this book focuses on two important types of social organizations—those in education and health care. Organizations in health care and education are of particular interest precisely because they each operate with key ethical assumptions, no matter how minimal, as part of the fabric of their work. The moral values of health care and educational organizations ought to influence the day- to-day operations of the organizations and function as more than a plaque in the hallway or a slide in a power point presentation. The challenge is that these organizations operate and function in secular societies that are, in principle, ethically diverse and morally pluralistic.

Exploring these two types of social organizations raises two different types of ethical questions. First, how can the organizations function and participate in such a diverse society. Second, recognizing the reality of these organizations moves us beyond simply the questions of individual citizens and government authority and can lead us to ask how we can think more deeply, and critically, about contemporary, postmodern secular society.

This book addresses the broad topic of organizational ethics in the context of secular, morally pluralistic societies, and argues why this topic is also an important way that one can address and discuss the role of ethics in postmodern societies. Organizations play important roles in the work life, social life, and community life of a postmodern society, and yet they are often neglected in our ethical reflections and arguments. Discussions about ethical issues focus, most often, on the relationship of government, law, and individual choices. However, organizations, at least in health care and education, are also actors that interact with individual citizens and government agencies and regulators.

Organizations bring people together in order to accomplish particular tasks, such as those required of education and health care, where moral values are interwoven into the practices of both. This volume focuses in particular on organizations in health care and education in that they provide excellent examples of services, in contemporary society, which are often embedded with moral values. Nevertheless, many of the book's insights about ethics and organizations can be applied to other organizations, beyond the fields of education and health care, as well. The book also examines ways in which organizations can structure themselves internally as a way

---

[3] Anne Lawrence, https://time.com/longform/boy-scouts-sex-abuse Web, *Business and Society: Stakeholders, Ethics, and Public Policy,* (New York: McGraw Hill, 2017.

[4] James Keenan, S.J., *University Ethics: How Colleges Can Build and Benefit from a Culture of Ethics,* (New York: Roman & Littlefield, 2015).

to strengthen their commitments to who they are, what they do, and how they accomplish their goals.

A reader might ask why one should bother with these questions, in view of an abundance of well-developed literature in the area of business ethics. There are at least two good reasons to pursue this particular line of inquiry. First, the areas of health care and education are two structures that are particularly important in multicultural, postmodern societies for the services they provide in diverse secular societies. However, while attempts have been made, neither area is readily adaptable to typical business models that are used to define and measure corporations.

Both health care and educational organizations are, as will be argued, laden with moral values. For example, the extensive literature on health care and ethics is a clear reminder of the existence of moral content in the practice of health care. The moral issues in education for example address basic, fundamental questions about both the goals of education and about how students are treated. However, there are often more subtle and foundational ethical issues in education other than questions about the appropriate and inappropriate boundaries in treating students. Often the very content and goals of education itself are founded in a moral vision of what society hopes education will achieve and the kind of people it will produce. Any educational curriculum, for example, will have a foundational set of assumptions about what it is to be an educated person in a society, and those assumptions drive the content and methodology of educational programs.

The moral dimensions of health care and education present particular challenges for those organizations and how they function in a postmodern society.

The chapters that follow develop, in more detail, how the framework of "organizational ethics" can be understood, while exploring the ways one might analyze ethical questions surrounding organizations in education and health care. Later chapters examine ways that structures can be developed, within organizations, which address ethical challenges for organizations in postmodern societies. The first part of the book investigates what it is to be an organization in the ethical context of a postmodern, secular society. Part One lays out the foundations and questions that underlay the proactive recommendations contained in the second part of the book.

However, before going on to develop this more in-depth analysis, it seems worthwhile to ask *why* we might pursue an analysis of organizational ethics. Readers may ask if we can even speak of "organizational ethics". Do organizations make moral decisions? Do organizations make moral mistakes? Do they make morally good decisions? If the answer to these questions is a resounding "no," there is no reason to pursue this project. However, it will be argued that organizations, particularly those in postmodern societies, can create a moral culture within themselves. Organizations can serve as important moral agents in postmodern, secular societies, and they can and should be held ethically accountable. Furthermore, the actions we need to examine include not only specific decisions made by an organization but also decisions on how the organization structures itself.

Most of the organizations in education and health care are labeled, in American society, as "non-profits" because they are distinguished from for-profit businesses and, as such, fall outside the purview of business ethics. As "non-profits", society recognizes that these organizations benefit society by giving them a special tax status. Nonetheless, these traditional non-profit organizations are embedded with several layers of morality. The services they provide to society have a vision and moral values embedded within them. Society in general engages in an act of trust in creating these organizations. Our assumptions about good health and good education are tied to our vision of what is a good human life. Second, the populations served by these organizations, students of all ages and/or the ill, are disadvantaged in some way and cannot be understood simply as consumers as we would normally conceive them. There is, generally, a level of vulnerability experienced by patients and students that differentiates them from those who fit into the normal consumer model. While structures for oversight by society have been put into place (See Chap. 8 on Accreditation), an assumption of trust has been extended to these organizations.

Our contemporary moral language and analysis focus most often on individuals or the actions and policies of governments. We use moral language to evaluate individual persons, individual acts, or specific individual laws and regulations. On those occasions when we do enter into ethical analysis beyond the individuals themselves, we typically examine businesses and how they comport themselves within the realm of business ethics, or we look at governments and their laws and regulations. We do turn, in education and health care, to broader analysis beyond the individual. However, those analyses are typically undertaken when addressing wide-ranging, broad, and sweeping acts.

Before turning to the question of how we might examine organizations from an ethical standpoint, we might first begin by asking *why* we should evaluate them. One reason to evaluate organizations comes from the reality of *moral failure*, which helps us to understand what is possible. If we can understand the boundaries of moral failure, we may find a clearer path for understanding the possibilities of moral success.

2.1 Examples of Organizations and Moral Failure

Readers, no doubt, recall glaring news headlines that have trumpeted examples of organizations and moral failure, both in the for-profit sector and in social services such as education and health care. However, to help support and illustrate this exploration I would like to point once again to two recent and ongoing examples of organizations and moral failure. As mentioned, two organizations that have exemplified moral failure are the Boy Scouts USA and the Catholic Church in the United States. In light of their shortcomings, both organizations have taken important steps to both understand and remedy the moral failures found within. Moreover, both organizations have been studied by a collection of experts and law enforcement agencies, and they have been, or are being, penalized for their actions and failures to act. Reforms have sought to address structural and cultural issues within the organizations that enabled such moral failures.

Important lessons from these two negative examples can be not only learned but used in the field of organizational ethics. One broad, general lesson is the importance of *trust* in organizations in postmodern societies. Organizations are clearly different from individual agents in that individual agents need to earn trust that is invested in them. However, organizations have many individual agents working in and for them. Trust in an organization is different from trust in an individual agent, as the basis of trust accorded to individuals in an organization is grounded on the fact that they are part of a trusted organization. There is no doubt that individual members of both organizations committed immoral actions. However, limiting the focus to individual actions alone does not provide an adequate explanation as to how people were able to commit heinous offenses. A more complete explanation needs to recognize that these individuals were trusted, because the organization they represented was trusted. Because these individuals were members of trusted organizations, they, the individuals, were trusted. The trust that exists toward an organization, or a group such as a group of professionals, is transferred to the individual agent. This relationship points to the need to develop a language and conceptual framework by which organizations can be understood and evaluated as moral agents.

Such a presumption of trust is certainly not a new development in Western society. Those engaged in the classical professions of the Western world—Law, Medicine, and the Clergy— have been viewed as trustworthy in society, because they are certified members of professions that have professional codes of ethics to which their members are held accountable. It is worth recalling how they have been understood, morally, as this may be of help as we think about organizations. It is worth remembering that engaging with professionals in the classical professions cannot be viewed as a normal commercial exchange. People do seek the help of lawyers, doctors, or clergymen, in part, because they have specialized knowledge. However, any expert can claim specialized knowledge! One element that has contributed to the special *ethical* understanding of the classical professions is that those seeking assistance are in need. Unlike when I need the assistance of an electrician or a computer expert, who surely has specialized knowledge, a person who seeks the help of one in a classical profession is vulnerable. It is not merely my computer that needs fixing; I need fixing. Moreover, because I am the subject of the exchange, that interaction is certainly different from a typical commercial transaction.

With that in mind, the classical professionals are bound by codes of ethics, which, in part, protect the patient, penitent, or client in their vulnerable states. Therefore, when members of these professions act immorally, and take advantage of the trust society invests in them, as has occurred in recent history, there is an organizational as well as individual failure. It is not only that the individual cleric, physician, or lawyer is guilty, but trust in the entire profession of a society is eroded. Nevertheless, what has been set out, thus far, is individual failure that can and often does erode trust in the larger organization. Not only are the particular actions morally opprobrious, but they undermine society's trust in the professions and organizations.

What can we learn from these moral failures? There are, I believe, a number of lessons that can be drawn, and much of this book is dedicated to developing lessons in thinking about organizational structures in a postmodern society. However, the first lesson, which ought not to be overlooked, is that we can and do think of organizations in moral and ethical terms.

Organizations are moral actors. While society will make judgments about individual agents, (e.g., this cleric, this physician) it can also can make moral judgments about entire organizations and groups of professionals.[5] What is the culture of an organization? How does it prepare members of the organization to think about ethical issues? What are the organizational tools for reporting ethical misconduct? What is the follow-up to such reporting?

2.2 Organizations and Morality in Contemporary Secular Society

Understanding the "obvious" is both an important and difficult task. As A. North Whitehead wrote: "It requires a very unusual mind to undertake the analysis of the obvious."[6] This chapter is not an extensive inquiry into organizations, bureaucracies, and accountability. Excellent scholarly work has been done on these topics.[7] Instead, the purpose of this chapter is to explore the obvious. I want to explore the language and concepts that can be used to understand the questions of ethics and organizations, concepts that allow us to discuss and analyze the moral failures mentioned in the first chapter. We have already identified examples of organizations and moral failure—in the American Boy Scouts and the American Catholic Church. It is worthwhile to explore how we can understand the role of organizations in postmodern, contemporary society as part of the foundation to explore how organizations, particularly in education and health care, can be evaluated. We need a basic, shared understanding of organizations and their bureaucracies and their role in contemporary society before we can explore the significant issues in the organizations of health care and education.

In his writing on postmodern society and ethics, H.T. Engelhardt, Jr. valuably examines issues surrounding the human person and government in postmodern society.[8] The reality of the postmodern condition, in secular societies, is explored more carefully in Chap. 3. However, it is worth noting here that we need to reflect

[5] David Crary, "Boy Scouts could be hit with more sex abuse claims", Associated Press, 24 April 2019.

[6] Alfred North Whitehead, *Science and the Modern World*, Preface, New York: The Free Press, 1925, Preface p. 4.

[7] Weber, Max. *The Theory of Social and Economic Organization.* Translated by A.M. Henderson and Talcott Parsons. London: Collier Macmillan Publishers, 1947.

[8] H. T. Engelhardt, Jr., *After God: Morality and Bioethics in a Secular Age* (Yonkers, NY: St. Vladimir's Seminary Press, 2017), *Bioethics and Secular Humanism* (Philadelphia: Trinity Press International, 1991), *Bioethics Critically Reconsidered: Having Second Thoughts,* (Dordrecht: Springer, 2012).

on the role and ethical decision-making of organizations as they fill a middle ground between individual persons in the rest of a society and government. Given the postmodern context of contemporary secular societies and questions of ethics this book does not attempt to morally assess the particular moral values of an organization. As with individual moral agents, in a postmodern society we need to evaluate, morally, organizations on their own commitments. However, I do think that laying out the elements for organizational identity is an important step that can serve as a starting point for such an exploration.

Organizations are influential parts of contemporary society, and they play a variety of roles and fulfill a wide array of functions. One might generalize and say that for much of human history families and kinship relationships have played a central role in organizing society. This history if particularly obvious in the West as a collection of agrarian societies. However, with the development of changes in economic, social, and political structures, organizations have come to play more important, central roles in how societies are structured in the West. One change often noted is that government and governmental organizations now play central roles in almost every other aspect of social life. This is especially true in the West. The rise of organizations has taken place primarily in the economic realm of life, as the economic sphere has moved beyond familial structures. The emergence of organizations in modern societies has grown much like the evolution of business organizations. Businesses have developed in size and complexity, from small start-ups to large multinational organizations. In the realm of business, we often examine the topics of "business ethics" and explore how businesses are organized and interact with one another and with the rest of society. However, organizations and organizational structures have transformed the way important parts of the "nonprofit" sector of social life are organized. This has been particularly true in the way modern and postmodern societies assign important roles in all major aspects of life, like education and health care. Yet, there has been little in-depth examination of the ethics of non-profit sector organizations.

The evolution of organizations in health care and education has also influenced the transformation of many traditional non-profit charitable organizations. While they can be described and analyzed in a variety of ways both health care and education have a moral foundation upholding the work accomplished by these organizations. The work of organizations in health care and education focuses on particular people, whether patients or students. Unlike a commercial exchange, it is *the person* of the student or the patient that is the object of the services involved. The services are not about an object but about a person, and this difference makes the exchanges in health care and education different from typical commercial exchanges involving a good, product, or service. Societies often view organizations in health care and education as fiduciaries for patients and those seeking education. Furthermore, the services that are offered by educational and health care organizations have at least a minimal moral dimension insofar as they are tied to an individual's vision about his or her own life and what it is to lead a good human life. So, while many of the questions about organizations in health care and education can be asked of any organization there will always be some level of moral commitment and dedication to moral values in the basic ideas about what it is to be educated or healthy. And, of course, in morally pluralistic societies it is important to recognize that the basic concepts of health and education will be freighted with a number of moral values.

However, before focusing on organizations in the non-profit sector, particularly in education and health care, it can be helpful to explore, generally, characteristics one often finds in *any* organization. An organization is an entity comprising multiple people, such as an institution or an association that has a particular purpose. There are different ways to identify organizations. However, it is safe to say, generically, that an organization is a group of people that has a vision and mission for a purpose. Organizations can be both formal and informal. In this book, however, we will be examining formal organizations. At the very general level an organization can have a purpose that includes creating a profit, such as a business organization. Alternatively, an organization can have a purpose that is not focused on profit-making. A non-profit organization, such as a charitable organization, is such an example. Therefore, use of the term "organization" does not tell us anything about the purpose of the organization or the type of organization it is.

2.2.1 *Civil Society*

Often discussions and arguments about ethics and policy focus on individual agents and the role of governments or their agencies. In this book we are developing another actor, the role of organization as moral actor. It is helpful to this analysis if we identify the role of "civil society" as a background for organizations and not limit our focus to the role of governments and government authority.[9]

Organizations play an important role in "civil society". Civil society is the "aggregate of non-governmental organizations and institutions that manifest interests and will of citizens".

The World Bank describes civil society as follows: "Broadly speaking civil society is commonly defined as 'the area outside the family, market and state', encompassing a spectrum of civil society actors and entities with a wide range of purposes, structures, degrees of organization, membership and geographical coverage."[10] While definitions vary across institutions and countries, the "civil society ecosystem" typically includes:

- Non-profit organizations (NGOs) and civil society organizations (CSOs) that have an organized structure or activity, and are typically registered entities and groups
- Online groups and activities including social media communities

[9] https://www.worldbank.org/en/about/partners/civil-society/overview

[10] Rachel Cooper, (2018). *What is Civil Society? How the term used and what is seen to be its role and Value in 2018,* UK Department of International Development, Brighton, Institute for Developmental Studies.

- Social movements of collective action and/or identity, which can be online or physical
- Religious leaders, faith communities, and faith-based organizations
- Labor unions and labor organizations representing workers
- Social entrepreneurs employing innovative and/or market-oriented approaches for social and environmental outcomes
- Grassroots associations and activities at local level
- Cooperative ventures owned and democratically controlled by their employees

Civil society includes the family and refers to a wide array of organizations: community groups, non-governmental organizations (NGOs), labor unions, indigenous groups, charitable organizations, faith-based organizations, professional associations, and foundations in the private sphere, referred to as the "third sector" of society, distinct from government and business.[11]

These changes and developments contributed to and illustrate the evolving role of organizations in our contemporary world. Furthermore, the evolving role of organizations was influential in changing and developing structures of education and health care. There is a variety of influences on how health care and education are organized. For example, in the United States, the influence of war and the care of wounded soldiers influenced how Medicine is organized.[12] However, the "industrial" economic model of organization has clearly been influential on both the models of delivery for both education and health care.

To understand and analyze how organizations act ethically in a postmodern society, it is important to understand how they have emerged in the modern world and the roles they have come to play in both education and health care. In most cases an organization is defined primarily by a particular purpose; in most cases, the purpose is shaped by the social structures of a society. Organizations frequently arise in response to the needs within a society or the perceived need to undertake something that is not being done or can be done better. A group of people forms an organization for a particular purpose, which is thought to be needed within a vision of society by the group. The organization, no matter how informal, has a structure, which aims to fulfill its purpose. Depending on the organization and its complexity, it will have a differentiated structure. In the best-case scenario, the differentiated structure should work in an integrated fashion to achieve the goal(s) of the organization.

It should be clear that organizations should not be thought of as some sort of distinct or distant platonic form. They are formed in response to a need. However, they are also responsive to the society around them, and if, over time, the need changes or disappears this means the organization will either redefine its identity and mission or possibly go out of existence. The development and history of an organization should be tied to the history and needs of a society.

[11] Who and What is Civil Society, Society World Economic Forum, https://www.weforum.org/agenda/2018/04/what-is-civil-society

[12] Paul Starr, *The Social Transformation of American Medicine*, (new York: Basic Books, 1982).

2.3 From the Personal to Organizations and the Bureaucratic

Most of the time, our analysis is about individual persons and their acts, or we talk about the actions and policies of governments. We do move beyond the individual paradigm when we address the questions of business ethics. However, for much of western history discussions and questions about ethics have been cast in terms of individual persons or individual actions. In more recent times, we have explored social actions and policies (e.g., war, civil rights).

However, we have not attended, outside of business ethics, to the ethical character of the actions of organizations.

Organizations, particularly in education and health care, often allow people to accomplish what individuals cannot accomplish on their own. It is important to remember that the development of bureaucracy in health care, for example, occurred in an era when Medicine in particular was growing in its ability to do more and more for people. The expansion of our knowledge in Medicine, and our ability to diagnose more and intervene more fueled an expansion of bureaucracy in health care. At the same time, the continuing expansion of knowledge and our standards of what it is to be educated was also accompanied by a desire to document and measure what was accomplished, which led to an expansion of the role of bureaucracy to document and measure what was accomplished. So, if we expand our analysis of ethics in health care and education to organizations, we need to explore the role of bureaucracy, as a conceptual category, in order to understand how organizations can structure ethical accountability.

This shift, from the personal to the organizational and bureaucratic, brings a number of distinct challenges for ethical analysis and language. One of the key challenges is to recast how we think about "responsibility" when we think of a bureaucracy and an organization. When a person is the actor or agent, the idea of responsibility is usually clear. However, the category becomes much less clear with organizations. In a similar way, we need to recast the notion of "trust" when we move from individual agents to organizations. In everyday discourse, we often think of trust in terms of individuals. However, when we trust an organization the individuals who are part of the organization benefit from our trust in the whole organization.

In thinking about bureaucracy, it is helpful to remember that the term "bureaucracy" developed from the French bureaucratic, which itself was formed by combining bureau ("desk") and -cratie (a suffix denoting a kind of government). The term "bureaucracy" originated in the French language: it combines the French word bureau – desk or office – with the Greek word κράτος (kratos) – rule or political power. The French economist Jacques Claude Marie Vincent de Gournay (1712–1759) coined the word in the mid-18th century. De Gournay is reputed to have said: "We have an illness in France which bids fair to play havoc with us; this illness is called bureaumania." On occasion he would invent a fourth or fifth form of government under the heading of "bureaucracy".[13] While the term is often used in reference to government and government service, it can be widely applied to all organizations in society. The evolution of bureaucracy, in any aspect of life, reflects a move away from associations of kinship and family.

Allen Buchanan identifies and discusses six features of bureaucratic organizations.

Following Buchanan's analysis, bureaucratic organizations are structured in a hierarchy. That is, there is a clear structure of organizational authority in a bureaucracy. Second, he argues that there is a complex division of labor with distinct roles in a bureaucratic structure. Third, those people who are in positions within a bureaucracy are usually identified as professional mangers or administrators. Fourth, what the organization produces is through the cooperation of a number of groups. Fifth, the day-to-day operation of the organization relies on established rules and policies.

The development of organizations as decision-makers and actors in education and health care, as well as other parts of social life, alters some of the most fundamental elements of moral discourse as we look to think about organizations as moral actors and agents. One key element in that discourse is the language of responsibility and accountability for decision-making. When we examine many moral issues, we focus on the individuals involved, and the moral analysis often examines the decisions and action of individuals, which is important to understanding categories of moral responsibility. What did a physician or educator do or say? What did the patient or student do? How did they respond? However, when we shift to organizations the lines are often less clear. There may not be a clear "actor" in an analysis. Moreover, if one looks to identify who has responsibility for an organization, to whom or to what should one look? The Board of Trustees or Directors? The Bureaucracy?

The term bureaucracy often suggests routines, constrained behavior and inefficiency.[14] "Bureaucracy" is a set of regulations drawn up by governments, or organizations, to control activity; the regulations are usually instantiated by a public set of standardized procedures. These regulations and procedures are known within the organization. There are four main concepts, which shape the notion of bureaucracy. These concepts are embodied within a bureaucracy as follows.

First, there is a well-defined division of administrative labor in a bureaucracy.

Second, a personnel system is consistent with patterns of recruitment and needs.

Third, there is a hierarchy of offices such that authority and status are differentiated and distributed among personnel.

Fourth, there are formal and informal networks that connect organizational personnel to one another and the flow of information and decision-making.

---

[13] It was coined in the mid-18th century by the French economist Jacques Claude Marie Vincent de Gournay, who never wrote the term down, but was later quoted at length in a letter from a contemporary—Baron von Grimm (1723–1807).

[14] Haridimos Tsoukas; Christian Knudsen (23 June 2005) *The Oxford Handbook of Organization Theory*. Oxford Handbooks Online. p. 149. ISBN 978-0-19-927525-0.

Modern bureaucracies arose as the economy was industrialized, and businesses reorganized themselves. Bureaucracies in government developed as state governments grew larger, through taxes; states began to take in more and more revenue and responsibilities; and the role of administrators increased.

2.3.1 A Theory of Bureaucratic Organizations

2.3.1.1 Mission

For many reasons the identity of an organization is central to any sort of ethical evaluation of the organization both internally and externally. This point is particularly relevant in secular, postmodern societies that are morally pluralistic. Identity and Mission are the key points from which we can move this exploration of organizations and ethics forward. Nevertheless, organizations, certainly in education and health care, need more than a mission. They are more than a collection of individuals who are gathered together to accomplish a mission. This is a case where the whole is more than simply the sum of its parts. Indeed, in health care and education, the organizations are needed to accomplish the goals of the organization. Any organization needs a structure precisely because it involves more than one person and because it is designed to endure over time. For a complete exploration of the ethics of organizations, we need to examine how we can ethically analyze the bureaucratic structures within organizations, as those structures will bear key responsibilities for the actions of the organizations.

Organizations exist in a changing, social context. The mission and identity of an organization will be foundational to what it is and how it functions within a society. However, as the social context around an organization changes and develops, so too will an organization's need to adapt and develop. This development should be aligned with the mission and identity of an organization and can be accomplished through a process of setting goals for the entity. The goals should aim to link the organization and its mission to its current, evolving environment.

2.3.1.2 Moral Responsibility

One of the keys to organizational leadership is "role-clarity", which is also important for ethical analysis of an organization and its actions. Achieving such clarity is often a challenge for new organizations, as they emerge and grow. However, role-clarity can also present a challenge for older, longer-term organizations, where roles have grown and developed incrementally over the years.

Developing clear understandings and clarity about roles and responsibilities is essential for establishing a culture of organizational ethics. An entity can seriously achieve a language of moral responsibility only if a clear understanding of roles and responsibilities exists; that way, the entity can assess how and in what cases moral decisions are made. It must be clear, within the organization itself and to the outside world, who holds the authority to make decisions and who (in which roles) bears responsibility for these decisions.

In any organization, the Directors or Trustees should have ultimate responsibility for the organization, given that they have ultimate responsibility for organizational governance.[15] However, part of their responsibility entails making sure the organization's structure, internal organization, and bureaucracy clearly define the various roles and ethical responsibilities within the organization. There are several reasons for this clarity of roles. One obvious reason is that such transparency serves to clarify the moral responsibility of the role itself. In a secondary virtue, role clarity helps to build an internal ethical culture within an organization: individuals become aware of the expectations of themselves and others and thus can hold one another accountable for not only work performed for the organization but the way in which that work is conducted.

Just as organizations should have in place procedures for the ongoing evaluation of employees, part of that evaluative process should include review of the moral commitments of the organization and where those responsibilities lie. However articulated in the mission of an organization, some sort of fiduciary responsibility should always be a part of education and health care organizations, given that these organizations interact with individuals when they are vulnerable or lacking in knowledge and understanding. Evaluations are essential to building an internal culture that is committed to the values of the organization and its fiduciary nature. The internal culture and structures are essential for an organization's ability to build relationships with other organizations and the world beyond it.

2.3.1.3 Trust

When thinking about organizations in health care and education, a background assumption is often made regarding the element of trust on the part of those who seek the organization's services. Ethics and trust are inextricably linked, particularly in a postmodern, secular society. Often our trust in an organization is based on a minimal level of "consumer" trust and consumer protection. However, organizations in health care and education offer more than simple consumer exchanges. The ultimate subject of an exchange with an organization is a person, whether a patient or student.

One of the problems in assessing organizations in health care and education stems from the diverse, pluralistic nature of contemporary secular societies. This is especially true, given the different expectations concerning what makes for a good health care system or a good university. It is not uncommon, for example, that in higher education, parents will examine a college or university's graduation and job placement rates, as well as costs, as they make decisions with their children. In the

[15] See Chap. 5 of this book.

United States, several publications have created special issues for ranking colleges and universities, as well as hospitals, nursing homes, and physicians. Such rankings are not surprising in a postmodern, secular society. In addition, our interest in ethics is often driven by concerns regarding whom we can trust in a diverse, pluralistic world where there is risk and uncertainty. Trustworthiness relates directly to postmodern ethics in at least two specific dimensions: integrity[16] and benevolence.[17]

2.3.1.4 Dealing with Vulnerable Populations

Many readers might quickly conclude that organizations should simply, in a postmodern world, follow good practices of informed consent in marketing themselves while, at the same time offering some form of validation that they are who they say they are. While this is a good starting point for moral authority in postmodern, secular societies, this starting point should be approached with some caution. There are some problems in using the commercial exchange model for education and health care. It should be noted that in health care and education we are often dealing with populations of patients, students, and families who are not necessarily informed consumers. They are sick, vulnerable, concerned, and sometimes ill-informed. While the baseline maxim of "caveat emptor" applies, outside supervision is needed to make sure that appropriate steps and measures are taken to ensure that patients, students, and families are fully informed of both the promises and risks they are undertaking. Their vulnerabilities or lack of knowledge often make it necessary to take additional steps and implement additional processes to assure informed consent. More steps are necessary so that patients, children, and families understand the choices before them and those which they are making.

2.3.1.5 Structures for Ethics: Accountability

Clarity of roles is foundational if there is to be a real, developed sense of moral responsibility within an organization. Therefore, clarity in the bureaucratic structures is a foundational building block for a moral culture. However, there are other structures that can be part of an organizational bureaucracy which can play a vital role in the moral culture of an organization.

One office or function is that of the compliance office. Organizations of all kinds, but particularly those in education and health care, are subject to an array of laws, rules, and regulations. These are often external to the organization. They are often issued by governments, federal and local, and accrediting associations. Further, it is often the case that the organization develops its own policies and rules, sometimes

---

[16] See Chap. 7 of this book.

[17] Francis Fukayama, *Trust: The social virtues and the creation of prosperity,* (New York, NH: The Free Press, 1995.

in light of external rules, which must be met. In response to this array of rules and regulations, it can be very helpful for an organization to employ an officer who is responsible for making sure the organization is complying with the wide array of rules and regulations.

Along the same lines, it is helpful for an organization to establish an independent office for *internal audits*. This can be a function done internally or externally. The only caveat is that if handled internally, the office or officers must be afforded clearly delineated independence. In addition, no matter how it is done, the Audit function should have a direct relationship with the organization's board. This relationship assures a certain level of independence and freedom for the audit function.

To operate as an ethical organization the organization needs to be sure, as well, that there are appropriate procedures and protections for "*Whistle Blowers*".[18] That is, there need to be both procedures and protections for employees within the organization who point out when the organization's procedures are not being properly followed.

*Annual evaluati*ons, throughout the organization, are not only a good business practice, but they are also a good way to help build an ethical organization. In all of this, an excellent, common practice for organizations is to have a good department of Human Resources. Such an office should do the obvious, basic tasks needed to fill and create positions, but it can do so much more for the moral functioning of an organization. It can be sure that position descriptions are appropriate and accurately written. It can foster a culture of compliance and evaluation and ongoing education on the changing environment in health care and education. It can also look for patterns within an organization (e.g., an office with significant turnover) and attend to helping to build and support the culture of an organization.

2.4 Health Care and Education as Moral Concepts for Organizations

Again, it is important to point out the obvious. Both health care and education are each a hybrid concept that, in reality, is often freighted with measurable, empirical data and at the same time linked to moral values. The whole field of bioethics is a testimony to the link between empirical facts (the patient has X disease and needs Y treatment) and value judgments. Does the patient want or value the treatment options that she or he has? In an analogous way, education is not just about the accumulation of information but of learning what information to value and why. This means health care and educational decisions will be influenced by the person's moral commitments and vision of the type of life she or he wants to live.

[18] https://agb.org/trusteeship-article/some-first-principles

It is important to recognize that the underlying moral commitments of an organization in education and health care should influence the particular ways in which an organization acts.

2.5 Organizations and Vulnerable Populations

The processes of informed consent, so often a pillar of bioethics, can serve the postmodern societies so well in ethical issues, controversies, and disputes. Moreover, from a foundational view, in a diverse, morally pluralistic society it can be argued that the model of informed consent is a good position from which to start.

However, we should also note that when dealing with organizations in both health care and education we are also dealing with two complicating factors that distinguishes these organizations from the normal consumer experience and model. First, both the areas of health care and education are more complex than the normal purchase of goods and services. So, morally, one will need to be attentive to the "informed" qualification for the practice of informed consent. Second, populations of patients, students, and families do not always fit the assumed model of informed consumers. Patients, students, and their families are often not well informed, and they are vulnerable in the midst of their own illnesses or concerns. Unlike the normal consumer exchange services in health care and education are about the person themselves and not about some object or service external to the person. Furthermore, sometimes people are not informed well enough to understand the complexities of a society's educational or health care systems and the implications for the choices they are making. One has only to look at recent examples of problems faced by the for-profit sector in American higher education. Therefore, while the baseline maxim of "caveat emptor" does apply, more protections will often be needed so that patients, children, and families understand the choices before them and the decisions they are making in regard to organizations.

2.6 Organizations and Social Sins

We are exploring, throughout this book, the different aspects of organizations as moral actors in education and health care. A significant portion of this investigation is focused on the internal structures of organizations in health care and education and their missions and identities. The Third section of the book examines more carefully how organizations function in the broader, secular, postmodern society.

It is assumed throughout this book that there is at least a dialogical relationship between the broader society and any organization in health care and education. The next chapter explores the framework through which we can talk about ethics in postmodern, secular societies. The cornerstone of secular ethics, it will be argued, is consent. Therefore, it follows that secular, pluralistic societies will have a wide range of actions that are permissible, as long as there is free and informed consent.

However, it should also be clear that any society, as a dialogical partner for an organization, will often have moral deficiencies which may be labeled as "social sin." This theme will be taken up more carefully in Chap. 9, which examines the way societies are organized and how we can talk about justice in secular, postmodern societies. For now, it is worth recalling historical examples such as systemic racial discrimination through practices such involuntary slavery or Jim Crow laws, the practice of "separate but equal" laws and the practice of redlining neighborhoods in the United States, as examples of social sin.[19] One might also consider laws and practices which have historically excluded women or regulated their behavior as other examples of social sin.

In postmodern, secular societies, it is no doubt difficult to identify what would constitute a "social sin" or wrongdoing. However, by the very skepticism that identifies a postmodern society, one can articulate certain basic moral parameters that are necessary for the minimal ethics necessary for such secular societies. This book will, hopefully, expand our tools for analysis by reviewing the foundational concepts for moral language in postmodern, secular societies and exploring how those concepts can be used to assess and analyze the actions of organizations.

2.7 Conclusions

This chapter began by identifying examples of moral failure by organizations. Starting with moral failure may seem like an odd place to start an investigation about moral integrity.

However, we begin this investigation with the assumption that, if we can recognize moral failure, there is reason to think that we can recognize and understand moral success.

To identify and understand ways to recognize moral success this chapter also began to explore some of the roles played by organizations in contemporary secular societies.

Organizations play important roles in secular societies, particularly in the areas of education and health care. While this book is focused on organizational ethics it will also develop our understanding of secular, postmodern societies insofar as it expands the population of moral actors in these societies. We will be able to speak of individual moral agents, the moral agency of government, and the moral agency of organizations.

[19] Plessy v. Ferguson, 163 U.S. 536 (1896), https://supreme.justia.com/cases/federal/us/163/537

The chapter also explored the questions of how bureaucracies in organizations can become a part of the way to understand the ethical character of an organization. Understanding the role of bureaucracy in an organization is important if one is to understand ethical accountability of and within an organization.

Organizations are important in contemporary society, particularly in health care and education. They allow both individual agents and society to achieve what is difficult, if not impossible, for the individual agent alone. However, organizations in education and health care often deal with vulnerable populations, meaning that the normal "consumer" model for moral exchanges in postmodern, secular societies cannot be easily applied. Most consumers of the services in education and health care are disadvantaged, as consumers in those fields. Further, organizations in education and health care frequently benefit from some level of pubic investment, and they are often the subject of public oversight. While a "market" model may benefit organizations in health care and education and society, it would be too simplistic to rely merely on a "market" model to resolve moral disputes when dealing with organizations in education and health care. Furthermore, organizations in education and health care often serve vulnerable populations who cannot be thought of in terms of the same model as a fully autonomous consumer. One also needs to be aware that organizations can be shaped, unknowingly, by the cultural or social biases of a culture and social practices in which they operate.

To understand how organizations can function, and be evaluated, in secular, postmodern societies it is important to be clear about how we can frame ethical language, and its use, in postmodern, secular societies—the goal of Chap. 3.

Summary of the Main Points

1. Examples of Organizations and Moral Failure
2. Organizations and Morality in Contemporary Secular Society
3. Moving Ethical Discussions From the Personal to Organizations and the Bureaucratic
4. Health Care and Education as Moral Concepts
5. Health Care and Education rely on organizations for delivery in many societies
6. Organizations and Vulnerable Populations
7. Organizations and Social Sin

Chapter 3
Ethics in Postmodern Secular Societies: The Context for Ethics and Organizations

This book attempts to analyze organizations as moral actors in the fields of health care and education. To accomplish this task this chapter will introduce a number of conceptual distinctions which can help with the analysis of this book. First it will make a distinction between morality and ethics. Ethical Appeals in a Secular Society. Then it will examine ethical appeals in a multicultural secular society. Then it will examine some of the challenges to thinking about organizational ethics in Post-Modern secular ethics. Finally it will examine the possibilities of structural bias in organizations and society

Before moving along in the analysis of organizations as moral actors it is important to explore the context in which they are actors. Specifically, this book addresses the questions that surround organizations, with particular identities, that live in the context of secular, morally diverse societies. Understanding this context is important if one is to understand the issues of organizational moral identity and the ways organizations might live out their identities. It can be argued that, in understanding the issues of moral identity for organizations, one can also arrive at a better and deeper understanding of postmodern, secular societies.

Health care and education are fields often viewed through moral lenses and that, for many people, are unarticulated. Consequently, organizations in health care and education, and the public policy that regulates them, can be fraught with moral conflicts. So that the reader can better understand the sequence of the chapters which follow, and the argument developed, it is important to be clear at the outset about key concepts which frame this investigation.

Most importantly we should be clear about what it is to talk about ethics and ethical language in *secular*, post-modern societies. Understanding any type of organization requires a complete analysis of the organization and the social context in which it operates. To assist this exploration of organizations as moral agents in health care and education, it is important to understand the social terrain and challenges for moral language and ethics in which they operate. We are examining health care and educational organizations that operate in societies which are secular, multicultural,

K. W. Wildes, S.J., *Organizational Ethics and Moral Integrity in Secular Societies*, Philosophical Studies in Contemporary Culture 29,
https://doi.org/10.1007/978-3-031-39097-5_3

and morally pluralistic. The questions of organizational ethics should be very different if posed in societies that are not secular and morally diverse, such as in nations with a particular religious affiliation or nations which do not see themselves as secular states.

Furthermore, understanding the "postmodern" context for ethics in secular societies is important, so as to help clarify the challenges faced when thinking about organizations and ethical issues in such societies. However, in identifying and thinking about the postmodern context for secular ethics, one can identify possible ways to resolve these challenges for organizations in postmodern, secular societies.

As I have argued elsewhere, moral language is complex, particularly in diverse, secular societies.[1] Moral words and terms may be similar, but they can have different stipulations and uses depending on the moral language in which they are used. Indeed, individuals can often use the same words or terms but intend different meanings. This means that in the common, secular realm moral terms can be more like Babel than a shared language.

In addition, part of the challenge about the use of moral language is that people rarely think about moral language as complex. People normally use moral language and its terms as part of their ordinary, daily language with others. However, this is one reason why moral language can become confusing, particularly in morally diverse, secular societies where people with different content-full moral views use the same words but with different contexts and meanings.

This book uses the term "morality" to refer to a first order moral language. Relatedly, another part of the complexity of moral language is that it can include many different aspects of moral decision-making. Moral language can include virtues, goals, ideals, and aspirations, as well as prohibitions, character virtues and flaws, and prohibited aspirations. Moral language conveys a matter-of-fact tone when it labels a particular action, but when it labels a particular act as "moral", it imparts a judgmental tone, in the fullest sense of the word. The complexity of moral language is such that it also contains a level of affective and emotional commitments, in terms of actions and characters. As part of the complex dynamics of morality, moral language also encompasses concepts of responsibility and accountability.

If we are reserving the term "moral" for the area of first order discourse, how are we to understand the use of the term "ethics"? Here I would stipulate the idea that "ethics" refers to the systemic development of a moral system. If morality is a first order discourse, ethics is a second order discourse. In a pluralistic society we may agree that the act of an intentional killing of a human being is wrong. But we may need a second level of ethical discourse to determine if such an act was morally wrong and to what degree. Was it intentional? Was it self-defense?

Was it premeditated? These are examples of the types of questions that ethical analysis must bring to the first order discourse.

[1] K Wildes, S.J., *Moral Acquaintances: Methodology in Bioethics*, (Notre Dame, IN: University of Notre Dame Press, 2000).

From all of this it follows that, as we need to find ways to think about how we can apply moral language and categories to organizations, we will need to articulate how we understand the meanings behind moral language, the rules of moral language and the use of moral terms, as well as consider how moral language can be applied to organizations. However, not only is moral language complex in terms of speaking about the moral agency of organizations, it can become even more complex in our contemporary secular societies because of political and sociological dialogues, ideas, and events we often celebrate like "multiculturalism". Moral language is a multifaceted phenomenon in secular, postmodern societies. This chapter argues that the reality of multiculturalism, often celebrated in contemporary, secular societies, presents an important challenge in thinking about ethics, not only because of the moral pluralism that is found in multicultural, secular societies but because of the secular nature of such societies.

One of the goals of this chapter is to lay out some basic conceptual and linguistic boundaries for moral language that can be helpful in thinking about organizations. Doing so will help in the exploration of organizational ethics in culturally diverse secular societies. To initiate this exploration, it is helpful to stipulate a distinction between morality and ethics, as well as define the concept of a secular and diverse society, if we are to grasp the challenges to ethical thought in such a society. In addition, this background is important in order to understand the challenges to establishing a "common" morality in a secular society.

3.1 Morality and Ethics: A Distinction for Clarity in Analysis and Argument

People often use the terms morality and ethics interchangeably, but such usage can contribute to the confusion that often follows, particularly in public discourse about ethical issues in secular societies. For the sake of clarity, analysis, and argument in this book it will be helpful to distinguish between the two terms. The term "morality" is rooted in the Latin term "mores", meaning custom. As it has evolved in Western usage the term morality is generally grounded in a vision of human life, which often conveys an understanding of the purpose of human life and how it is best lived. Morality, as a way of living, is sustained within a community, which shares a vision of human life, and the community is bound together, in part, by that vision. Oftentimes, the vision of a community is not confined to a moral vision; rather the vision of a community is a vision about a way of life in which morality is embedded. Often the vision of human life in a community is a comprehensive vision about the purpose of human life and the ideals of human life. Such a vision usually includes a moral way of proceeding. The moral code is embedded within a vision of what it is to be a flourishing human being; there is a vision of what common life is like and how it is to be comported.

The arguments in this book stipulate that the term "ethics" should be used as a way to identify a systematic articulation of a moral view. An ethical system attempts to free the content of a morality from the particulars of a way of life and a way of living. In what follows it is argued that moral philosophy, in the Modern Age, sought to find ways to free morality from the particulars of religious "faith" or customs and develop a way to articulate ethics that transcended any particular way of life or custom.

This distinction of morality and ethics is more than simply an academic stipulation or nicety. In deploying this distinction, the language and domain of ethics allows us to analyze comparatively what people assume in their day-to-day morality. It allows us, in undertaking ethical analysis, to take a step back from our ordinary assumptions and examine them analytically. The distinction takes on critical importance in developing policy for education and health care in a secular society that is diverse and multicultural. Such a society may have a number of different communities living within, each with its own moral vision and way of life. Social organizations like those in education and health care are affected by these different communal moralities. Therefore, it will be important for social organizations like health care and education to identify ethical language and concepts that transcend the different moralities and enable them to function in such secular, diverse societies.

One challenge, for any specific community, is to determine how the community can maintain its particular moral vision of human life, how that vision can be developed, and how a vision can be shared especially with those outside of the community of faith. It is not difficult to observe that contemporary secular, multicultural societies pose challenges for any moral community and the efforts of the community to maintain, live out, and share its moral identity with others outside the community who do not share the same framework and assumptions. In addition, at the same time, such multiculturalism and pluralism in secular societies pose a challenge to how one thinks about ethics in such societies. This is a particularly troublesome question when one asks about the relationship of morality, public policy, and law in a secular society. Many of the moral communities found within secular nation-states transcend national boundaries. For example, one has only to think of religious communities such as Catholics, Jews, and Muslims, who have distinctive ethical codes and who transcend the boundaries of nation- states. These communities have particular identities that are not tied to any one nation but can be found in many different nations, particularly those that are secular. These communities not only have identities as communities, but they have moral identities as part of their culture and identity. At the same time, many secular states celebrate "multiculturalism" and "diversity", and so they also celebrate these moral differences. Through canons of civility, toleration, and respect, this communal diversity can exist and work together in the secular nation-state without war and disruption.

3.2 Understanding a "Secular" Society: The Context for Moral Pluralism

Contemporary secular societies often struggle with the confluence of a number of tensions, which are culturally driven, that do not always fit together coherently. On the one hand, they celebrate diversity and multiculturalism. On the other hand, people in these societies will often mourn the lack of community or highlight the absence of "community". This tension is particularly evident in moral discussions in secular societies that cross the boundaries of moral communities. Morality, as has been argued, is tied to a sense of community as part of a way of life. What seems to be overlooked is that when we celebrate multiculturalism and diversity, we are also acknowledging the potential for diversity in morality and the possibility of many moralities.

Oftentimes there are organizations, particularly in education and health care, which serve society in general and transcend particular communities; yet, at the same time, both health care and education are often rooted in moral visions, and organizations in education and health care often face the challenge of how to maintain their particular visions and work in a diverse society. What is good health care? What is good education? The answers to those questions go beyond the medical interventions for patients or what is taught to students. Indeed, often those questions surrounding medical interventions implicitly involve the value-laden questions and assumptions about good health.[2] In a similar way, questions surrounding educational programs involve value-laden assumptions about what it is to be an educated person.

A secular society that celebrates multiculturalism and diversity will also present challenges for organizations, and organizational systems that deliver health care and education. While both areas serve populations in terms of specific services in education and health care, both of these areas deliver their services based on underlying moral assumptions about the good life. Both fields of education and health care make assumptions about what it is to be a human person who is educated and healthy. So, one challenge for these social structures will be how to address the moral dimensions of education and health care as they serve diverse populations.

In many ways, these organizations provide a new and different dimension in which to understand and wrestle with the tensions and challenges of what it is to be a multicultural, postmodern, secular society. To begin with, in many cases, both health care and educational organizations are organizations that are supported by the wider secular society, and they are organizations whose services are often integral to such societies. Yet, the services they deliver have moral assumptions running through them. Both education and health care make underlying foundational assumptions about what it is to be a healthy, educated human being. In developing

---

[2] H.T. Engelhardt, Jr., and K. Wildes, S.J., "Health and Disease: Philosophical Perspectives", *Encyclopedia of Bioethics*, ed. Warren T. Reich (New York: Simon & Schuster MacMillian Publishing Company, 1995), pp. 1101- 1106.

systems of health care and education, often unarticulated, underlying views about human life and flourishing exist. The challenge, in postmodern secular societies, is how to build systems of education and health care that serve the celebrated diverse population.

This understanding of morality, as communally grounded, presents a real conceptual and practical problem for a contemporary secular society. In secular societies, which celebrate diversity and multiculturalism, there will be a challenge to finding a "common" morality. Often Christians have assumed that because of their beliefs about Creation, the Incarnation, and the presence of the Holy Spirit, God's moral law was discoverable in the world by non-Christians through the use of reason alone. It is no wonder that the assumptions of the Natural Law tradition took such deep roots in Christian moral thought. Influenced by this tradition of Christian moral thought and Enlightenment rationality the Western world certainly has lived with the hope of finding a common morality. From the ancient world to the present time, thinkers in the West have sought to find ways to address moral issues in ways that can transcend the boundaries of local communities and speak to different cultures and communities. Realistically, these efforts have often been undertaken when one tribe or nation imposed its morality on other tribes or nations. Often a tribe or nation would assume its morality to be superior to that of other tribes and cultures.

However, people have sought to find ways to transcend the cultural boundaries of morality without a fundamental appeal to force. Plato and Aristotle, for example, each developed methods of thinking about ethics that would appeal to a notion of "reason" that transcended a particular culture and place. The Stoics broadened this search for universal moral knowledge by systematically rooting it in natural reason that was shared by all men. They sought to ground morality in reason, which was common to all men. This thinking heavily influenced the Romans, whose empire spanned the globe and was, in contemporary terms, "multicultural". By appealing to Reason, and Natural Law, the Romans could frame a legal system that was universal (e.g., prohibiting murder) and transcended tribal law, while allowing different tribes and nations to also maintain their own laws and customs (e.g., Jewish Old Testament Law). The Stoic line of thought was baptized by Church Fathers like Justin Martyr and became a part of Christian theology and philosophy.[3] St. Justin Martyr wrote in the second century: "In moral philosophy the Stoics have established right principles, and the poets too have expounded such, because the seed of the Word was implanted in the whole human race."[4] The Natural law tradition assumed that there is a human nature which has certain inherent rights and duties and that these can be known by human reason. As determined by nature, the law of nature is implied to be objective and universal; it exists independently of human understanding, and of the positive law of a given state, political order, legislature or society at large. One can argue that this line of thought continues to this day in the language of human rights.

[3] Runar M. Thorsteinsson, *Roman Christianity and Roman Stoicism: A Comparative Study of Ancient Morality*, (New York: Oxford University Press, 2010) and see As St. Justin Martyr (Second Apology VIII, 1).

[4] Justin Martyr, *Second Apology* VIII, 1.

While taking different forms the aspiration of a natural moral law was found in ancient Greek philosophy, including Aristotle, and was referred to in Roman philosophy by Cicero. Late Christian philosophers such as Albert the Great and Thomas Aquinas expounded upon it in the Middle Ages.[5] Modern natural law theories are rooted in developments in the Age of Enlightenment, combining inspiration from Roman law with philosophies like social contract theory. Natural Law was used to challenge the divine right of kings and became a way to justify the social contract, positive law, and government—and thus legal rights—in the form of classical republicanism. It also became a way to challenge the legitimacy of uses of power and coercion. One can argue that the concept of natural law is foundational for the concept of natural rights.

Indeed, many philosophers, jurists and scholars use natural law synonymously with natural rights (Latin: *ius natural*), or natural justice.

One can argue that, because of the intersection between natural law and natural rights, the hope of the natural law tradition has been intellectually foundational for certain key documents in the Modern Age. The United States *Declaration of Independence* (1776), the *Declaration of the Rights of Man and of the Citizen* (1789) of France, the *Universal Declaration of Human Righ*ts (1948) of the United Nations General Assembly, as well as the European *Convention on Human Rights* (1953) of the European Union all have their roots in the aspirations of the natural law tradition of moral thought.

The dilemma for contemporary secular societies is that, on the one hand, these societies celebrate "diversity" and "multiculturalism". On the other hand, many people in the contemporary, secular world want to be able to argue that there is a basis for ethics which transcends cultures and national boundaries. Therefore, on the one hand we want to respect and, indeed, celebrate diversity and multiculturalism, while, on the other hand, we want a universal foundation for moral judgments and policy.

As others and I have argued, the "postmodern" dilemma for ethics is evidenced in cultural diversity and pluralism.[6] In the Modern Age, ethical thought mimicked the evolution of scientific thought and sought to find ways to address morality that transcended the foundations of faith and religion. This hope, however, was not unique to modernity. Indeed, one can argue that there are aspirations of morality transcending tribe or nation that are rooted in the ancient world. The Natural Law tradition of the ancient Romans, for example, was a method to identify ethical principles that transcended the different tribes, cultures, and mores of the Empire. But the challenge now is to examine how one can speak of ethics in a postmodern age. Therefore, it seems important to set out an understanding of Modernism in ethical thought to understand better the challenges of the postmodern era and the grounds for ethical thought.

---

[5] Ernst Troeltsch, *The Social Teaching of the Christian Church*, Vol. II, (Louisville, KY: John Knox Press, 1992).

[6] H. Tristram Engelhardt, Jr., ed., *Global Bioethics: The Collapse of* Consensus, (Beverly, MA, M & M Scrivener Press).

One can argue that the Modern Age kept these broader aspirations and sought to free ethical thought from religious thought. The next section of this chapter shows how the Modern Age sought to free ethical thought from the ethics of particular communities in order that such thought would have universal appeal. This movement was part of the larger secularization of the west. One can make the argument that in the Modern Age, after the Wars of Religion, and the establishment of Science, how we came to think about ethics shifted significantly. In an age of religious fragmentation and pluralism, the Western world needed to find ways to talk about ethics that transcended religious communities and churches. Consequently, moral philosophy regained a position in public discourse, which it had not held, in the West, since the ancient philosophy of Aristotle and Plato.

3.3 Ethical Appeals in a Multicultural Secular Society

It is important to understand, in any argument, the terms that are being deployed so that the arguments can be clear and appropriately evaluated. There is a danger in using a term like secular or secularization when discussing and exploring moral pluralism in our contemporary world, because the term "secularization" can have a number of different specifications; it is therefore important to specify how the term is being used.[7] At times, terms like secularization have been made into slogans, as they are understood to represent a particular point of view that is anti-religious. Secularism is often understood as being hostile toward religion. However, that need not be the case.

Secularism has been understood in a number of ways. Indeed, it is a term that is polyvalent.

H. T. Engelhardt, for example, identifies seven different senses of secularity.[8] In contemporary societies, secularism is often interpreted as an overt hostility to religion, religious thought, or religious communities. Moreover, both secularists and religionists use this sense of the term as well.

However, for this work we can stipulate that the term secularism be used to refer to a social and political structure, like the United States, which is neutral toward the views of particular communities and religions. It is true that the term can and has been used in other ways, such as an assumed hostility to religious thought or sentiments. However, in the analysis undertaken in this book it is most helpful to use an interpretation that understands the "secular" as neutral in terms of religious sentiments and values.

In a secular society, which is neutral toward different communities and beliefs, there is the very real possibility of different moral views on social and ethical policy

---

[7] H. T. Engelhardt, Jr., *Bioethics and Secular Humanism: The Search for a Common Morality*, Trinity Press International (1991).

[8] H. T. Engelhardt, Jr. *After God: Morality and Bioethics in a Secular Age* (Yonkers, NY: St. Vladimir's Seminary Press, 2017), Also, refer to note 6.

issues. The phenomenon of moral pluralism is complex. If one thinks about morality as tied to a way of life, different communities in a secular society will have differing ways of life within that society.

Communities may not be extremely different. As has been argued, elsewhere such communities with different moral commitments can be moral acquaintances.[9] When people use the phrase moral pluralism, they could simply be identifying disagreement at the level of moral judgment, or they could be identifying much more significantly different views.

Understanding the secular context of contemporary society is important for understanding the context of organizational ethics. If one understands a secular society as one where different moral communities can live peacefully, we will have to find ways in which different communities can engage, and disagree, about moral issues. We need to develop a framework for secular societies that will allow peaceable argument. It is particularly important to understand how, in a secular ethnically diverse society, ethical issues can be addressed in public policy and law.

In popular culture "secularism" is often understood to be hostile toward religion. In principle, however, that need not be the case. Secularism is a term that can be used in a number of ways. Indeed, it is a term that is polyvalent. H. T. Engelhardt, for example, identifies seven different senses of secularity.[10] However, the term secular can be used to refer to a social and political structures, like the United States, that are neutral toward the views of particular communities and religions. In such a social context, there will be social space for different views on moral issues.

3.3.1 Secularization and Moral Pluralism

Secularism has been understood in a number of ways. Indeed, it is a term that is polyvalent. H. T. Engelhardt, for example, identifies seven different senses of secularity. In our contemporary society, secularism is often interpreted as an overt hostility to religion, religious thought, or religious communities. Moreover, both secularists and religionists use this sense of the term as well. However, for this work I want to stipulate that the term be used to refer to a social and political structure, like the United States, that is neutral toward the views of particular communities and religions. This is a legitimate use of the term and I think it is a sense of the term that best fits with the dreams and aspirations of the United States.

In a secular society that is neutral toward different communities and beliefs there is a very real possibility that there will be different moral views on social and ethical policy issues. The phenomenon of moral pluralism is complex. If one thinks about morality as tied to a way of life, then different communities will have differing ways

---

[9] Kevin Wm. Wildes, S.J., *Moral Acquaintances*: (Notre Dame, IN: University of Notre Dame Press, 2000).

[10] H,T, Engelhardt, *Bioethics and Secular Humanism*, see note 7.

of life. Communities and their moralities may not be extremely different. As I have argued, elsewhere such communities will be moral acquaintances. When people use the phrase moral pluralism, they could simply be identifying disagreement at the level of moral judgment, or they could be identifying much more significantly different views.

The secular context of society is important as it provides the context for organizational ethics in these societies. If one understands a secular society as one where different moral communities can live, peacefully, then we should be able to find ways in which different communities can engage, and disagree, about moral issues. A secular society will develop a framework that will allow peaceable argument and disagreement. This is particularly important for understanding how ethical issues can be addressed in public policy and law in secular societies. There is a danger in using terms like "secularization" and "moral pluralism" in our contemporary world as often times these terms have been made into slogans, as they are understood to represent a particular point of view. Again it may be important re restate the obvious which is that secularism is often understood as being hostile toward religion. However, that need not be the case.

There are different ways to characterize and define the Modern Age. However, for the purpose of this argument, we will focus on the Modern project, in the West, in terms of ethical thought. The evolution of ethical thought follows the evolution of secularization in the West. The Renaissance and the Wars of Religion in the West were important influences on the Modern project in ethics. The rediscovery of reason, apart from Faith and a religious context, was a central element in the Renaissance and the beginning of the Modern Age. The appeal to Reason opened up the possibility to think about political and moral authority as separate from religious authority and without the need to invoke any religious authority.

Over time, philosophers moved beyond reason alone, and some sought a foundation for ethics in human feelings and intuitions. In all, the shift away from divine revelation to reason, or feelings, or intuition, moved the focus of ethical thought to the human, rather than the Divine.

This focus on the human, outside of a particular religious authority or a religious tradition, was crucial at a time when religious authority was often at the center of controversies and wars. One can argue that the move to establish knowledge, which appealed to reason outside of religious authority, led to the beginnings of modern science as well as the full realization of the secular state, whose authority was grounded "in the world".

In this search we are led to the goal to establish a basis for ethics that did not appeal to God, religious authority, or custom and, at the same time, transcended local communal boundaries. The efforts to establish this kind of morality often turned to reason, intuition, sensibility, or feeling in one form or another. The hope was to find a basis for ethics that would be something that was common to human beings and could be known to them but which transcended communal boundaries. This shift led to a focus, in ethics, on philosophical ethics rather than theological ethics and an appeal to a common starting point; most notably reason or experience.

3.3.2 *Philosophical Appeals*

With the fragmentation of Western culture and the religious warfare which followed, the Western world had to look for ways to ground ethical thought, which transcended religious belief. So, in many ways the western world returned to its past and sought to ground ethical thought in reason. As I have explored extensively elsewhere, a variety of models has been developed to frame ethical analysis, and these models have been based on different aspects of moral decision-making.[11]

3.3.2.1 Consequentialism and Utilitarianism

A common and familiar way to think about ethical evaluation is to examine the consequences of an action. Consequentialism is a school of thought that was significantly developed by the Utilitarian thinkers as a basis for creating social policy and law.

The Classical Utilitarianism, as propounded by Bentham and Mill, was concerned with legal and social reform. If anything could be identified as the fundamental motivation behind the development of Classical Utilitarianism, it would be the desire to see useless, corrupt laws and social practices changed. Accomplishing this goal required a normative ethical theory employed as a critical tool. What is the truth about what makes an action or policy a morally good one, or morally right? However, developing the theory itself was also influenced by strong views about what was wrong in their society. The conviction that, for example, some laws are bad resulted in analysis of why they were bad. In addition, for Jeremy Bentham, what made them bad was their lack of utility, their tendency to lead to unhappiness and misery without any compensating happiness. If a law or an action does not do any good, then it is not any good.[12]

3.3.2.2 Deontological Approaches

The word deontology derives from the Greek words for duty and science (or study) of (logos). In contemporary moral philosophy, deontology is a kind of normative theory regarding which choices are morally required, forbidden, or permitted. In other words, deontology falls within the domain of moral theories that guide and assess our choices of what we ought to do (deontic theories), in contrast to those that guide and assess what kind of person we are, and should be as is done in virtue

[11] Kevin Wm. Wildes, S.J., *Moral Acquaintances*: (Notre Dame, IN: University of Notre Dame Press, 2000).

[12] Driver, Julia, "The History of Utilitarianism", The Stanford Encyclopedia of Philosophy (Winter 2014 Edition), Edward N. Zalta (ed.), https://plato.stanford.edu/archives/win2014/entries/utilitarianism-history

theories of ethics. In addition, within the domain of moral theories that assess our choices, deontologists—those who subscribe to deontological theories of morality—stand in opposition to consequentialists.

Deontological approaches such as provided by Kant (1785)[13] and Ross (1930)[14] are commonly characterized by applying usually strict moral rules or norms to concrete cases. Religious approaches, such as those of the Catholic Church, and non-religious deontological approaches, such as Kantian-oriented theories, are prime examples of applying moral rules. For example, the conservative position of the Catholic Church justifies that one should not abort fetuses, under any circumstances, including in cases of rape,[15] and forbids the use of condoms. Furthermore, the Catholic Church regularly defends its strict religious position in end-of-life cases to prolong human life as long as possible and not to practice euthanasia (or physician-assisted suicide) because human life is sacred and given as a gift from God. In this respect, religious approaches are necessarily faced with the objection of speciesism, if they claim that it is sufficient to be a member of the human species in order to be protected. Kantian-oriented approaches, instead, are not necessarily faced with this objection because—at least, in the original version—moral status is assigned according to "rationality" and not according to "membership of the human species". Other neo-Kantian deontological approaches, however, might emphasize "human dignity" and hence run into serious troubles with regard to the objection of speciesism as well. In other words, there is a fundamental disagreement inherent in the notion of human dignity—roughly, the idea that there is something special about human beings—and the ascription of moral status to non-human nature such as animals and plants.

Kantian-oriented deontological approaches (or Kantianism) generally adhere to the basic Kantian ideas of respect for persons and human dignity; both central ideas are rooted in the human being's capacity to act autonomously. Kantianism has been adopted in order to provide a justification for strict truth telling in medical contexts: for example, in cases of terminal cancer, bedside rationing, and medical experiments. This development can be seen as a counter- movement against previous malpractice. The former practice consisted in not telling the truth to the patient in order either not to cause additional harm or not to undermine the goals of the medical experiments (for example, the Tuskegee Syphilis Study). In the late 20th century, this changed by virtue of acknowledging the patient's right to be told the truth about his or her health condition. Likewise, this was the case regarding the patient's involvement in research studies— including research with placebos—in order to enable the patient to make adequate autonomous decisions (that is, individual informed consent).

[13] Immanuel Kant, *Critique of Practical Reason*, (New York: Classic Books, 2010).

[14] W. D. Ross, *The Rights and The Good*, (Oxford: Clarendon Press, 2002).

[15] John Noonan, *Contraception: A History of Its Treatment by the Catholic Theologians and Canonists* (Harvard University Press,1965).

The second formula of Kant's Categorical Imperative[16] has been successfully used in different medical contexts in order to avoid abuses. In particular, it is often used to avoid abuses in research experiments on human subjects. The sad examples of the Tuskegee Syphilis Study and the Human Radiation Experiments clearly show the dangers of researchers acting in a highly dubious and immoral way (see *The Belmont Report* 1979).[17] Additionally, deontological approaches have been used in the fields of animal ethics[18] and environmental ethics,[19] offering a thorough examination of the strengths and weaknesses of Kant's ethics concerning a vast range of important bioethical issues in contemporary applied ethics.

3.3.2.3 Contract Theory

Another approach to thinking about ethics in contemporary pluralistic societies is in terms of contract theory.[20] The method of using contracts argues that there is a contract between the larger society and the professions, in this case education and health care professionals. The key assumption underlying this method is that we can construct what the moral and ethical points and foundations are for such a contract. Then, in light of the contract and social agreement there are boundaries for the professional to work and expectations for society.

One problem with this approach is that it presupposes that we can identify what the moral content will look like. However, if we look at contemporary examples, we quickly discover that it is challenging to identify such moral content for the professions. In health care, the issues of abortion or physician-assisted suicide are good examples of moral controversies which exist not only in society but also within the health care professions. In education, current controversies involving what models of education constitute a "good" education or those involving the content of education make it clear we cannot assume, in our society, that professionals alone can construct a model. One has only to think of the different theories in science, and the controversies they cause, to see where problems with contract theory lie.

---

[16] ,---"Act in such a way that you treat humanity, whether in your own person or in the person of any other, never merely as a means to an end, but always at the same time as an end".

[17] The National Commission for the Protection of Human Subjects in Biomedical and Behavioral Research, *THE BELMONT REPORT: Ethical Principles and Guidelines for the Protection of Human Subjects of Research*, Office of Secretary of Health and Human Services, Washington, DC,, April 18, 1979.

[18] Tom Regan *The Case for Animal rights*, (Los Angeles: University of California Press, 1983).

[19] Paul W. Taylor, *Respect for Nature: A Theory of Environmental Ethics* (Princeton University Press, 1986).

[20] In bioethics probably the best example is Robert Veatch, *The Basics of Bioethics*, 3rd Edition, (New York: Routledge, 2016).

3.3.2.4 Virtue Theory

Alasdair MacIntyre argued for a very different approach to thinking about practical moral issues. Rather than focus on the outcomes, as Utilitarians do, or the rules of moral reason, as are found in Deontology, MacIntyre argued for a return to another method of ethical thought found in the ancient world; he argued for the need to return to thinking about virtues.[21] That is, simply put, rather than focus on rules or principles or weighing outcomes we should focus our thought on the character of moral agents and the virtues that we seek in such agents. If we focus on virtue and character, we need not focus on other elements like rules, obligations, and comparing or measuring outcomes.

3.3.2.5 Casuistry

The appeal to casuistry as a method of moral deliberation makes sense to many, particularly in the Anglo-American world. Case-based reasoning, or casuistry, is familiar in law and legal studies in Anglo-American law and in moral thought as well. The method is also rooted historically in Catholic moral theology and confessional practice. The method works by matching contemporary cases and problems with cases that have been studied and analyzed in the past and then using the past models of resolution to resolve the present cases and controversies.[22]

There are practical and conceptual challenges in using this methodology, however. First, there is the problem of developing an adequate description of a particular action that is necessary for the method to proceed. For example, while people may agree on a physical description of an action (e.g., Joe hit Sam) other parts of the description are equally important morally. Was the action premeditated and intentional? Was it accidental?

Beyond the questions surrounding the description of the action there are further challenges for this method of thinking, in a diverse, morally pluralistic society. How are we to know the categories of actions, which are morally problematic? Different moral traditions may have very different views about what is or is not appropriate or prohibited.

3.3.2.6 Summary Observations

In the face of religious, cultural, or other moral differences, we can view the search for a secular bioethics as a search for a secular or civil religion that might bind the sentiments of citizens who are at least nominally divided. It is a search to ground moral claims in reason without appealing to a religious foundation. These

[21] Alasdair MacIntyre, *After Virtue*, (Notre Dame, IN: University of Notre Dame Press, 1981).

[22] K. Wildes, S.J., "The Priesthood of Bioethics and the Return of Casuistry", *Journal of Medicine and Philosophy*, 18 (February 1993), 33–49; Albert R. Jonsen, Stephen Toulmin, *The Abuse of Casuistry: A History of Moral Reasoning*, (Berkeley: University of California Press, 1988).

aspirations have a consanguinity with the aspirations of the Stoics and natural law theorists, and with the aspirations that led to the modern philosophical or Enlightenment project. As the West entered the Modern Age, it was wrought by deep religious controversies and bloody wars. Just as individuals then hoped to discover a reason-based, content-full understanding of proper conduct and to develop a secular moral authority that could be acknowledged across confessional lines, so too, theorists now hope that secular bioethics can provide a content-full morality to guide public policy decisions and to yield a secular moral

authority. Because health care is a cooperative venture that potentially brings together an array of differing moral visions, it highlights the phenomenon of moral pluralism. Health care is delivered in a setting of complex institutions that brings together a diversity of health care professionals, engaged in ventures that are sponsored by both public and private resources and that fulfill a variety of different goals or visions. The men and women involved in the practice of health care often have conflicting understandings of the rights and obligations of professionals, patients, and society. These different interests and moral points of view form the background for the moral controversies of health care and bioethics in our secular pluralistic society. Bioethics has emerged as a discipline seeking to resolve such controversies in this secular, morally pluralistic setting.

It is important to remember the context in which health care organizations and educational organizations operate. First, in the United States and many countries, health care operates in a secular context. That is, as was noted before, a secular context is not tied to any particular religious point of view. Historically, the Western world has sought a grounding for ethics which was free of any particular religious foundation. This quest for a secular foundation for ethics can be seen in philosophy from the Stoics to the philosophies of the Enlightenment.

However, because health care is a cooperative venture that potentially brings together people with, potentially, an array of moral visions, it has highlighted the phenomenon of moral pluralism. Furthermore health care is delivered in a setting of complex institutions that often brings together a diversity of health care professionals, as well as patients, all engaged in ventures that are supported by both public and private resources and that fulfill a variety of different goals or visions. The men and women involved in the practice of health care often have conflicting understandings of the rights and obligations of professionals, patients, and society.

These different interests and moral points of view form the background for the moral controversies of health care and bioethics in our secular pluralistic society. Bioethics has emerged as a discipline seeking to resolve such controversies in this secular, morally pluralistic setting.

This model can work well and is a familiar way of thinking in the Anglo-American world. The challenge, for health care and education, as I have argued elsewhere is identifying the paradigm cases in a society that is diverse and multicultural. As noted elsewhere[23] each of these methods falls short in a society that is truly

[23] *Moral Acquaintances: Methodology in Bioethics*, (Notre Dame, IN: University of Notre Dame Press, 2000).

morally pluralistic, and even the choice of any model can itself be problematic. Consent of individual agents becomes a key to sorting out particular moral issues and reaching some form of resolution. A challenge now, in thinking about organizations, is how to identify that type of moral authority in the lives of organizations.

3.4 Ethical Challenges for Organizations in Education and Health Care in Postmodern Society

In a postmodern, secular society, health care and educational organizations face several broad challenges. First, there are challenges that are internal to these organizations. They face questions about how, in the society that is morally and culturally diverse, they can develop their own internal cultures to support their identities and missions and how this is accomplished. Second, they face challenges as to how to maintain their organizational identities and missions in a society that is morally and culturally diverse.

It is important to remember the context in which educational organizations, health care organizations, health care professionals, and patients operate. First, in the United States and many countries, health care operates in a secular context, as we have seen. Health care and education present some distinct challenges in the contemporary, secular world. One challenge is simply the ongoing progress in both education (knowledge) and Medicine, as both areas continue to open up new questions, possibilities, and problems for society. The ongoing development of medicine and knowledge often raises ethical issues that need to be addressed. Addressing these issues can be further complicated by another challenge, not unique to health care, which is that the cooperative enterprise often involves moral/ethical issues. Therefore, health care delivery often involves people with different moral views working together. Moreover, in many instances, they are working together on cases that have moral dimensions. Health care and education are different from most businesses where people with different moral views can work together with no problem. However, in health care many cases involve ethical questions in that many of even the most routine decisions have moral dimensions. Therefore, the questions of moral pluralism are important practical questions if we are to develop ways for people to work together.

One of the fundamental challenges for health care organizations and educational organizations in contemporary secular society is the reality of moral pluralism. This reality is a challenge for health care and medical practice for two broad reasons. First, while health care is essentially scientific and often perceived that way, it is threaded with social and moral values. This means that in contemporary secular society health care decisions are rarely simply "medical". They are often more than "applied science". One has only to think of contemporary moral controversies around the beginning of life and reproduction, or the moral controversies about death and end of life issues, to see examples of the moral challenges which health care faces. In a similar way one can examine the controversies that surround different standards for models of education, in terms of both content and method, to find other examples of the effects of moral pluralism, given that different models of morality can lead to different models of education.

However, the questions of moral pluralism are further complicated for health care and education, since both are often delivered through institutional and cooperative ventures (See Part III, particularly Chap. 11). This often involves more than a person going out and buying a service. Rather, the delivery of the service involves others, most notably physicians and health care professionals but also HCOs, including hospitals, clinics, and insurers. In a similar way, educational organizations may provide a variety of services in a number of different settings.

They obviously serve their own students. Nevertheless, they may also be involved with other educational centers and outreach programs.

However, determining the role of an organization, in ethical terms, can be difficult. In some situations, organizations are part of the context. However, in other situations, they are present as actors and agents. Decisions made by the organization will shape and affect the ethical decisions that are made in the clinic or the research arena, or the classroom. Organizational decisions shape the context for the care patients will receive or the education that will be offered to students. How might we think about the moral responsibility of organizations in health care and education? We use the term "organization" to cover the wide variety of health care organizations, such as hospitals and clinics, as well as research institutions and insurance plans. In a similar way educational organization can be traditional schools, colleges, universities, or professional programs in continuing education.

The purpose of an organization is a central factor in thinking through these ethical and policy issues for organizations. It can be argued that the purpose of an organization is the defining element that makes an organization different from an aggregate. Organizational purpose is crucial to evaluating the actions of organizations. Purpose defines the collective action of an organization. People organize themselves together in hopes of accomplishing some sort of task that either cannot be done by an individual alone or is, at least, very hard if not impossible for the individual to do. The purpose of an organization is also a key to how the organization structures itself and defines the roles that individuals play within the organization. In the world of organizations, purpose can be articulated in a number of ways, but it is often articulated in a mission statement. Such statements can be merely ornamental. They appear hanging in the hallway, opening a website, or appearing in a glossy annual report. However, an organization mission statement can be much more than ornamental, for they not only articulate the purpose of the organization but also help to establish the boundaries of the culture of an organization and its way of proceeding. They can help to define the internal culture and structure of the organization and its external relations.

There can be many factors which contribute to any moral dilemma. First there are the facts and realities of the situation. But value judgments enter into what gets counted as a fact of a situation and how it is described. The purposeful nature of the actions of an organization makes their actions different from other "circumstances" in which bioethical decisions are made. Often when we are making bioethical decisions there are elements that shape those decisions, and they are simply "just there." A patient has a particular disease. The options for the patient are A and B. Our choices are made in these circumstances. However, other elements are not as self-evident. For example, a patient's insurer may limit the range of treatment options for a patient, or it may be that an HCO has set certain boundaries regarding the procedures it will or will not perform. In an analogous way a student or student's parents may have expectations about what constitutes "education", and these expectations may be different from those of governing boards or an organization. The questions of organizational ethics are about those sorts of policy decisions and moral accountability. A simple example is to think about the different decisions that may be involved in a patient's treatment and how those decisions are made, depending on each patient in terms of one's temperament, family situation, and insurance. And, in considering treatment decisions it is worthwhile to be aware that treatment decisions often involve many agents aside from the patient and physician. In many treatment decisions the health care organization will be involved in their decisions about the menu of treatments offered, as will a patient's employer in the type of plan purchased for a patient.

For an organization "mission" is a term that is crucial; this subject is developed more carefully in Chaps. 5 and 6. For an organization the idea of "mission" incorporates the purpose of an organization (e.g., providing a clinical service or educational programs) and more. A mission statement often articulates not only the purpose of the organization, but it may also address what motivates the mission, include information on the population it serves, and delineate the manner by which it will pursue its goals. An organization is defined not only by its purpose (e.g., clinical services) but also by its moral commitments that should be reflected in its culture, its motivation, and the kinds of services it offers. It can be helpful to use the language of "mission" to bring together the purpose and the moral commitments that are central for an organization. Mission will also stand as a central element for understanding organizational integrity.[24]

Integrity is as crucial a concept when talking about assessing an organization's mission as it is when talking about individual human beings. However, integrity is often a concept that is used without clarity. The word is used very freely these days in many different occupations. In recent years, there have been many political campaigns, national and local, in which the integrity of the candidates has been an issue. In the wake of recent business and accounting scandals integrity has also become a watchword for many people in business. In the clergy scandals in the Roman Catholic Church, one often hears repeated concerns about the integrity of individuals and institutions. Those concerns are not only about individuals, but they are also about the integrity of the institution. In many cases the mistakes, or the sins, of a

[24] Kevin Wm. Wildes, S.J. "Institutional Integrity: Toleration, Approval, and Holy War or 'Always True to You in My Fashion'", *Journal of Medicine and Philosophy* 16 (April 1991), 211–220.

person may have a much broader effect as they are seen, by a larger society to represent the organization.

The language of integrity is often linked to discussions of trust, as integrity is an essential element to both building and maintaining trust. For organizational trust to exist it is important to know how an organization understands itself, and that self-understanding is essential to assessing an organization. Moreover, the value of integrity is often tied to the failures and breakdown of trust. One can argue that concerns about integrity have arisen as trust in social institutions, including government, religion, the professions, and business, has declined. With the decline in trust, it is not surprising that talk of the need for integrity has increased. The concern for integrity is a crucial link between what constitutes an organization and the common purpose that is the central element of any organization. Organizational integrity, particularly in health care and education, is a crucial element in organizational ethics.

It is important to understand integrity in order to understand why it is important for an organization to articulate its mission and how mission is integrated into the work of the organization. This book argues that, too often, when the word "integrity" is used, too much is assumed. Yet, because the word is so much a part of our moral vocabulary, people do not realize how much they are assuming about the word and its applications. Understanding the concept of integrity helps us to think about navigating the terrain of health care in a morally pluralistic society. The process of reflecting on integrity and the values to which an organization is committed sets the groundwork for understanding how compromise, cooperation, and toleration are possible. After examining the concept of integrity, we can think about how and why one might talk about integrity in health care. Once these issues are set out, a discussion about integrity in a secular, morally pluralistic society can begin. This context is very important for an organization. Both education and health care are moral enterprises and cooperative enterprises. People need to work together, as should organizations. Part of the discussion on integrity within organizations must involve an examination of the cooperation of organizations with other organizations in health care and education that may be using different moral frameworks.

3.5 Structural Biases in Organizations and Society

The second section of this book examines common ways to articulate and structure the identity of an organization and ways that an organization can help to maintain its identity over time. The third section of this book examines more carefully some of the different ways we often think about how organizations can have some type of formalized relationship with other organizations to accomplish their missions.

However, it is worth reminding the reader now that the structures of an organization, or even the structures of a secular society, are not "value-free".[25] That is, the structures or procedures of a society or organization will themselves reflect the values of those who created the organization and its structures. So, there is no reason to think that social enterprises and organizations like health care and education will be free of the values and biases of those who create them, simply because the organizations rely on "procedures". The way organizations are structured should reflect the moral vison, commitments, and values of the organization. And organizational structures can be impediments to ethical discourse, as the structures may limit the scope and degree to which an organization can engage with other organizations outside itself.

In the United States, for example, the American Civil War did not end racial bias. The period after the War, known as "Reconstruction", and the period that followed Reconstruction saw the development of a number of social practices that replaced chattel slavery with segregation under a policy of "separate but equal". The segregation included real estate and banking practices, such as "redlining" to segregate and control demographics in a town. There were also laws and legal practices that suppressed voting rights and enshrined positions such as "separate but equal"[26] into the structures of American life and how it was organized.[27] Such social practices and laws were a part of the way American society organized itself based on prejudice and assumptions about race.

These historical examples remind us of the need for a constant critical examination of structures and processes within an organization and those within a society, given that the structures themselves are not "value-free". Rather, the way an organization or society is organized and structured reflects moral assumptions and values of the individuals and society that established the structures for organizations. And, there are numerous examples of structures that enshrined certain values and moral commitments that can be seen as morally opprobrious. The "Jim Crow" laws and practices along with the juridical doctrine of "separate but equal" are examples of this problem in American history. The procedures themselves, in those cases, were morally objectionable. So, it is important that organizations and secular societies critically examine the structures that are in place, not only for their efficiency and effectiveness but also for the goals they are trying to accomplish and the moral values they embody.

A procedural basis for ethics and policy is not "value free". Rather, the appeal of a procedural ethic, for an organization or society, is that it should make the basic, minimal assumptions in terms of value commitments; furthermore, those values should be able to be articulated.

---

[25] Kevin Wm. Wildes, S.J., *Moral Acquaintances: Methodology in Bioethics*, (Notre Dame, IN: University of Notre Dame Press, 2000.

[26] *Plessy v. Ferguson*, 163 U.S. 537 (1896) was the U. S. Supreme Court decision which was foundational to the segregation practice of "separate but equal".

[27] American Academy of Family Physicians. Institutional Racism in the Health Care System https://www.aafp.org/about/policies/all/institutional-racism.html

3.6 Summary and Conclusions

In light of the moral failures of organizations, examined in Chap. 2, this chapter has sought to outline the grounds for applying ethical language to organizations in post-modern, secular societies and the different moral appeals that can be found in morally and culturally diverse secular societies. This chapter has examined a distinction between morality and ethics in a Secular Society and it has examined different ethical appeals in a multicultural secular society. From there the chapter moved on to examine organizational challenges in post-modern, secular, ethics and the way structural bias can be present in organizations and society.

We have examined in this chapter the basic foundations for ethical language in a postmodern, secular society, which is, in principle, open to diverse moral communities. This chapter has further examined the ethical foundations for secular societies, though legal and policy practices can interfere with free, moral exchanges and, in some circumstances, enshrine immoral practices, such as the "separate but equal" laws and policies and Jim Crow practices. As such we need to be mindful that organizations can participate in social sin as much as they can participate in accomplishing good.

In light of the reality that moral language is not only concerned with individual agents and the state, the quest to expand the scope of morality within society is turning this investigation toward organizations and how we can adapt and use ethical language and concepts to evaluate their actions.

Summary of the Main Points

1. Distinguish between morality, as a way of life, and ethics as systematic appeals which transcend cultures in a secular society
2. There are a variety of possible ethical appeals in a multicultural secular society
3. Multiculturalism and different ways of thinking about ethics presents challenges for organizations which have moral identities in a Post-Modern secular society
4. One needs to be aware of structural bias in organizations and society

Chapter 4
Organizations in Postmodern Society

The first two chapters of this book explored some of the fundamental challenges for ethical discourse in secular, postmodern societies and how such societies, because of their secular nature, are open to cultural and moral diversity, which can lead to Babel in moral discourse. In secular societies where there are different moral views, there will be fundamental questions about the *ethical* justification for the use of government power and authority to regulate ethical issues in such morally diverse, secular societies. Because of their secular character, such societies will be open, in principle, to moral pluralism, while moral pluralism in the society will affect organizations such as those in health care and education, which have moral dimensions in their work. The use of government authority, by itself, is simply the use of power and not a moral argument.

Other writers have addressed the challenges of navigating diverse ethical claims in secular societies by focusing on the role of government in regulating certain human behaviors, decisions, and actions. However, this book takes up the questions of how we should consider organizations, at least those in health care and education, as moral actors. The book has argued that organizations present an additional set of conceptual and ethical challenges, given that organizations are a different type of moral actor than either individual agents or the state. They are not individual moral agents, nor are organizations the government behaving as a moral actor with constitutionally limited moral authority. The ethical challenges faced by organizations are distinct from the questions that are normally asked about government regulation of certain behaviors of individual agents.

A key starting point in the argument of this book contends that organizations can be moral actors if they so choose (Chaps. 2 and 3). Organizations can be committed to a set of moral values that shape the moral character and the work of the organization. This means that if organizations choose to be committed to certain moral values, they must confront ethical challenges within the organization and the consciences of those who are members of the organization. At the same time

K. W. Wildes, S.J., *Organizational Ethics and Moral Integrity in Secular Societies*, Philosophical Studies in Contemporary Culture 29,
https://doi.org/10.1007/978-3-031-39097-5_4

organizations may face ethical challenges, depending on the identity and character of the organization, in how they deal with other organizations and society in general. An organization will face the challenge of maintaining its own identity, moral commitments, and mission while complying with government and social oversight and working with other organizations.

Organizations in health care and education, unlike many organizations, are likely to face particular moral challenges, in view that the work of these organizations carries some level of moral commitments. How we think about education and health care involves underlying assumptions about what it is to be a flourishing human person. While these assumptions are not always well articulated I will argue that organizations in health care and education should be understood as moral actors, because they operate from underlying assumptions about human flourishing. Organizations in education and health care are shaped by a commitment to moral values grounded in assumptions about what it is to be a flourishing human being. Educational organizations make assumptions, even if unarticulated, about what it is to be an educated person, while health care organizations make assumptions, also often unarticulated, about what it is to be a healthy human being. So, these types of organizations are guided by assumptions, perhaps unarticulated, about ideals of human life. Furthermore, organizations in health care and education make moral decisions, based on the values of the organization, and act, through policy, regarding individuals, other organizations, the government, and sometimes society as a whole. However, before we can analyze these organizations as moral agents, we need to develop a conceptual framework and moral language that will allow us to think and talk about the ethical nature of organizations in the areas of education and health care.

4.1 From the Personal to Organizations and the Bureaucratic

When we focus on organizations as moral actors, we need to think about how we might apply to organizations concepts that are often a common part of moral language. One of the first ethical concepts that must be rethought is the concept of responsibility. The reasons for rethinking the concept of responsibility in relationship to moral language is, to some extent, obvious. No matter the framework of moral analysis that is used, the concept of responsibility for choosing actions is essential to the ethical analysis and language. With the idea of responsibility in mind, one immediate problem for organizational actions is to consider how the concept of responsibility can be applied to an organizational agent. The risk is that without some way to talk about responsibility the category gets lost. If everyone is responsible then no one is responsible, and no one is accountable for the moral choices that are made, whether they are considered right or wrong.

4.1.1 A Theoretical Understanding of Bureaucratic Organizations

This shift in ethical discourse from the personal to the organizational and bureaucratic brings a number of distinct challenges to the analysis of ethics and organizations. One of the key challenges is to recast how we think about ethical "responsibility" in the decisions of organizations. The concept of responsibility, no matter how it is stipulated, is a central concept in the languages of ethics and morality. When a person is the actor or agent, the idea of responsibility is usually clear. While there may be circumstances that mitigate an assessment of responsibility, such as the freedom of the agent or the knowledge of the agent, we know how to focus our analysis. However, the category of responsibility becomes much less clear when we begin an analysis of organizations and organizational actions.

Often it is helpful to go back to basics to help maintain some clarity for questions like these. Often, when we think about ethical issues in the contemporary, secular world we often think about such issues in terms of individual agents or in terms of government actions regulating the actions of individual agents. When we think about ethics and organizations we need to expand our categories because organizations do not act like individual agents. They act through corporate decision-making and policies. It may be helpful to recall the discussion of bureaucracies in Chap. 2 to understand how organizations act through bureaucracy, rules, and policy.

The development of organizations as decision-makers and actors in education and health care, as well as in other parts of social life, shifts some of the most fundamental elements of moral discourse. One key element in that discourse is the language of responsibility, agency, and accountability for decision-making. When we examine many moral issues, we focus on the individuals involved, and the moral analysis often examines the decisions and actions of individuals, which is important to understanding categories of moral responsibility. What did a physician or educator do or say? What did the patient or student do? How did they respond?

However, when we shift to organizations the lines of moral analysis and decision-making are often less clear. There are often many actors involved in a decision or specific choice.

Therefore, it follows, in undertaking an ethical analysis of organizational choices and decisions, one needs to examine the whole decision tree, within an organization, to determine how a particular choice was made and who had responsibility for making the decision.

4.1.2 Moral Responsibility

If we address the moral quality of the choices made by organizations, we need to also find ways to speak of moral responsibility in organizations and bureaucratic structures. In secular, postmodern societies, the consent of moral agents plays a central, foundational role in the ethical language; implicit in consent is the idea of responsibility for an action or a choice. As we focus on organizations as moral agents it will be necessary to assess how we can talk about ethical responsibility in the choices of organizations. This means it will be necessary for every organization to be clear about the lines of authority and decision-making, within an organization, and which members of the organization can authorize and give consent for actions by the organization. This means the lines of authority within the structure of every organization, no matter its moral values, should be clear so that there is no uncertainty regarding who can authorize actions and resources and who bears responsibility for ethical choices.

In postmodern, secular ethics we work from a basic assumption of the importance of consent as a key to moral authorization for actions between moral agents. However, when we think about consent and organizations we need to expand and clarify our categories. In thinking about how consent can play a pivotal role in an organization, it becomes clear that, among other things, one of the keys to ethics in organizations is "role-clarity." This means employees must fully understand their roles within an organization and what they are authorized to do on behalf of the organization. Such clarity within an organization is essential for understanding who has the authority to give consent, on behalf of the organization, in any given agreement or arrangement. Achieving such clarity is often a challenge for organizations, given that they develop and grow, and with development and growth, roles within an organization develop and change. For *any* transaction, it is essential for an organization to be clear about who has the appropriate authority to authorize the transaction. It will be particularly important to be clear on whom has that authority for any type of moral commitment and who has responsibility for such commitments.

4.1.3 Trust

Normally, when we talk of trust in moral language the object of trust language is most often a person. "Because of past dealings with Mr. X, I trust that he will do the right thing." However, when dealing with organizations the level of trust, or distrust, is, most often, not personal. Rather it is based on one's experience of the organization or the experience of others whom we trust. So, I do not know this particular agent of the organization, but I trust them because of past experience(s) I have had with other agents of the organization, the thinking goes. The experience of trust is transferred from past experiences of the organization to the agent with whom I am dealing now. Because I trust the organization, I assume a level of trustworthiness in the agent with whom I am dealing.

4.1.4 Consent and Integrity

In postmodern, secular societies, others and I have argued that moral authority is grounded in the free and informed consent of the agents involved.[1] However, when one considers the actions of an organization one needs to reimagine how the categories of identity and consent can be understood, given that we are no longer examining an individual agent.

If one is to think about how an organization can function ethically in a morally diverse secular society, one needs to begin with the identity of the organization. What is the organization? What does it seek to do? Why does it try to do what it does? How does the organization understand itself and announce itself to the broader secular society?

At the same time, an organization should be clear about its moral commitments and the values it holds. In being clear about its identity, an organization also needs to be clear about the moral values that are part of its identity and guide it and its decisions about how it will fulfill its mission and maintain its identity. If an organization is to live with a sense of integrity, it needs to be mindful of its identity, values, and mission and live out these commitments.

Integrity, as I have argued elsewhere, is a second order moral virtue.[2] Integrity, by itself, is empty of content and, by itself, can be reduced to a notion of consistency. However, in a moral language the concept of integrity is built on the assumptions, values, and commitments that a person or organization has made. To make this procedural understanding of integrity concrete, think of a movie or story in which one of the central characters is a criminal. While we may morally disapprove of the criminal's moral values and illicit projects, we often admire the criminal for his or her tenacity and ingenuity in the pursuit of his or her goals and projects. In *The Godfather*, for example, one may admire the Don for his resourcefulness and persistence in his commitment to his goals and projects even though one may disapprove of his methods or the goals themselves. Morally we may abhor the values a person holds, while intellectually we admire the person for dedication to those values. It is this sense of integrity, as a second order virtue, on which we lean in exploring institutional identity.

Clarity about an organization's basic identity, purpose, and moral commitments is an essential foundation and necessary condition for the organization to function with integrity and for the organization to participate, ethically, in the broader, multicultural society. Such an environment is also very important for members of the organization and those who freely join the organization. People should be given the opportunity to have a clear understanding of what they are joining and the moral commitments of an organization when they become members. One of the most important elements for the allowance of moral exchanges in a morally pluralistic,

[1] H.T. Engelhardt, Jr., *The Foundations of Bioethics*, (New York, Oxford University Press, 1996).

[2] K, W. Wildes, S.J., "Institutional Integrity: Toleration, Approval, and Holy War or 'Always True to You in My Fashion'", *Journal of Medicine and Philosophy* 16 (April 1991), 211–220.

secular society is the agreement of moral agents. That agreement is best captured by a process of free and informed consent.

If one is to think about how an organization can function in a morally diverse, secular society, the identity and value commitments of an organization are an essential starting point for any discussion or moral evaluation of the organization and its activities. What is the organization? What does it seek to do? Why does it try to do what it does? What are the organization's values and ways of proceeding? At the same time, an organization also needs to be clear about its moral commitments and values. In being clear about its identity, an organization also needs to be clear about the moral values that guide it and its decisions about how it will fulfill its mission and maintain its identity.

Clarity about an organization's basic identity, purpose, and moral commitments are all essential for the organization's ability to maintain its own integrity and for its ability to participate, ethically, in the broader, multicultural society with integrity.

The concept of responsibility is an important element in Western moral language; developing clear understandings and clarity about roles, and responsibility, within an organization, is essential to organizational ethics and developing a concept of responsibility. One can seriously achieve a language of moral responsibility when speaking of organizations only if a clear understanding of roles and responsibilities exists; it is this clarity that enables one to assess how and where moral decisions are made. An organization needs to be clear, to itself and to the outside world, who has the authority to make decisions and who (which roles) bear responsibility for these decisions.

In any organization the governing board, whether it is called a Board of Directors or a Board of Trustees, should have the ultimate responsibility for an organization. The role of the governing board is more carefully developed in Chap. 7. However, part of a Board's responsibility is to make sure the organization's internal structure and bureaucracy are clear on the different roles and ethical responsibilities within the organization and how they are carried out.

There are several reasons for making sure this clarity of roles exists. One obvious reason is that it clarifies moral responsibility for the role itself. However, a secondary reason for clarity about roles is that such clarity helps to build an ethical culture within an organization: individuals are aware of the expectations of others within the same organization and can hold one another accountable for their work in the organization and the way they conduct their work.

Just as organizations need to have some process, or processes, for ongoing evaluation of employees, part of that evaluative process regarding role fulfillment should also include elements of morality and ethics. Such evaluations are essential to building a culture within an organization that is ethical in its dealings with other organizations and the world beyond the organization.

These processes are also essential to building an internal culture that values the ethical commitments of the organization.

Such clarity about roles and responsibilities is important not only so that the organization will function well but also as an essential element and foundational for the ethical analysis of an organization. Only with such clarity can there be a real, developed sense of moral responsibility and accountability within an organization. In sum, clarity in bureaucratic structures is a foundational building block for the moral culture of an organization. However, there are other structures within an organizational bureaucracy that can play a vital role in the moral cultural of an organization.

One other important office or function in an organization is a *compliance office*. Organizations of all kinds, particularly those in education and health care, are subject to an array of laws, rules, and regulations. Those who are external to the organization often monitor compliance with these rules and regulations. This work often involves governments, federal and local, and accrediting associations. It is often the case that the organization develops its own policies and rules, sometimes in light of external rules, which must be met. It can be very helpful for an organization armed with a wide array of rules and regulations to employ an officer who is responsible for making sure the organization is in full compliance.

Along the same lines, it is helpful if an organization has some sort of an independent office or officer, within the organization, that is authorized to conduct internal audits. Here we are arguing for the idea of an audit function that goes beyond simply monitoring the money and resources of an organization. Such an internal audit function would allow for the examination, internally, of how different offices operate within an organization. These different offices, from fundraising to student services, should be examined to make sure they are meeting the needs of the organization and to help assess how well the organization is serving its target audience. The audit function can be an internal or external function. The only caveat is that if internal, the office(r) must be strictly independent from the organization. Additionally, whether internal or external, the Audit office(r) must have a direct relationship with the organization's Board of Directors or Trustees as a way to assure its internal independence and freedom, which is necessary in order for it to carry out this critical function.

To operate as an ethical organization in a postmodern society means not only that an entity must be clear about its identity and moral values but also that it must create a culture, within the organization, in a manner that allows the organization to adhere to its own standards, as well as the legitimate demands of society. One of the points of having an audit function is to provide assurances that an organization is doing what it should be doing and is what it says it is. While the audit function is key to the ordinary operation of an organization, it is also important that an organization have some form of protection and process for members of the organization who may become "Whistle Blowers". Simply put a whistle blower is a person who exposes secretive information or activity, within a private or public organization, that is deemed illegal, unethical, or not correct.

Annual evaluations, throughout an organization, are not only a good business practice, but they can also be a good organizational mechanism for building an ethical organization and monitoring and supporting the ethical culture of the organization. In all of this, an excellent, common practice for organizations is to have a good department of Human Resources. Such an office should do the obvious, basic tasks needed to fill and create positions, but it can do so much more for the moral functioning of an organization. It can be sure that position descriptions are appropriate and well defined for each position. It can foster a culture of compliance and evaluation and ongoing education on the changing environment for health care and education. It can also look for patterns within an organization (*e.g.* an office with significant turnover) and help to build and support the desired culture of an organization.

The shift in ethical discourse from the personal to the organizational and bureaucratic is an expansion of the parameters of ethical discourse in the secular, postmodern society, which brings a number of distinct challenges to how we think about the ethics of organizations. One of the key challenges is how to recast how we think about "responsibility". The concept of responsibility, no matter how it is stipulated, is a central concept in the languages of ethics and morality. When a person is the actor or agent, the application of the idea of responsibility is usually clear. While there may be circumstances that mitigate an assessment of responsibility, such as the freedom of the agent or the knowledge of the agent, we usually know how to focus our analysis on the question of responsibility. However, the category of responsibility becomes much less clear when we begin an analysis of organizations and organizational actions.

Organizational actions are the actions of the organization and, in most cases, not the act of individual. But, how do we assign responsibility within an organization? We want to avoid the risk that if everyone is responsible, no one is responsible.

4.2 Role Clarification: Moral Responsibility in Organizations

The concept of responsibility is a key element in Western moral languages, and so developing clear understandings and clarity about roles, and responsibilities, within an organization is essential for moral language and organizational ethics. If we are going to talk about ethics and organizations, we need to be able to include some account of responsibility. Without an account of responsibility in an organization, one runs the risk that if something is seen as everyone's responsibility, it is no one's responsibility. The key to seriously achieving a language of moral responsibility in an organization is tied to a clear understanding of roles and responsibilities within the organization so that one can assess how, where, and why moral decisions are made and who has responsibility for making the decisions and for carrying them out. These functions are frequently separated within an organization, and yet, both are essential to a moral assessment. An organization needs to be clear, to itself and to the outside world, on whom has the authority to make decisions and who (which roles) bears responsibility for these decisions. Also, an excellent organization has in place a procedure for the assessment of decisions after they have been made, so that the organization can assess the decision's procedures and execution as well.

In any organization the organization's governing board (see Chap. 7) will have the ultimate responsibility for the organization or those to whom the Board delegates authority.

However, one responsibility of the Board will be to be sure that the internal structures of the organization are clear about roles and responsibilities within an organization.

One of the key responsibilities of the governing board is to be sure that roles, responsibilities, expectations, and accountability, within the organization, are clear.

Just as organizations should have some process, or processes, for the ongoing evaluation of employees, part of that evaluative process regarding role fulfillment should also include the appropriate elements of morality and ethics. Such evaluation is essential to building an ethical culture within an organization for its dealings with other organizations and the world beyond the organization. However, using such processes is also essential to building an internal culture that values the ethical commitments of the organization.

In an organization there should be clarity about internal roles, and responsibilities. Such clarity is important not only for the proper functioning of an organization but as an essential element and as foundational for an ethical analysis of an organization. Only with such clarity can a real, developed sense of moral responsibility and accountability exist within an organization. In sum, clarity in bureaucratic structures is a foundational building block of a moral culture.

Additionally, there are other structures that can be part of an organizational bureaucracy and play a vital role in its moral culture.

One important office or function within an organization is a *compliance office.*

Organizations of all kinds, particularly those in education and health care, are subject to an array of laws, rules, and regulations. Others who are external to the organization often monitor these rules and regulations. They often come from governments, federal and local, and accrediting associations. Then, it is often the case that the organization develop its own policies and rules, sometimes in light of external rules, which must be met. In response to this array of rules and regulations, it can be very helpful for an organization to have an officer who has the responsibility to be sure that the organization is complying with the wide array of rules and regulations.

To be an ethical organization in a postmodern society is to create a culture, in the organization in a manner that allows the organization to adhere to its own standards as well as the legitimate demands of society. One of the points of having an audit function is to assure people that an organization is doing what it should be doing and what it says it is. While the audit function is key to the ordinary operation of an organization, it will also be important that an organization have some form of protection and process for members of the organization who may become Whistle Blowers. Simply put a whistle blower is a person who exposes secretive information or activity that is deemed illegal, unethical, or not correct within a private or public organization.

Annual evaluations, throughout an organization, are not only a good business practice but they can also be a good organizational mechanism for building an ethical organization and monitoring the ethical culture of the organization. In all of this, an excellent, common practice for organizations is to have a good department of Human Resources. Such an office should do the obvious, basic tasks needed to fill and create positions but it can do so much more for the moral functioning of an organization. It can be sure that position descriptions are appropriate and well done. It can foster a culture of compliance and evaluation and ongoing education on the changing environment for health care and education. It can also look for patterns within an organization (e.g. an office with significant turn over) and attend to helping to build and support the desired culture of an organization.

It follows that there is no single theory for ethical responsibility within an organization. Each organization will vary in its history, mission, and structure. However, each organization will have the opportunity to assign ethical decision-making, and responsibility, throughout the structure of each particular organization.

4.3 Moral Responsibility and Role Clarification in Organizations

One of the key elements in any moral language is the idea of "responsibility," a concept that can be easily lost when examining the work of an organization. Organizational actions can be hard to evaluate ethically on the grounds that they are actions that require an organization and not only a particular person or group of persons. However, an ethical evaluation poses the risk that if everybody is responsible, no one is responsible. On the other hand, if an action requires the support of the whole organization, we are back to the problem of everyone being responsible. Since we know that the idea of responsibility is a key element of moral language, we need to push our analysis so that we can talk about the concept of moral responsibility in an organization.

If we are using moral language to speak of an ethical evaluation of an organization's actions, there needs to be some way to identify who bears moral responsibility for the actions or inactions of an organization. Just as we need to develop clarity about particular role and job expectations within an organization, so too an organization should develop clarity around responsibility for ethical actions in the organization. This is why role clarity within an organization on how decisions are made and who has responsibility for the decisions that are made is crucial. What is the internal process for making decisions? Who has the appropriate authority to make decisions for the organization? Who has responsibility to implement decisions, and how they are implemented? Finally, how are decisions assessed? The decision-making process will, to some extent, often be spread across different parts an organization. However, there ought to be clarity for how decisions are made and who has responsibility for making, implementing, and monitoring them. This also means that ethical responsibility will be spread, in many cases, across the organization; therefore, the organization will need to reimagine the notion of responsibility to mirror the structures of decision-making.

4.4 Consent and Integrity for Organizations

If one is to think about how an organization can function in a morally diverse society, one needs to begin with the identity of the organization. What is it? What does it seek to do? Why does it try to do what it does? At the same time, an organization also needs to be clear about its moral commitments and values. In being clear about its identity, an organization also needs to be clear about the moral values that guide it and its decisions about how it will fulfill its mission and maintain its identity.

Clarity about an organization's basic identity, purpose, and moral commitments are essential foundations and very important for the organization to participate, ethically, in the broader, multicultural society. One of the most important elements for moral exchanges in a morally pluralistic, secular society stems from the agreement of moral agents. That agreement is best captured by a process of free and informed consent where two agents clearly lay out the parameters for actions and decisions and who may, or may not, consent to the terms of the agreement.

One of the keys to the proper function of any organization is "role-clarity" where it is clear, within the organization, who has responsibility for what and who has the appropriate decision-making authority. Achieving such clarity is often a challenge for new organizations, as they emerge and grow. However, it can also be a challenge for older, longer term organizations where roles have incrementally grown and developed over the years. The concept of responsibility is a key element in Western moral language and so developing clear understandings and clarity about roles, and responsibility, within an organization, is essential to organizational ethics and developing a concept of responsibility. The only way one can seriously achieve a language of moral responsibility is if there exists a clear understanding of roles and responsibilities so that one can assess how and where moral decisions are made. An organization needs to be clear, to itself and the outside world, who has the authority to make decisions and who (which roles) bear responsibility for these decisions.

In any organization the governing board, whether it is call a Board of Directors or Trustees, should have the ultimate responsibility for an organization and the role of the governing board is more carefully developed in Chap. 7. However, part of the Board responsibility is to be sure that the organization's structure and bureaucracy is clear on the various roles and ethical responsibilities within the organization.

There are several reasons in making sure there is clarity in the roles people fill. One obvious reason is that it clarifies moral responsibility for the role itself. However, a secondary virtue is that it helps to build an ethical culture in an organization as people know the expectations of each other and can hold one another accountable for their work in the organization and the way they conduct their work.

Just as organizations need to have some process, or processes, for ongoing evaluation for employees, part of that evaluative process about role fulfillment should also include elements of morality and ethics. Such evaluation will be essential to building a culture within an organization which is ethical in its dealings with other organizations and the world beyond the organization.

However, using such processes is also essential to building an internal culture that values the ethical commitments of the organization.

In an organization there needs to be clarity in the roles within an organization. Such clarity is important not only so that the organization will function well but also such clarity is an essential element and foundational for an ethical analysis of an organization. Only with such clarity, can there be a real, developed sense of moral responsibility and accountability within an organization. Therefore, clarity in the bureaucratic structures is a foundational building block for a moral culture. However, there are other structures, which can be part of an organizational bureaucracy that can play a vital role in the moral cultural of an organization.

One important office or function in an organization is that of the compliance office.

Organizations of all kinds, particularly those in education and health care, are subject to an array of laws, rules, and regulations. Those who are external to the organization often monitor these rules and regulations. They are often employed by governments, federal and local, and accrediting associations. It is often the case that the organization develops its own policies and rules, sometimes in light of external rules, which must be met. In response to this array of rules and regulations, it can be very helpful for an organization to have an officer who has the responsibility to make sure the organization is complying with all the rules and regulations.

Along the same lines, it is helpful for an organization to have an independent office empowered to perform internal audits. Here, we are arguing for the idea of an audit function that goes beyond simply following the money and resources of an organization. A function for internal auditing is designed to examine, internally, how different offices operate within an organization. These different offices, from fundraising to student services, need to be examined to make sure they are meeting the needs of the organization; the internal auditing function helps to assess how well the organization serves the people it seeks to serve. The audit function can be internal or external. If internal, the office(r) must have clearly demarcated independence to perform the job. In addition, whether internal or external, the Audit function must have a direct relationship to the Board of Directors/Trustees to assure its internal independence and freedom in carrying out this critical function.

Annual evaluations, throughout an organization, are not only a good business practice, but they can also be a good organizational mechanism for building an ethical organization and monitoring and supporting the ethical culture of the organization. In all of this, an excellent, common practice for organizations is to have a good department of Human Resources. Such an office should do the obvious, basic tasks needed to fill and create positions, but it can do so much more for the moral functioning of an organization. It can be sure that position descriptions are appropriate and clearly developed and understandable within the organization. . It can foster a culture of compliance and evaluation and ongoing education on the changing environment for health care and education. It can also look for patterns within an organization (*e.g.* an office with significant turnover) and help to build and support the desired culture of an organization.

This shift in ethical discourse from the personal to the organizational and bureaucratic, brings a number of distinct challenges in the analysis of the ethics of organizations. One of the key challenges is to recast how we think about "responsibility" within the context of an organization. The concept of responsibility, no matter how it is stipulated, is a central concept in the languages of ethics and morality. When a person is the actor or agent, the idea of responsibility is usually clear. While there may be circumstances that mitigate an assessment of responsibility, such as the freedom of the agent or the knowledge of the agent, we know how to focus our analysis. However, the category of responsibility becomes much less clear when we begin an analysis of organizations and organizational actions.

Allen Buchanan identifies and discusses six features of bureaucratic organizations.

Following Buchanan's analysis, bureaucratic organizations are structured in a hierarchy. That is there is a clear structure of organizational authority in a bureaucracy. Second, he argues that there is a complex division of labor with distinct roles in a bureaucratic structure. Third, there are those who are in positions within the bureaucracy that are usually identified as professional mangers or administrators. Fourth, what the organization produces is through the cooperation of a number of groups. Fifth, the day-to-day operation of the organization relies on established rules and policies.

The development of organizations as decision-makers and actors in education and health care, as well as in other parts of social life, shifts some of the most fundamental elements of moral discourse. One key element in that discourse is the language of responsibility and accountability for decision-making. When we examine many moral issues, we focus on the individuals involved, and the moral analysis often examines the decisions and actions of individuals, which is important to understanding categories of moral responsibility. What did a physician or educator do or say? What did the patient or student do? How did they respond?

However, when we shift to organizations the line or moral analysis and decision-making are often less clear. There are often many actors involved in a decision or specific choice.

Therefore, it follows, in undertaking an ethical analysis of organizational choices and decisions one needs to examine the entire decision tree, within an organization, to determine how a particular choice was made and who had responsibility for the decision.

If one is to think about how an organization can function in a morally diverse society, one needs to begin with the identity of the organization. What is it? What does it seek to do? Why does it try to do what it does? At the same time, an organization also needs to be clear about its moral commitments and values. In being clear about its identity, an organization also needs to be clear about the moral values that guide it and its decisions about how it will fulfill its mission and maintain its identity.

Clarity about an organization's basic identity, purpose, and moral commitments are essential foundations for the organization to participate, ethically, in the broader, multicultural society. These foundations shape the organization, ethically, both internally and externally in the wider, secular society. One of the most important elements for moral exchanges in a morally pluralistic, secular society involves the consent and agreement of moral agents. That agreement is best captured by a process of free and informed consent.

One of the keys to organizational leadership is "role-clarity". Achieving such clarity is often a challenge for new organizations, as they emerge and grow. However, it can also be a challenge for older, longer-term organizations where roles have incrementally grown and developed over the years. The concept of responsibility is a key element in Western moral language and so developing clear understandings and clarity about roles and responsibilities, within an organization, is essential to organizational ethics and developing a concept of responsibility. The only way one can seriously achieve a language of moral responsibility is if there exists a clear understanding of roles and responsibilities so that one can assess how and where moral decisions are made. An organization needs to be clear, to itself and the outside world, who has the authority to make decisions and who (which roles) bear responsibility for these decisions.

In any organization the governing board of the organization, whether it is called a Board of Directors or Trustees, should have the ultimate responsibility; the role of the governing board is more carefully developed in Chap. 7. However, part of the Board's responsibility is to ensure the clarity of the various roles and ethical responsibilities within the organization's structure and bureaucracy.

There are several reasons for making sure there is clarity in the roles people fill in an organization. One obvious reason is that it clarifies moral responsibility for the role itself.

However, a secondary virtue is that it helps to build an ethical culture in an organization: workers know the expectations of each other and can hold one another accountable, not only for their work in the organization but also the way in which they conduct their work.

Just as organizations need to have some process, or processes, for the ongoing evaluation of employees, part of that evaluative process regarding role fulfillment should also include elements of morality and ethics. Such evaluation is essential to building a culture within an organization that leads to ethical dealings with other organizations and the world beyond the organization. However, using such processes is also essential to building an internal culture that values the ethical commitments of the organization.

In an organization there needs to be clarity in the roles within an organization. Such clarity is important not only so that the organization will function well but also such clarity is an essential element and foundational for an ethical analysis of an organization. Only with such clarity, can there be a real, developed sense of moral responsibility and accountability within an organization. Therefore, clarity in the bureaucratic structures is a foundational building block for a moral culture. However, there are other structures, which can be part of an organizational bureaucracy that can play a vital role in the moral cultural of an organization.

One important office or function in an organization is that of the compliance office.

Organizations of all kinds, particularly those in education and health care, are subject to an array of laws, rules, and regulations. Others who are external to the organization often monitor these rules and regulations. They often come from governments, federal and local, and accrediting associations. Then, it is often the case that the organization develop its own policies and rules, sometimes in light of external rules, which must be met. In response to this array of rules and regulations, it can be very helpful for an organization to have an officer who has the responsibility to be sure that the organization is complying with the wide array of rules and regulations.

Along the same lines, it is helpful for an organization to have some independent office for internal audits. The function for internal auditing would be an audit function which examines, internally, how different offices within an organization function. These different offices, from fund raising to student services, need to be examined to be sure that they are meeting the need of the organization and it helps to assess how well the organization serves the people it seeks to serve. The audit function can be a function done internally or externally. The only caveat is that if done internally, the office (r) needs to have clear independence. In addition, no matter how it is done, the Audit function needs to have a direct relationship to the Board of Directors or Trustees to assure its internal independence and freedom so it can carry out this critical function.

I. Developing the Language of Consent and Responsibility for Organizations

We know, from other explorations about ethics in postmodern, secular societies that consent between different moral agents plays an important and central role for establishing moral authority in a morally diverse society. As we move to think about organizations as moral agents in such societies, we need to think about how we can we understand key ethical concepts, like consent either for individual moral agents or by organizations as moral agents. In morally and culturally diverse societies, indeed any society, one should begin with the identity of the organization and its moral commitments no matter how thick or thin they might be. The identity of an organization is foundational for moral analysis of the organization and its actions. What is the organization? What does it seek to do? Why does an organization try to do what it does? All of these questions are important for understanding the moral commitments and goals of an organization. Most importantly, for ethical discourse, an organization also needs to be clear about the moral commitments and values, whatever they may be, which ground the organization as a moral actor. These elements of purpose, goals, and values are essential if one is to think about and evaluate an organization as a moral action.

This type of clarity about an organization's basic moral commitments is very important not only for the identity of the organization, but it is also important for those who participate in the life of an organization or those who collaborate with it. One of the most important elements to ground such exchanges of moral agents in such a secular society comes from the agreement of moral agents. That agreement is best captured by a process of free and informed consent. For an organization, it is important that the organization be clear in its own mission and identity as they will be foundational to its moral identity. These important elements for organizational ethics are further developed in Chap. 5.

As has been argued, in a secular, morally pluralistic society, there will often be many different moral views, each of which may have its own moral language. So, it will be a challenge to think about moral language when we examine the moral choices of an organization. However, in western societies the use of content-full moral language is built on the use of the concepts of responsibility and agency, which are essential to any moral language. Different content-full moral views will often advocate different ways to specify the concepts of agency and responsibility. Nonetheless, these concepts are used, and organizations must specify how they are being used. Different moral views will not only, potentially, hold different moral rules and values, but they may also hold different methods and ways of thinking about moral controversies and their resolution.

Most of the time, when we use moral language and think about ethics, we think, write, or speak about the actions and choices of individual persons in response to other people or in terms of their relationship to the government. In addition, when we engage in moral discourse, we often deploy the concept of responsivity as part of moral language. One of the important shifts that must take place when we speak of organizations as moral agents is how we can use the concepts of moral agency like choice and responsibility, which are so important to moral language. We need to recast the important concepts of moral language, such as freedom and choice, which are so important to our understanding of moral responsibility when we examine organizations.

At times, in some particular areas, we do reflect and think about the relationship of ethics and organizations such as governments or businesses, and when we do we move beyond the paradigm of individual actions. This shift is particularly evident in the entire area of business ethics, which provides a valuable example for thinking about organizations. However, for much of western history, understandably discussions and questions about ethics have been cast in terms of individual persons or individual actions. At times, particularly in recent history, we have explored the ethics of collective, social actions and policies. The Civil Rights movement and the Civil Rights legislation in the United States are examples of collective reflection and structural action to address organizational issues. And, it can be argued that the Civil Rights legislation, beginning in 1964, changed both the organization and ways of proceeding for the United States. The same may be said of the particular topics in the area of business ethics, in regard to the identities and the actions of organizations.

If we think through the shift laid out in this book, and agree that organizations in education and health care should be considered as moral actors, then we need to reconsider and redevelop some of the basic concepts that are deployed when we use moral language in terms of organizations. There are good reasons for this development of moral language. Organizations, particularly in education and health care, often allow people to accomplish far more than what an individual can or cannot accomplish on their own. Organizations are, most often, more than simply the sum of their parts. Organizations bring together resources, and, in so doing, they create opportunities for individuals that go beyond those to which they, as individuals by themselves, were limited.

This shift, from the personal to the organizational and bureaucratic, brings about a number of distinct challenges in thinking about ethical questions and the use of ethical language and concepts. One of the key challenges is to recast how we think about the concept of "responsibility", which is so important to any moral language. In most Western moral views, the concept of responsibility plays a central role in moral language. No matter the content of a moral worldview, when a person is the actor or agent, the idea of responsibility is usually clear.

However, the category of responsibility becomes much less clear when we speak of the agency of organizations.

Two key elements in moral discourse are the concepts of responsibility and accountability for moral decision-making. When we examine many moral issues, we focus on the individuals involved. What did a physician or educator do or say or do? What did the patient or student do? How did they respond? However, when we shift to organizations the line for responsibility is often less clear. There may not be a clear "actor" in an analysis. Moreover, if one looks to identify who has responsibility for an organization, to where should one look? The Board of Trustees or Directors? The bureaucracy? This is one reason why, in law and in ethics, we often speak of the organization as being the responsible agent and why it becomes very important, in the life of an organization that roles and responsibilities be clear. This is not only important for organizational structure and efficiency, but it is also important for ethical clarity. So, when we investigate organizations the notion of responsibility needs to be assigned, somewhere, within the organization.

4.5 The Ethical Importance of Information

As has been argued throughout this book, particularly in Chap. 3, free and informed consent are crucial practices for moral authority in a postmodern, secular society. In exploring organizations in health care and education it is important to expand out categories and think beyond limited physical notions of consent, in view that so much of what transpires in education and health care involves non-physical aspects of human life. Organizations in health care and education are both built around personal information involving patients and students. A person's information is not separate from these organizations but is a part of them. Consent from the individual is crucial to justify morally the sharing and use of information. So, it is morally important to think about how personal information is used, shared, and protected. The misuse of information – the use of information without a person's consent – is tantamount to assault.

This is a morally important consideration in organizations in industries such as health care and education, where information is often shared freely within the organization and with other organizations such as partners, reporting organizations, or insurers. So, just as organizations pay careful attention to how patients and students are treated, they equally must show care for the information about patients and students for whom organizations are fiduciaries.

4.6 Organizational "Sin"

In this exploration of ethics and organizations it is important to note that organizations should be held accountable for at least two types of moral failures in morally pluralistic, secular, postmodern societies. I refer to these organizational failures as organizational "sin".

Organizations operate in a social context. They are not individual moral agents, as has been argued, and nor are they the whole of society. This means that in secular, postmodern societies it is conceivable that a variety of similar organizations with differing moral visions can exist side-by-side, based on the fact that postmodern, secular societies can, in principle, be morally pluralistic. This is certainly true for organizations in education and health care, which we have been examining! In turn this means that an organization needs to be clear about what the organization is and what it offers the society surrounding it. This goes back to the mission and identity of an organization as foundational to the organization itself and its participation in secular society. The first type of organizational failing, for any organization, is the failure to be clear about what it is and the values it holds for those who are members of the organization, those who use its services, and the society around it. This is important for the internal functioning of the organization, but it is also important so that the organization can fulfill a basic necessary condition for secular societies – free and informed consent. While educational and health care organizations may be similar to others in the same fields, each organization nonetheless should articulate its distinct identity and its own moral commitments, both to itself and to those outside the organization. The organization needs to clearly express its identity and commitments to those who are members of the organization, those who use it services, and the society around it.

Each society, however, may have its own procedures for verifying that organizations are what they say they are, as well as ways for certifying organizations that operate in a certain society. In this way members of a society will be able to trust that organizations are what they say they are. With that in mind, it would seem that there are two ways by which we might categorize organizational "sin" or moral failure.

We can categorize the failings of organizations by labeling them as either internal or external failings. What does this categorization mean? As argued in Chap. 3, organizations that operate in secular, morally pluralistic societies must clearly communicate their identities to the larger, morally diverse society. To participate in the broader, secular society it is important that an organization express its identity clearly and be able to validate that it is what it says it is to others outside the organization, in the wider, secular society. Practices in society such as accreditation and truth in advertising, as investigated in Chaps. 7 and 8, are practices designed to validate the integrity of the organization for the broader secular society. These types of external practices, like accreditation and certification for organizations in health care and higher education, testify as to whether or not an organization is telling the truth about itself.

However, it should be clear that in postmodern, secular societies one clear moral failing of an organization is the failure not to tell the truth about itself and its moral commitments.

Now, there is no doubt that organizations which represent themselves as part of a particular community can make moral mistakes, in light of the commitments of the particular community with which they identify. This book draws on examples from the Roman Catholic community; certainly, one can think of examples of an educational or health care organization that self-identifies as Roman Catholic and engages in positive or negative actions that go against the tenets of the wider community. So, if an organization claims, as part of its identity, a relationship with a wider community, the wider community will have the burden to evaluate such claims. The appendices of this book provide some examples of criteria for membership in particular health care and educational associations.

However, in a secular, morally pluralistic society there is one moral failure that has to do with the integrity of any organization (See Chaps. 7 and 8); this moral failure is rooted in an organization's identity and moral commitments. The moral values of an organization, in postmodern societies, should be grounded in the organization's mission and identity. Given the moral pluralism of secular, postmodern societies this means that there can be, potentially, a range of moral values embodied in different organizations. So, while educational organizations may be largely similar, individually they may be committed to different moral values, resulting in a type of dissimilarity among educational organizations, even though they may seem alike.

In light of the moral pluralism in postmodern, secular societies there are several types of moral failures, or "sins," that can be articulated. The first kind of organizational sin is the failure of an organization to articulate its identity and the moral values to which it is committed. This failure affects the organization itself and its ability to operate ethically in a postmodern, secular society, essentially because there is no way for people to know the moral commitments of the organization.

A second type of failure is the failure of the organization to live out the values to which it claims to be committed. This is the moral failure of organizational hypocrisy. Examples of racism, in some organizations, can demonstrate this type of failure. For example, if an organization in health care or education announced that it was committed to the care or education of people, but subsequently excluded certain people on the basis of race alone, that would be an example of organizational hypocrisy. On the other hand, if an educational organization adopted a mission to educate students in a particular religious tradition, and announced that mission to the public, the organization would be free, ethically, to determine who attended the school and what the curriculum would be. The examination of an organization's identity, and its fidelity to its identity, is part of the examination that takes place in external accreditation and evaluation, as explored in Chap. 8. Organizational hypocrisy undercuts the ability of the organization to enter into agreements with individuals, other organizations, or society in general, since the honesty of the organization cannot be trusted.

With that in mind, there is one clear way in which an organization can fail in terms of its values. That is when an organization fails to live out its own identity and moral values. An example of an organizational failure or sin is when a health care or educational organization, whose identity and mission focus on serving the underserved, fails to serve that population while having the needed resources. Because they create, articulate, and monitor their identities, organizations have a great deal of freedom in setting out who they are and how they do and will operate. At the same time, they carry the obligation to monitor themselves and make sure they are living out their identities.

4.7 Conclusions

The goal of this chapter has been to move the investigation of organizational ethics forward by thinking about organizations as moral actors in postmodern, secular societies. In the first two chapters, we reviewed an analysis about the possible roles for organizations in moral dilemmas and began to explore how organizations can be thought of as moral agents. This was done mindful of the challenges for ethical analysis in the context of postmodern secular societies that are potentially morally pluralistic. The third chapter developed key concepts in moral language for organizations, like the concepts of moral integrity and consent. It explored the importance of both integrity and consent, while also exploring some possible ways those concepts might be used by and applied to organizations.

To continue this examination of organizations as moral actors, it is important that we enter into a more nuanced examination of the extent to which common moral language in secular, postmodern societies might be developed for the analysis of the moral characters and actions of organizations.

Summary of the Main Points

1. From the Personal to Organizations and the Bureaucratic
    (a) A Theoretical Understanding of Bureaucratic Organizations
    (b) Moral responsibility
    (c) Trust
    (d) Dealing with Vulnerable Populations
    (e) Structures for Ethics: Accountability
2. Organizations and Vulnerable Populations
3. Organizations and Social Sin
4. Consent and Integrity
5. Role Clarification: Moral Responsibility in Organization
6. The Ethical Importance of Information
7. Organizational "Sin"
8. Conclusions

Chapter 5
Recasting Moral Language for Organizations in Secular Societies

The first chapters of this book, in Section One, explored the terrain for ethical discussions and arguments generally in postmodern, secular societies. Most of the time these arguments have been about the role of government in regulating particular individual behavior, such as assisted suicide. The debate about the role of government, and the moral limits to government authority, is important for apprehending questions about understanding and judging the moral character of organizations.

These chapters also explored why postmodern, secular societies are particularly challenging, in an ethical sense, for organizations in health care and education. The challenge in this investigation seeks to expand the cast of characters in the discussion of ethics in a secular society. Normally, we look at individual agents and the limits on the moral authority of the state to regulate behavior. However, this investigation includes the role of organizations in the areas of health care and education. Organizations in education and health care are different types of moral actors than individual agents, which extend beyond the individual actor. Organizations in health care and education make decisions, through policies that are implemented, which direct the choices of particular actors. For example, employers and insurance companies set limit to treatment options and decisions while educational organizations limit the range of choices available to students. However, these organizations are different from the state. While there are public organizations in education and health, even those that are private organizations need to account for themselves, in some way, to public, governmental agencies. These organizations are sort of a 'middle-man' between the individual actor and the broader governing authority. In fact, government agencies often regulate these organizations. So, in society they fall somewhere between individual agents and the authority of the state.

No matter how they are conceived, organizations in health care and education will have at least some minimal level of ethical commitment in the work they do, given that their clients are, in some way, vulnerable human beings. To think about organizations as moral actors, in a morally diverse, secular society, means that we need to rethink moral language and concepts, like consent and responsibility, and

K. W. Wildes, S.J., *Organizational Ethics and Moral Integrity in Secular Societies*, Philosophical Studies in Contemporary Culture 29,
https://doi.org/10.1007/978-3-031-39097-5_5

think about how such language can be applied to organizations. This work is the focus of the current chapter.

There are two ways that one can outline the geography of moral pluralism for organizations in secular societies. The first way is to examine how an organization can address moral pluralism internally (see Chaps. 6 and 7). It will be important for an organization, with a particular moral identity, to examine how that identity is transmitted and nurtured by the organization. The second challenge involving the moral identity of an organization will be how an organization, with a particular moral identity, can operate in a diverse, morally pluralistic, secular society (see Part Three of this book).

We already know, from the examples in Chap. 2 as well as from daily news reports that organizations themselves can fail to act ethically. The possibility for moral failure by an organization can happen in any society at any time. But, the possibilities for the moral failure of organizations are increased in a contemporary, postmodern, secular society, given the nature of the moral diversity in such societies. In the midst of such cultural and moral diversity and fragmentation, it is easy for an organization to lose its way. The experiences of diversity and fragmentation challenge us to reimagine how we think about organizations, moral pluralism, and ethics in secular societies.

This book so far has reviewed important ideas about moral pluralism in secular, postmodern societies. Many ideas about moral pluralism have been explored, in depth, by authors such as H. T. Engelhardt, Jr.[1] Chapter 3 of the book further examined some of the key challenges posed by moral pluralism in a postmodern, secular society. In addition, it was argued that the questions and issues raised by Engelhardt and others about pluralistic secular societies are important issues not only in exploring the relationship of individual, agents and the regulatory authority of government and society through policy, and law, but in identifying questions about the roles and actions of organizations, as moral agents, in such morally diverse societies.

The reality of moral pluralism in secular societies, and the implications of that reality, is important if one is to understand and evaluate organizations, particularly in light of some of the earlier examples of moral failure by organizations in those societies. As we know, organizations play important roles, as moral actors, in the non-profit spheres of contemporary life of postmodern secular societies. It is important to think about how these societies can develop the moral language and concepts to support moral and ethical analysis, which includes organizations. In this chapter, we will begin to explore some of the key ethical and moral concepts and language that can be used to assess how organizations can function ethically and act in such societies. The book focuses generally on organizations, but it is particularly focused on organizations that are often characterized as "non-profit" or "charitable"

[1] H. T. Engelhardt, Jr., *After God: Morality and Bioethics in a Secular Age*, (Yonkers, NY: St. Vladimir's Seminary Press, 2017); *The Foundations of Bioethics*, (New York: Oxford University Press, 1996); *The Foundations of Christian Bioethics*, Swets & Zeitlinger Publishers, 2000.

organizations in health care and education. These non-profit and charitable organizations are often the beneficiaries of social trust in diverse, pluralistic, secular societies. And the assumption of social trust raises questions for any society as to how organizations should both merit and maintain such trust.

One of the foundations for trust in any organization might be captured in the slogan "truth in advertising". Is the organization what it says it is? Does the organization do what it promises to do? Another key element of trust in educational and health care organizations is tied to how the organization thinks about and handles the information of students, patients, and families that use the services of an organization. As argued later in this chapter, a person's information is part of who that person is; questions surrounding how information is conveyed, used, managed, and protected should be thought of in the ethical terms of consent, while the use of information, without consent, should be understood in terms of battery.

We know that organizations, both for-profit and not-for-profit, play important and central roles in contemporary secular societies and that organizations are central actors in the areas of education and health care in contemporary secular societies. The reality of organizations in contemporary, postmodern societies was investigated and identified in the first two chapters of this book. Now, the book is focusing on the roles that organizations play in the delivery of services in the areas of education and health care. Both areas are important to human societies for many reasons, as they deliver critical social goods and services that are significant to individuals and to society in general. However, attempts to understand and analyze organizational actions are complicated in that both education and health care have at least minimal moral commitments underlying and shaping the work they do. Those moral commitments present challenges both for organizations and secular society, making it necessary to think through how such organizations can maintain their moral identities and function in a morally pluralistic, postmodern society.

Thus far, this book has argued that organizations in education and health care are important structures in contemporary secular societies, as they are central for both the development and the delivery of critical social goods. The use of organizations as vehicles through which to deliver different forms of education and health care stands in contrast to how those goods and services were provided in western societies in past eras, when endeavors in health care and education were organized primarily at the local level and were often formed around family members and churches and other local community structures. Since the Industrial age began and extending through the Modern era, organizations have come to play important roles in both the development and distribution of goods and services in both health care and education. This shift toward the ever-increasing role of organizations is not limited to the areas of education and health care but has occurred throughout the economic sphere of life in the western world during the Modern Age as well. Organizations have been an important part of both economic and social life in the Modern Age, and they continue to play important roles in the postmodern age as well.

One can argue that this shift, away from the local and familial and toward organizations, is neither good nor bad in itself. The shift toward organizations simply reflects a reality of contemporary societies. An assessment of the value of such changes can only be made in light of how one views the goals of education and health care. Calling attention to this shift highlights, at this point, the reality of where we are in contemporary, secular societies. This shift raises, however, important questions for how we can think about moral issues and use moral language when questions and issues involve organizations.

In light of the historical and ongoing development of organizations in both health care and education, we need to think through how to navigate the ethical issues raised by moral pluralism in the delivery of services by these organizations, given that in such instances the organizations are moral agents. Organizations in education and health care are intermediate structures in society, which are related to, but distinct from, the structures of the family and the state. They fill a social space between the family and the state. Yet, the development of an organization often includes some sort of role for family involvement, along with oversight by various agencies or branches of government. Organizations, at least in health care and education, fill the "in-between" space between families and the local units of government. This also means that organizations in health care and education need to be responsive on both the local and other governmental and social levels.

Organizations, particularly in education and health care, often allow for the accomplishment of what individuals or smaller, familial models cannot deliver on their own. In the Modern and contemporary ages both education and health care have witnessed an extraordinary growth in knowledge, as well as in technology skills that allow us to utilize the growing knowledge base. We can actually do things with what we know! It is important to understand that important changes are not only about the growth of knowledge but also about our ability to disseminate and deploy that knowledge.

However, if we shift our ethical analysis to organizations we need to explore and examine the role of bureaucracy, as a conceptual and ontological category, if we are to understand how organizations can implement ethical accountability. The shift in analysis, toward organizations, means that we need to return to the questions of how to reimagine the use of some of the basic outlines and contents of moral language. Most notably, in exploring the uses of moral language, we need to think anew about how we use the language of responsibility in talking about organizations.

While this shift toward the role of organizations is a necessary condition to explain the problems and questions we are exploring, this shift alone does not fully explain the problems and challenges we face in health care and education in contemporary secular societies. By itself, the shift toward organizations is not a sufficient explanation. We need to identify, explore, and understand a second shift in society but in the context of organization ethics as explored earlier in Chap. 3: the challenge of multiculturalism and, with it, the reality of moral pluralism in moral ethical discourse. Organizations, no matter their identities, require that people work together. In education and health care, we often find people with different moral views working together on projects that reflect a moral vision.

5.1 Organizations and Moral Pluralism in Secular Societies

After examining the secularization of postmodern society in Chap. 3, it is easier to understand why western secular societies, in particular, have become more culturally and morally pluralistic, while society as a whole has become more fragmented in its moral views. Today, these societies frequently celebrate cultural diversity. However, we need to remember that because morality is rooted in culture, multiple moralities will often exist in secular societies that celebrate cultural diversity. Moral diversity can be not only about the particulars in content- full moral views, but such diversity is also often about even the methods by which we think about morality.[2] In light of this diversity in ethical analysis, I have argued elsewhere, there is no "view from nowhere."[3] Multiculturalism, so often celebrated in contemporary secular societies, leads to a variety of ways to identify, analyze, and evaluate ethical dilemmas. In most cases, generally, the resolution of moral dilemmas can be found through the consent and agreement of those involved. Of course, when one of the parties involved is a government agency or organization, one has to evaluate whether the use of the law and regulation, as a form of force, affects the ability to consent or compromises it. The focus on consent, however, raises important questions for organizations and their actions in postmodern, secular societies, in view that organizations act on behalf of their members.

The development of the role of organizations in education and health care, coupled with the moral and cultural pluralism of postmodern secular societies, creates challenges in these societies regarding how to evaluate and regulate these organizations morally. In morally pluralistic societies, questions often center on how to address moral pluralism within an organization and how organizations, with moral identities, can interact in and with a morally pluralistic society and its organizations. Later, this book will explore some of the important organizational structures that can be used to support the identity of an organization and help it live out its moral identity. However, before moving to those significant areas it is important in this chapter to emphasize the conceptual and linguistic issues presented by moral pluralism in a secular society and to clarify key concepts in moral language, such as integrity and responsibility, so that they may be adapted and used in the analysis of organizations in a postmodern society.

5.2 Recasting the Language of Consent and Responsibility

In secular, postmodern societies, there are key elements that are necessary to construct a grammar for ethics. The key element, in postmodern, secular societies is the procedure of free and informed consent between moral agents. The practice of free

[2] See note 1.

[3] Thomas Nagel, *The View From Nowhere*, (New York: Oxford University Press, 1986).

and informed consent is foundational to an ethical assessment in postmodern, secular societies, which can be morally diverse. In thinking through the conceptual structure for organizational ethics in postmodern, secular societies it will be important to translate the practice of free and informed consent to organizations. If we can accomplish this task, we can lay the groundwork for how organizations interact, morally, with other organizations and with individual agents.

The first element that needs to be reimagined is the element of consent and how it can be understood for interactions with and by organizations. In reimagining the notion of consent, and how it can be deployed with organizations, we can also begin to develop the framework that will allow us to understand how the concept of responsibility can be utilized for organizations.

If one goes back to understanding the moral grammar of secular ethics one finds that consent plays the crucial role in ethical decisions in secular societies.[4] The challenge with organizations will be in determining and identifying who is the appropriate person *in authority* to make decisions. This, of course, is a determination that will need to be made by each organization. However, it should be clear, within an organization, who has the proper authority to make the appropriate decisions.

Two of the key components of moral discourse are the components of agency and responsibility. These components are more difficult to analyze when one looks at the actions and policies of organizations, as we need to be clear about whom is invested with the appropriate authority to make decisions and who has responsibility for implementing decisions. In every case assigning these roles and responsibilities will depend on the organization itself in light of its distinct culture and history.

5.3 Recasting the Concepts of Consent and Integrity for Organizations

If one starts with the importance of consent, as a key hermeneutic for understanding post- modern, secular ethics, then it becomes important, in organizational ethics and actions, that the organization be clear about who in the organization is in the proper role of authority to make decisions for the organization. The important piece to remember is that consent still plays a central role in assessing the ethical actions of an organization. However, what needs to be very clear in order for an organization to act, or not act, is identifying who is the appropriate person or persons in authority to make decisions.

As I have argued elsewhere, integrity is a second order virtue that needs the first order commitments of the individual, or the organization, to measure whether the

[4] H. Tristram Engelhardt, Jr. and Kevin Wm. Wildes, "In The Beginning: The Emergence of Secular Bioethics", in *Advances in Bioethics: Bioethics for Medical Education*, eds. R. Edwards and E.E. Bittar, (Stamford, CT: JAI Press, 1995.

agent is acting with integrity.[5] It follows then that the first step will be for an organization to articulate its values, goals, and objectives both for the organization itself and for the wider, diverse, secular society. It is only in light of these articulated goals and values that one can assess the integrity of an organization. As I have argued elsewhere, one may not approve of the values of an organization, but one can still assess whether or not the organization is living with integrity. One may think, for example, of an organization like the Ku Klux Klan, where a person can disapprove of the values of the organization and indeed the organization itself and still conclude that the organization is living with integrity, given its values.

What is important to remember is that the concept of integrity, by itself, is an empty virtue. It relies on the other, content-full virtues to which an agent is committed to give it meaning. So, for example, one may have integrity as a soldier, because a person lives out the values and virtues of a soldier. Or, one might have the integrity of a public servant, because a person lives out the virtues esteemed of the public leader. The concept of integrity is empty by itself and needs to be tied to the topic or role that is in question. The same line of thought can be applied to the use of the term integrity when it is applied to an organization. Our ability to assess the integrity of the organization will depend on the organization's values and commitments.

The key goals here are, first, for an organization to be clear about its own values and moral commitments. Second, the organization must be clear in communicating its values to those who join the organization. Finally, it must communicate its values to those outside the organization (particularly other organizations with which it might enter into relationships).

5.4 Responsibility and Role Clarification

One of the key challenges, when talking about ethics and organizations, is the question of how to make determinations about responsibility when an organization takes action. We know that, in addition to consent, part of moral language is agency for particular actions or decisions. This question about decision-making, and moral agency, is more complicated for organizations. How do we determine who makes the decisions, for taking action, on behalf of an organization?

One can argue that there is no "platonic form" for organizational decision-making.

Rather, each organization should make its own determinations, given the identity and history of the organization with regard to the procedures for how decisions are made. And, decision- making processes should be consistent with the history, mission, vision, and culture of the organization. Also, the decision-making processes should be known within the organization.

[5] Kevin Wm. Wildes, S.J., "Institutional Integrity: Toleration, Approval, and Holy War or 'Always True to You in My Fashion'", *Journal of Medicine and Philosophy* 16 (April 1991), 211-220.

And, we know in the practical order of events, that agency, and with it responsibility, can be easily lost when we examine the actions of organizations. In one sense, if everyone is responsible, then no one is responsible.

So, managerial ideas about role clarification should take on an ethical dimension as well when examining how we can talk about moral responsibility within organizations. The idea of having an organizational structure that is clear on the roles of individuals is important as part of having a good, efficient organization. But it is also important in terms of determining responsibility for decision-making, which, in turn, can be part of the ethical evaluation of an organization and how it operates.

5.5 The Ethical Importance of Information

In exploring the actions of organizations in health care and education it is important to think about all of the facets of what transpires in education and health care. As this book has pointed out, normally when we think about the notion of "consent", we do so in terms of the physical touching of someone, and this notion certainly applies in education and health care organizations. However, the concept of consent, which is crucial to ethics in morally diverse, secular societies, involves more than simply acts of physical contact. We need to move beyond a limited understanding of consent in both education and health care. Both of these areas involve a broader understanding of the person. While some aspects of the human person are physical, many aspects of the person, particularly those involved in education and health care, involve non-physical aspects of human life, particularly in the areas and ideas of personal or shared information, which are so much a part of education and health care. Both health care and educational organizations have access to and utilize personal information about patients and students.

Because of the importance of personal information, in education and health care, it is worthwhile to utilize a broader notion of property and rights, one drawn from Hegel,[6] to think about personal information. A person's information is not separate from the individual, especially in health care and education: in those areas, information that is personal is part of the person. This intimate relationship of personal information with the patient or student means that we need to think about how personal information is used, shared, and protected and the role of a person's consent in using personal information. The misuse of information, that is the use of information without a person's consent, is tantamount to assault or theft.

This view of information is a morally important consideration for organizations and particularly important, morally, for organizations in health care and education, where information is often shared freely within an organization and with other organizations, such as partners, reporting organizations, or insurers. So, just as

[6] *Hegel's Philosophy of Right*, Introduction, Trans. T.M. Knox, (Oxford University Press, 1967), 14–34.

organizations have moral obligations to pay careful attention to how patients and students are treated, organizations must equally demonstrate care for how information about patients and students is handled. The organizations have a fiduciary role to play in regard to a patient or student's information.

5.6 Conclusions

The goal of this chapter has been to move the conversation about organizational ethics forward. In the first two chapters, we reviewed the roles of organizations in moral dilemmas in postmodern, secular societies and began to think about organizations as moral agents. In the third chapter we examined the challenges for ethical analysis and moral language for organizations in secular, postmodern societies that are morally pluralistic. These key moral concepts, like integrity and consent, have been explored so that we might think about how those concepts can be used and applied to organizations. This exploration of moral language for organizations, hopefully, has cleared the ground so that we might move forward in this exploration of organizational ethics. The next chapter continues to explore how we might think about how moral language can be used in the bureaucratic structures of organizations. With the language and concepts to discuss and analyze the internal moral values of an organization, we can move on to think about how organizations, with moral identities, can participate in secular, pluralistic societies.

The first part of this book, Chaps. 2 through 5, have examined the different ways we can think about organizations in secular, postmodern societies with morally diverse cultures. In light of what has been done up until this point we now need to examine, in the next part of this exploration, how organizations can both develop and sustain their moral identities and cultures as they operate in a secular, postmodern society.

Summary of the Main Points

1. Organizations and Moral Pluralism in Secular Societies
2. Recasting the Language of Consent and Responsibility
3. Recasting the Concepts of Consent and Integrity for Organizations
4. Responsibility and Role Clarification
5. The Ethical Importance of Information

Part II
Internal Structures and Strategies for Organizational Integrity

Chapter 6
Organizational Integrity: Founded in Organizational Identity

This book has argued so far that secular, organizational ethics needs to be understood within the context of a postmodern, secular society. Such a society, because of its secular nature, is potentially a society that is culturally diverse and morally pluralistic. The diversity of moral thought and the reality of moral pluralism means that in postmodern secular societies the only common moral justifications are those which are grounded in the free, informed consent of moral agents.[1] Within the social and epistemological context of moral and cultural pluralism in postmodern society, this book has also begun to explore the roles organizations play, *as moral agents*, in secular societies, particularly in the areas of education and health care.[2] And we need to explore how we can think of organizations, as moral agents, in morally diverse, secular societies.

While many ethical issues in the postmodern world can be addressed through the free and informed consent of individual agents, there are other ethical issues in these societies that can only be viewed, adequately, through the lenses of organizations and organizational decision- making. Decisions are made by organizations in terms of policies and actions that direct many of the decisions made by individual agents. In this way, organizations can be moral agents.

The first part of this book argued that many of the ethical issues in health care and education can only be completely understood, as ethical issues, if we include organizations as moral actors. Many issues, whether they are faced in the clinic or the classroom, cannot be completely understood if one examines only individual agents involved, such as students, teachers, patients, and physicians. While these actors are important a more complete ethical analysis needs to include the role of organizations, given that they have made decisions, carried out in policy, which affect the interactions of faculty and students or physicians and patients.

---

[1] See Chap. 3 of this book.

[2] See Chaps. 4 and 5 of this book.

K. W. Wildes, S.J., *Organizational Ethics and Moral Integrity in Secular Societies*, Philosophical Studies in Contemporary Culture 29,
https://doi.org/10.1007/978-3-031-39097-5_6

What takes place in the classroom not only involves the teacher and the student but also the school, as well as a myriad of outside organizations that influence the curriculum, educational goals, and the classroom.

6.1 The Moral Nature of HCOs and Educational Organizations

The practices of organizations in both education and health care are complex in a number of ways. Many of the practices in diverse, secular societies often assume and use a "market model", not only in commercial exchanges but involving other areas in the life of a society, like health care and education. However, in our policy rhetoric about education and health care we often forget that, in very important ways, the operations of health care and education do not always fit well within an ideal market model. Patients, students, and families cannot always be regarded as fully informed consumers and decision makers, which, ethically, is such an important part of the market model in postmodern societies. Patients and students, as well as their parents, certainly should be important to the decision-making process, but to be a part of this process, they need to be informed. However, patients and students and their respective families may be limited, by illness or lack of experience, in their understanding of what they are engaging in. They may be disadvantaged and not fully informed consumers. Also, they may be disadvantaged by sickness, illness, or ignorance. In addition, organizations in education and health care can vary a great deal in the choices they offer patients or students. Health care and educational organizations are not cookbooks, where one simply applies the recipes. Just as there are different cookbooks for different cuisines or styles of cooking, there are different models and ideals of what it is to be healthy or to live with illness, or what it is to be educated. In addition, there are different models for what it is to be an educated person; and, different schools are often not simply different places, but they hold different models of what an educated person is. These organizations are more than vehicles for simply passing on knowledge or applying rules for healing. Such processes often involve complex scientific data, or complex technology in the diagnostic process and in the delivery of care, while, of course, both education and health care are fields that require assessment and judgment. However, organizations in these industries are also complex, because the practice of health care and education are not exclusively scientific. Medicine is not simply applied biology and chemistry, nor is education simply learning an assemblage of facts. Health care and educational practices are scientific, but they also come with moral values and commitments. In an analysis of the ways in which people can be educated, our choice of a model of an "educated" person is imbued with moral values and commitments. An ideal of what it is to be educated includes, at least implicitly, assumptions about the values and purpose of education. Some ideal, often unarticulated, underlies the model of what it is to be an educated person. In health care, determining what is "appropriate" care is often a matter that involves scientific knowledge and judgment, including moral judgment as well. The nature and context of health care and education make the questions of moral integrity vital. Both education and health care encompass intellectual challenges, in that these are areas where there is a true blending of scientific data with moral values. Much of medical knowledge rests on well-constructed scientific understandings of the world.

One of the challenges for health care and education policy in diverse, secular societies is that both health care and education are produced, developed, and delivered in a social terrain that is public and morally pluralistic. The public dimension of health care and education in a morally diverse society can be difficult to negotiate, given that there are many competing senses of the moral good and varying specifications of health and disease. The lack of a common, coherent, content-full, and shared view of the good has led fields like bioethics to reflect on issues of pluralism, communal values, individual values, and public order. The pluralism that exists in accounts of the good life, and theoretical accounts of the moral life, may be described in a variety of ways. Nonetheless, no matter how described, they present challenges for the development of public policy.

In other work, thinkers like Engelhardt, Jr., have developed a set of views about the underlying issues of moral pluralism in health care that can also be applied to education. It can be argued that moral pluralism in diverse, secular societies reflects much deeper questions about the relationship between moral epistemology and methodology. There are different ways to interpret the pluralism and its implications. I have argued that, in a secular society, it is possible to think of a secular society as a meeting of moral acquaintances. This analysis of moral pluralism and secular society can be extended to thinking of the roles of health care organizations and educational organizations.

Both health care and educational organizations make some commitments to some set of ethical values, which are often in play in diverse, secular societies. We have already explored the possible diversity of moral pluralism in secular societies. In light of the reality of such diversity, it is important for organizations in these two areas to articulate their purposes and identities.

Such an articulation of values and identity is a necessary condition if there is to be ethical dialogue. Mission is a statement of the purpose of an organization, and it has both internal and external impact in health care and education. Mission integrity is concerned with the internal life of an organization and with how the organization comports itself in the public arena. Integrity should form a backdrop for decision-making by the organization, and it should play a role in terms of how the organization presents itself to the public. These organizations fall into a middle ground between the two levels of public and communal discourse, for while their heritages and identities are tied to particular visions of human life, they are also "public". They are open to use by the general population, and they are subject to the laws and rules governing health care and educational organizations. In an age of moral pluralism, with conflicting demands and needs of patients, health care professionals, laws, and funding, it becomes increasingly difficult for such institutions to structure organizational life strictly from the point of view of the tradition they represent or their own particular moral visions. The tension, which develops, comes from the two goals of maintaining identity and functioning in the public domain in morally pluralistic, secular societies.

There are at least three alternative ways for any organization to proceed when facing challenges to its identity and moral commitments. One possibility is that it could completely withdraw from the sphere of public finance and regulation. This alternative is often not feasible for practical reasons. In addition, it may not be desirable. However, even if it were achievable, the organization is still not immune from the tensions and demands of pluralism and public regulation. One can imagine the case of an adult, competent Jehovah's Witness requiring a treatment that would involve blood transfusion. Arriving in the emergency room of St. Valentine's Roman Catholic Hospital, which has a commitment to the preservation of life, the Witness refuses the blood required for the treatment. How should the institution respond? One can easily imagine a set of cases in which a health care institution, with a particular sense of its moral identity and mission, such as St. Valentine's, could be situated in a remote rural setting. How can it deal with the demands of someone outside its tradition when there is no alternative health care setting for that person?

A second alternative might involve an organization that could, over time, simply loses its "identity". This seems a more likely possibility in the practical order. Many believe this is what has happened to numerous religiously inspired colleges and universities in the United States.

However, one can argue that such a scenario would be a tragic loss not only for the organization but also for the secular society. By its conception, the public sphere of a secular society tends to be impoverished in comparison with the content of the moral views of particular moral communities. The richness of secular society is found in the variety of moral viewpoints that meet and contend with each other in the public realm. If organizations give up their identities, the public, secular arena becomes impoverished in the discussion of moral issues.

There is a third alternative, which is the alternative of preserving organizational identity while engaging in the fabric of the secular, pluralistic society in which the organization is located. This is the messy alternative, in that it is not as clear-cut as the first two. This alternative involves the concepts of integrity and compromise and a distinction between "toleration" and "approval". The existence of this alternative, however, depends on how one conceptualizes the notions of integrity and compromise.

While questions of integrity and identity are clearly important for some organizations, such as those with religious identities, these questions are important for health care organizations and educational organizations as well. The importance comes for two different reasons. One reason is the reality of moral pluralism in secular societies. Addressing this pluralism is important so that a health care organization or educational organization can honestly deliver services and work with other organizations. The second is that views of health, disease, health care, and education are influenced, in part, by one's moral views and commitments. In a secular society, one can imagine a wide range and variety of health care and educational organizations. In order for these organizations to flourish and for a secular ethics based on consent and permission to develop, all health care and educational organizations need to articulate in some way their self-understandings.

In analyzing and addressing ethical questions in education and health care, a key question, for any moral and ethical analysis, concerns how we can give an account of the moral integrity of organizations in health care and education in postmodern, secular societies. In consideration that it is hard enough to assess the integrity of individual moral agents, how are we to think about, and assess, the moral integrity of organizations?

To assess the integrity of any moral agent, whether an individual or organization, one needs to begin with the identity of the moral agent, since the concept of integrity relies on the identity of an agent for content.[3] The identity of an organization becomes the key to understanding and assessing the integrity of any organization. The identity of the organization should be the Rosetta Stone for assessing how an organization acts morally toward its employees and those who engage its services. We know how easy it is for individual people to deceive themselves, particularly in the moral life, and this problem of self-deception is potentially even more prevalent, troublesome, and complicated when one examines an organization, simply because there are a number of points of decision-making within an organization.

One way to approach this question is to begin by thinking analogously about an individual moral agent and next think about how an organization, as a moral agent, can confront the problem. A common challenge for any moral agent is how to maintain one's personal identity and moral integrity as a moral agent in a diverse, pluralistic society. This problem can also present an even more complicated challenge when we analyze organizations as moral agents.

The focus of this chapter is on how an organization can articulate and maintain its identity and act with integrity in the broader context of a secular, morally pluralistic, postmodern society. It is easy to imagine, in such diverse societies, how an organization can lose its identity in the surroundings of such a pluralistic, secular society. Therefore, practical questions arise as to how we can verify the authentic identities of organizations and how we can assess if organizations are actually living out their identities. As argued in the previous chapter, the moral identity and commitments of an organization should be articulated clearly, in some way, for those people who are members of the organization and for those people and organizations outside of it so that they are left with a clear sense of with what and with whom they are dealing. A statement of organizational identity should be tied to the organization's statement or understanding of its mission or purpose. For an organization the identity, mission, and purpose ought to be inextricably bound together.

The identity of an organization is often understood in a limited way to mean only the purpose of an organization. However, there are broader implications for understanding an organization's identity. An organization's identity addresses not only it purpose but speaks to the culture of the organization; in this way, the identity of the

[3] Kevin Wildes, S.J., "Institutional Integrity: Toleration, Approval, and Holy War or 'Always True to You in My Fashion'", *Journal of Medicine and Philosophy* 16 (April 1991), 211-220.

organization permeates it and influences not only what the organization is but how the organization operates. The identity of an organization should have its starting point in its purpose, but purpose alone is insufficient to understand the identity of an organization. The purpose of an organization ought to shape the way an organization operates. Using a Jesuit turn of phrase at this point may be helpful. The purpose of an organization is more than what is meant in a narrow sense; the purpose of the organization ought to influence an organization's *way of proceeding*. It should not be assumed that all health care organizations, or all educational organizations, for example, are alike and have the same mission or way of proceeding to realize their missions. To borrow from Aristotle's language of classifications these organizations may be of the same genus, but they exist as different species within the genus. So, for example, one might think of Catholic health care or Catholic education as species in the larger genus of either health care or educational organizations. And, one could go on to argue that within Catholic education or health care, for example, there are different sub-species that speak to the different goals and styles of education. Jesuit education, for example, is different from other species of Catholic education.[4]

If, as was argued in Chap. 3, consent and agreement are foundations for understanding ethics in contemporary, morally diverse secular societies, the identity of an organization will be central to an organization operating ethically in the morally diverse society. An organization should be able to explain the reasons for its moral vision or commitments. In an ethically and culturally diverse society people will often have different views and may choose not to use the services of a particular organization. However, to function ethically as an organization in a postmodern, secular society the vision and moral commitments of an organization should be well articulated in a public statement of mission, vision, or purpose. Such a statement will be the foundational to judging the integrity of an educational or health care organization.[5]

However, the moral identity of an organization needs to go beyond simply a public statement of mission or purpose and the values of the organization. A mission statement or a statement of purpose for an organization needs to become more than a statement. Such a statement needs to become integral to the leadership and the culture of the organization and how it operates. In so doing the mission and identity of an organization become part of the fabric and bureaucracy of an organization. In this way, a mission statement not only articulates the purpose and mission of an organization but also helps to shape the organization's culture and *way of proceeding*.[6] Such a statement and articulation of organizational vision should lay out the foundation on which to build the culture of the organization; hopefully, in this way

[4] https://www.americamagazine.org/issue/care-person

[5] H.T. Engelhardt, Jr., and K. Wildes, S.J., "Health and Disease: Philosophical Perspectives", *Encyclopedia of Bioethics*, ed. Warren T. Reich (New York: Simon & Schuster MacMillian Publishing Company, 1995), pp. 1101-1106.

[6] John W. O'Malley, Ignatius Special Way of Proceeding, *America* magazine, July 31, 2006.

the culture will be integrated with, and reflect, the mission and purpose of an organization.

It has been argued in Chaps. 3 and 4 that, in the practices of contemporary health care and education entities, organizations provide the context for many day-to-day decisions that are made. Organizations are moral actors. Guidelines within organizations pertaining to national, state, or local funding or benefactor policy are given shape, in part, by organizational policy. When reviewing decisions, in terms of health care or education, the organizational context should be kept in mind. However, determining the role of health care or educational organizations can be difficult. Organizations speak through their policies and procedures. Policy decisions made by the organization shape the range of ethical choices that are then made available in the clinic or the classroom.

Ideally, the mission and identity of an organization should articulate the purpose of an organization, and this foundational statement ought to be a key part in decision-making by the organization. Any organization ought to ask itself how decisions and actions align with its mission and identity. In contemporary secular society, there can be a wide variety of ways that one can articulate the purpose of a health care or educational organization. Given the diversity of moral views in postmodern, secular societies, there can be a number of ideals of what it is to be a healthy or educated person. Therefore, when looking at a particular health care organization or educational organization it is important to first ask and understand *what the purpose of the organization is*. From that starting point one can investigate the policies of an educational organization or health care organization and the relationship of the policies to the organization's mission and identity. It can be argued that the purpose of an organization is the defining element that makes an organization different from a mere aggregate. Purpose is what should define the collective action of an organization, and purpose is what makes the action of an organization something different from an aggregate. People organize themselves together in an organization in the hope of accomplishing what an individual alone cannot do.

6.2 Integrity: Identity, Vision, and Mission

Organizations often articulate their goals and objectives in such forms as mission and vision statements of the organization. However, such statements need to be more than simply "statements," as they often speak to both the purpose of the organization and the manner by which the organization will proceed to operate both internally and in society. For example, included in this book, in the appendices, is a document entitled "*Characteristics of Jesuit Colleges and Universities*". The document provides an example of how one group of educational organizations, the Association of Jesuit Colleges and Universities, thinks about the identities and characteristics that define the organizations which are members of the Association. The document provides a framework for the particular mission statements of the different Jesuit colleges and universities in the Association. This document on the characteristics of an organization speaks to not only the mission of Jesuit educational organizations but also to the culture and lived reality that is aspired to in such organizations. Each of the institutions can articulate its own mission in light of its history and the characteristics of what it is to offer a Jesuit education.

When people talk about a mission statement of an organization, they often also talk about a *vision statement*. The mission and vision statements serve different purposes in the life of an organization but are often confused with each other. While a mission statement is more general and describes what an organization wants to do, a vision statement outlines and articulates how that mission is seen in the immediate and near-term future. The vision statement should balance out the more global mission statement with the particular needs and circumstances confronting the organization in the present. Each statement should be part of the strategic planning process of the organization, but each statement will have a different objective. These statements may be written for organizations, or they can be written for particular departments within an organization.

A mission statement is a concise statement for the organization's reason for existence. It describes the organization's purpose and its overall intention. The mission statement supports the vision and serves to communicate purpose and direction to employees, customers, vendors and other stakeholders.

What is the organization's purpose?
Why does the organization exist?

A *vision statement*, however, looks from the present moment to the future and creates an image of what the organization wishes to achieve. A vision statement should be both inspirational and aspirational and should challenge members of the organization to think about how to realize the mission in the contemporary context. Questions for what a vision statement should consider might include:

What problem is the organization seeking to solve? Where is the organization headed?
If we achieved all strategic goals, what would we look like ten years from now?

Organizations will often take another step and develop a *values statement,* which lists the core principles that guide and direct an individual organization and its culture. In a values-led organization, the values create a moral compass for the organization and its employees. It guides decision-making and establishes a standard against which actions can be assessed. These core values are an internalized framework that is shared and acted on by leadership. When drafting values statements, questions to consider might include:

What values are distinctive or unique to our organization?
What values should guide the operations of our organization?
What conduct should employees uphold?

By itself a statement of values is not sufficient for most organizations if the statement is nothing more than a wall hanging in the foyer of an office. In conjunction with a statement of values, a *code of ethics* should articulate a way to implement the foundational values into practice and, in so doing, articulate a way of proceeding for the organization. In a postmodern, secular society an organization's code of ethics takes on additional import, as it articulates for people within the organization and for other organizations the moral values by which the organization operates. These statements not only articulate the moral commitments of an organization, but they also become the basis for articulating how an organization operationalizes its values. Such a statement should outline the procedures that are in place within the organization to ensure the values are upheld. When creating such codes of ethics and procedures one might consider questions such as:

What are common ethical issues in our industry?
What should someone do if he or she sees a violation of our values?

For an organization to have an effective values statement, it must fully embrace its values and ethics at all levels of the company and use them daily to guide its attitudes, actions, and decision-making. An organization must build a culture, which reflects its values and commitments, and find the best ways to orient new members of the organization to the values and culture, as well as ways to renew the foundational commitments for older members of the organization.

To further articulate the identity of an organization, a Mission statement is often accompanied by statements on the Vision or Values of an organization. Values and Vision statements help to further an understanding of the organization's mission by articulating the values that will help to guide the development of the mission; a vision statement seeks to articulate the mission in the present and near-term social context of the organization. These types of statements should play an important role in how the organization structures itself and defines the roles that individuals play within the organization. While a Mission statement should articulate the purpose of the organization, accompanying statements about the values and vision of the organization should articulate how it will operate and how it will apply the mission to the contemporary circumstances in which an organization finds itself, respectively.

The purposeful actions of health care organizations and educational organizations should be exactly that: *purposeful.* The actions of an organization are different from other "circumstances" that influence many decisions. Policies are not mere accidents of a decision, but they are tied to the mission and identity of an organization. Frequently when making ethical decisions in education or health care those decisions are shaped by elements that are simply "just there." A patient has a particular disease. The treatment options for the patient are A or B.

Decisions about treatment are made in the context of the circumstances. However, other elements often exist that are not simply a given; they are decided. For example, a patient's insurer may limit the range of treatment options for a patient, or the health care organization may have limits and priorities regarding certain types of treatment. Or, in education, the funders (government or private) may have issued guidelines or regulations pertaining to the educational programs offered. In addition, the questions of organizational ethics concern those sorts of policy decisions and moral accountability.

For an educational organization or a health care organization, "mission" ought to be a term that is fundamental to the operations of on organization and used to differentiate a particular organization from other health care or educational organizations. It incorporates the purpose of a health care organization (*e.g.*, providing a clinical service) and more. Mission statements often identify what motivates the mission and something about *how* the mission will be accomplished. The appendices in this book, "*Characteristics of Jesuit Education*" and "*Ethical and Religious Directives,*" provide a basis for a health care organization or an educational organization defined not only by its purpose (*e.g.*, clinical services or primary education for the disadvantaged) but also by how its mission, identity, and moral commitments are reflected in its culture, its motivation, and the kinds of services it offers *and how it offers them.* The language of mission can help to bring together the purpose and moral commitments that are central for an educational organization or a health care organization. An organization's mission and identity should be foundational for understanding and evaluating the organization's integrity.

Integrity is a word that is often used freely these days in many different occupations and about many different types of organizations. In recent years, the integrity of candidates in many political campaigns, national and local, has been an issue. In the wake of recent business and accounting scandals integrity has also become a watchword for many people in business. In scandals involving the clergy, there has also been a repeated concern about integrity. The language of integrity is often linked to discussions of trust and often to the failures and breakdown of trust. One can argue that these concerns about integrity have arisen as trust in social institutions, including governmental, religious, professional, and business, has declined. The concern for integrity in an organization provides a crucial link between what an organization is and hopes to be and its central purpose. Organizational integrity, particularly for health care organizations and educational organizations, is a crucial element in organizational ethics.

This chapter is built on an examination of the concept of integrity. It is important to keep the concept of integrity in mind in order to understand how a health care organization or an educational organization can live within and adapt to a changing environment and still maintain an integrated sense of mission. It will be argued that, too often, when the word "integrity" is used, too much is often assumed. Yet, because the word is so much a part of our moral vocabulary, we do not realize how much we are assuming about the word and its applications.

Understanding the concept of integrity will help us think about navigating the terrain of health care in a morally pluralistic society. The process of reflecting on integrity and the values to which an organization is committed sets the groundwork for understanding how compromise, cooperation, and toleration are possible. After examining the concept of integrity, this chapter turns next to how and why one might talk about integrity in health care or education. Both health care and education are comprised of not only moral but cooperative enterprises. Part of the discussion of integrity in health care or educational organizations must involve an examination of cooperation with other organizations in health care and education, which may be working out of different moral frameworks.

6.3 Integrity and Compromise[7]

While the goal of this chapter is to open up discussion of integrity in educational organizations and HCOs, it will be helpful to continue to explore the notion of integrity based on the individual person in order to achieve this goal. In this way, we will have a clearer sense of the idea of integrity before tackling the more complicated notion of organizational integrity. When we think of integrity, we usually think of it in terms of an individual maintaining his or her moral commitments. The allocation of time, talents, and other resources, are key resources which indicate what a person values. Therefore, we need to make choices about how best to implement moral visions in this imperfect world with the resources that one has.

As situations of conflict emerge in a person's life, this hierarchy is crucial to determining which resolutions are acceptable without one having to abandon the fundamental moral tenets that constitute one's conception of the moral life. Such ordering leads to a prioritization. If there is an internal conflict of values that demands a compromise, one will have to decide which commitments are most central to knowing what can, and cannot, be given up in effecting a compromise. The second point is that this model of integrity can lead to the development of a model of compromise.

Many people understand integrity simply as consistency. That view is straightforward, but it misses out on any depth of understanding; simply put, integrity is more complicated than consistency. A person has a set of moral commitments, no matter how they are articulated (principles, rules, virtues), and the person seeks to stick to those commitments. The opposite of this notion of integrity is any idea of compromise. This construal of integrity involves a number of views and assumptions that need to be challenged.

One might ask why the model of consistency is incomplete. For one thing the consistency model by itself is too simple. For example, it does not give a way to think through conflicting moral commitments. One can see the problem of conflict within the lives of individual moral agents. One does not even have to open up the complicated issues of moral pluralism and diversity. Most people have confronted the problem of conflicting moral demands, such as the decision to keep or break a promise to one person in order to respond to the request of another person. Much of our moral thinking is shaped by conflicting demands and trying to judge what is the right thing to do. On the other hand, one can understand the simplicity of the integrity as consistency model by reflecting on the difficulties of applying a rule. First, people often assume that rules can simply be applied to particular cases. People often have no sense that it is often difficult to figure out what is the right rule to apply to a particular situation. Wittgenstein pointed out that rules do not tell us when

[7] Kevin Wildes, S.J., "Institutional Integrity: Toleration, Approval, and Holy War or 'Always True to You in My Fashion'", *Journal of Medicine and Philosophy* 16 (April 1991), 211-220.

and how they should be applied.[8] One often finds examples of this problem in sporting events when a controversy ensues over a call made by a referee or judge. Such calls are often controversial; no matter how much we use instant replay, as it is a human judgment about 1) whether or not there has been an infraction and 2) which rule was actually violated. In health care, one might think of examples from end of life care. An individual may have a commitment to the preservation of life. However, consistency, understood as always doing the same thing, would lead to a mindless vitalism and a misuse of resources.

Moral controversies are often contentious, because they can be described in different

ways and because different rules can be applied, depending upon the description. One has only to look at numerous cases of decisions at the end of life to see how differently the same case can be described. Therefore, while consistency is an element of integrity, consistency alone does not give a full picture of integrity. Moral controversies often involve competing moral commitments and a decision to choose among them or to rank them. If we assume that integrity is a second order virtue, with the task of ordering our moral lives, then consistency alone will not give a full account of integrity.

Integrity can be conceived, however, in a much broader and richer way than a model of consistency; that is, people have values, both moral and non-moral, which they wish to maintain and projects they wish to pursue. These projects and commitments shape their lives.[9] This sense of integrity is not simply a matter of narrow consistency in one's life. Rather, it usually reflects a ranking of goals and values, which leads to a balancing of different projects and to the directing of commitments over time. Integrity requires dealing with conflicting demands. Integrity requires *judgment.*

The dynamic or moral judgment and discernment takes us back to the first point about integrity: that is, its relationship to first order moral commitments. The exercise of integrity will involve a judgment and discernment of the balancing and ordering of the first order moral commitments and a decision about how they should be applied in different circumstances. Why should there be compromise at all? We live in an imperfect world. There are numerous ways to account for its imperfections, but one key element is that imperfections are rooted in the finitude of the world.

The recognition of compromise is the recognition that the practical world, the world of ethical decisions, is limited and finite. It is not some ideal world in which every moral value can be fully realized. Rather, it is a world of limits, where one has

---

[8] John McDowell, "Wiggenstein on Following Rules", *Synthese*, 1984, Vol. 58, #3, pp. 325-363.

See also, H.T. Engelhardt, Jr., and K. Wildes, S.J., "The Four Principles of Health Care and Post- Modernity: Why a Libertarian Interpretation is Unavoidable", in *Principles of Health Care Ethics,* ed. Raanan Gillon (New York: John Wiley & Sons, 1994), pp. 135-147 and K. Wildes, *Moral Acquaintances.*

[9] J.C Smart, and B. Williams 1973, *Utilitarianism: For and Against,* (New York: Cambridge University Press, New York, 1973), pp. 98-99; B. Brody, and H.T. Engelhardt, *Bioethics: Readings and Cases,* (Engelwood Cliffs, NJ: Prentice Hall, Inc., 1987), pp. 26-28; B. Brody, *Life and Death Decision Making*, (New York: Oxford University Press, 1988), pp. 36–37.

limited options. Therefore, individuals and organizations must compromise. However, to enter into the give and take of compromise one needs a sense of the moral values to which one is committed and a ranking of these values. Without a sense of the central value commitments, a person or an institution will not stand for anything. Without some ranking of the values, a person or organization will not know which values can and cannot be compromised.

Applying this understanding of integrity means that an organization would need to articulate an understanding of its "mission" (that is, its values and projects) in order effectively to preserve its moral integrity. Such a public statement would inform interested parties how the institution sees itself and why it is in "business". Such a statement ought to shape the business practices it adopts. Such an articulation can do even more, however. It can help the institution understand its own commitments and their foundations, as well as their relationship one to another. With this view of integrity, an institution can move beyond identifying itself simply by what it will not do to a positive view of what it is trying to achieve; such institutional self- understanding allows for the possibility of compromise. Not all of the commitments of an organization, in its mission, are univocally valued. Some are less fundamental than others. This understanding of integrity is a crucial first step for thinking about institutional identity, and it lays the foundation for a way to avoid the Scylla and Charybdis of a loss of self-identity or a withdrawal from the public context. In a secular society, with different moral values and visions, there are different views of what is morally appropriate medicine and health care. If an institution is to make its way in this world, it is important for it to have a vision of its moral commitments and their ranking.

The importance of such reflection is made evident in legal cases such as that of Beverly Requena. Mrs. Requena, suffering from amyotrophic lateral sclerosis (ALS), asked not to undergo artificial feeding or administration of fluids. St. Clare's, the hospital in which she was a patient, developed a policy stating that the institution would not participate in the withholding or withdrawal of artificial feeding or fluids. The policy, however, was established *after* Mrs.

Requena's admission to the hospital. St. Clare's has sought to honor her request by transferring her to a nearby hospital. Mrs. Requena asked that she not be compelled to leave St. Clare's in view that she had been there for fifteen months and had established relationships of trust with the staff.

In the deciding this case, the courts supported Mrs. Requena's request to remain at St. Clare's and refuse the artificial feeding and fluids. One of the reasons for the court's decision was the hospital's failure to develop and announce a policy in a timely fashion. The Appellate Court wrote:

> An equitable consideration here is that Beverly Requena had no notice of St. Clare's policy against withholding artificial feeding or fluids until July of 1986. The balance to be struck here is between the hospital's right to enforce its regulation and fundamental rights of the patient. Under the circumstances we find no waiver or estoppel against Beverly Requena who had *no notice of the regulation prior to her admission or for 15 months thereafter.*[10]

---

[10] Superior Court of New Jersey, Appellate Division, *Re Requena*, 442–486, decided October 6, 1986.

The court seems to support the hospital's right to have such regulations, but it held that the institution was responsible for its failure to communicate its moral commitments in a timely fashion. In writing about the effects of moral pluralism on the practice of medicine, Alasdair MacIntyre has offered some remarks that are appropriate to Requena and the issues of organizational identity and integrity.

> Where a community of moral and metaphysical beliefs is lacking, trust between strangers becomes much more questionable than when we can safely assume such a community. Nobody can rely on anyone else's judgments on his or her behalf until he or she knows what the other person believes. It follows that nobody can accept the moral authority of another in virtue simply of his professional position.[11]

While MacIntyre's remarks are focused on the importance of patient autonomy and patient- directed activity, the remarks implicitly address the need for persons and HCOs to spell out what they believe.[12] The practice of health care in the terrain of moral strangers means that the consent and agreement of participants is crucial to the justification of any choice or practice. Institutional statements of moral commitments are a means for honest participation in the pluralistic world of medicine. Such statements, and the process of formulating them, can also enable the organization to take a positive, proactive stance in the world rather than assuming a reactive, defensive stance to unfolding events.

6.4 Organizational Conscience

In light of this understanding of the concept of integrity it should be clear that organizational integrity depends on an organization's identity. Moreover, an organization's identity embodies the fundamental moral commitments of an organization. However, if secular societies can be places that are morally pluralistic with conflicting and competing moral visions, one needs to think about how to cooperate with others who have different moral commitments/agendas. In situations where people, with different moral visions, must work together around a moral project, such as that involving health care or education, they need to think about compromise and cooperation. One can develop the idea of compromise further by articulating the ways in which an organization can live in a morally pluralistic world that involves cooperation with others who hold very different views. A range of responses is available to institutions and organizations that have particular moral identities. At one end of the spectrum, they can withdraw from the secular arena. At the other end

[11] A. MacIntyre, "Patients As Agents" in S.F. Spicker and H.T. Engelhardt, Jr., (eds.), *Philosophical Medical Ethics: Its Nature and Significance,* (Dordrecht, the Netherlands: D. Reidel Publishing Company, 1977), p. 210.

[12] A. MacIntyre, "Patients as Agents" in S.F. Spicker and H.T. Engelhardt, Jr. (eds.), *Philosophical Medical Ethics: Its Nature and Significance (*Dordrecht, the Netherlands: D. Reidel Publishing Company, 1977), p. 210.

of the spectrum, they can lose their identities. Alternatively, they can engage the world around them and try to maintain their fundamental identities.

Conscience is usually discussed in reference to individuals. James Childress, for example, has written extensively on individual conscience.[13] One can argue, however, that conscience can apply, analogously, to institutions and organizations. It can be further argued that, given changes and developments in contemporary health care and education, an ethical analysis will be inadequate if it examines only individuals and fails to look at institutional practices and questions. Indeed, several years ago Ezekiel Emanuel[14] challenged the bioethics community to turn its attention from particular cases and principles to institutional arrangements and structures.

This shift to the examination of organizations and structures must be made for ethical reasons in both education and health care. The institutional and social structures that support and surround health care and education will not allow us to ask ethical questions as if they existed only at the level of individual choice. Too many of the ethical issues of the clinic are well beyond the control of the individuals involved. The issues of bioethics have moved beyond the bedside, the clinic, and the stand-alone hospital. These changes call for an important shift in the moral imagination to situate ethical questions in the web of institutional patterns and relationships. Institutional conscience is an important tool in this development.

In writing about conscience, James Childress has noted that appeals to conscience involve appeals to moral standards, but conscience itself is not a moral standard. Like "integrity" or "wholeness", conscience needs content.[15] For an institutional conscience, the articulation of a mission is central. Within the broad parameters of organizational mission, one can begin to think about moral integrity. That is, does the organization live out its moral commitments? Such a living-out need not be thought of as simply unimaginative consistency. Circumstances, contexts, and problems change and develop. So too integrity involves creativity and fidelity.

Developing an understanding of mission should give an institution the criteria to develop the tools to evaluate mission effectiveness and shape and implement institutional conscience. For example, one might look at the *Ethical and Religious Directives* (included in the appendices of this book) for Roman Catholic health care institutions in the United States as setting[16] out a broad framework in which Roman Catholic institutions can articulate their mission. The ERD are best known, perhaps, for the prohibitions they contain—*e.g.*, against abortion, euthanasia, and sterilization. However, an equally important part of the ERD is the positive vision articulated for Catholic health care institutions.

[13] James Childress, "Appeals to Conscience." *Ethics* (1974) 89: 315–335.

[14] Ezekiel Emanuel (1995).

[15] Kevin Wildes, S.J., "Institutional Integrity: Toleration, Approval, and Holy War or 'Always True to You in My Fashion'", *Journal of Medicine and Philosophy* 16 (April 1991), 211–220.

[16] United States Conference of Catholic Bishops, *Ethical and Religious Directives for Catholic Health Care Services*, (Washington, DC: United States Catholic Conference, 2019).

6.5 Tools for Organizational Identity

Assuming that an institution or system can articulate a mission, we need to ask how that mission is implemented. How can a vision become real? It is essential to the development of institutional conscience that, whatever form a mission takes, the mission has a common ownership within an institution. The mission supplies the vision against which institutional structures and procedures can be evaluated.

While it may vary, according to culture and history, from organization to organization, every organization will need some sort of planning process to articulate its *goals*, in light of its mission and identity. The goals of an organization ought to be rooted in its mission, identity and plan. But the goals ought to be particular events that can be measured and which are rooted in the vision of the organization.

A critical tool for the integrity and conscience of an institution is the budget. A budget should be understood as a planning document. It is an articulation of an institution's mission. For example, if an institution says in its mission statement that it is committed to care of the poor, but makes no line-item commitment to care of the poor, one can say that the institution either is in deep self-deception or is lying.

Along with a budget, an institution's planning processes and strategic plan are important to its mission, identity, and conscience. There should be an integration of an organization's mission, identity, and planning. Just as individuals plan according to life goals and objectives, so too health care institutions and systems need to deploy a planning process. A measure of the conscience of an institution is the degree to which the moral commitments of the institution are part of its strategic planning. They ought to shape the long-term goals and the means that are used to achieve them.

The process of planning involves a process of self-study and evaluation. One could well imagine a hospital ethics committee or some analogous structure that reviews the practices and policies of an institution. The focus would be on not only patients and particular issues of clinical care but also the overall moral culture of the institution, including, for example, advertisement.

In this whole process, the role of the institution's trustees/directors is crucial. They have a special role in the articulation of institutional mission and identity and a special responsibility to call and lead the institution in fidelity to that mission. While others may be more concerned with the day-to-day details of patient care and institutional management, the duty of trustees is to ask for accountability for broader questions of institutional identity and life.

If there is to be development of an institutional moral identity and conscience, there needs to be an ongoing process of education to shape the culture of the institution. Education is important for ongoing renewal and adaptation. It is also important for consent. That is, the members of the institution, patients, workers, and professionals, need to consent to the mission. They need to be aware of the culture of the institution they are joining. Of course, there is rarely a "perfect fit" of individuals and institutions. Another crucial tool, therefore, will be the provisions made for the protection of individual conscience.

The changing character of health care raises a new area of investigation and discourse for bioethics: institutional ethics. I have argued that there can be an institutional moral identity and an institutional conscience. The mission of the institution shapes institutional conscience, and this conscience is implemented by the structures of the institution, such as budgeting and planning. Internal practices provide a way to measure what an institution really is, and institutional structures provide a way to evaluate how well an institution lives out the mission it announces.

There is a scale of possible responses that organizations can make to the situations, and the demands, organizations encounter in a pluralistic society. The scale ranges from approval to condemnation with a number of responses of toleration that are found in between the two extremes. Health care and educational organizations give their approval to events in acts such as public statements and institutional honors. For example, when a university bestows an honorary degree, or a hospital gives an award, it is usually for some work that a person has done or will do for the institution. There is a sense, however, that such honors "endorse" not only the work that has been done but also *the person.* That person is honored as a model for the institution. In another example, one might think of St. Valentine's having a hospital chaplain available day and night to care for the spiritual and sacramental needs of any patient or staff member. The hospital commits its resources to such a service and may highlight that in its literature and advertising material. The work of the chaplain touches the core of St. Valentine's hospital's mission. His work is one that has the hospital's endorsement and approval.

At the other end of the scale of responses, one finds the response of condemnation and what might become a "holy war". Here an institution not only withholds approval but expresses strong disapproval by putting all of its resources to work to resist the challenge, refusing to cooperate in any way. For example, if a local law required St. Valentine's to perform abortions, one could well imagine the hospital utilizing its resources to fight such a requirement in every possible political and legal arena. A religious university, faced with a law that required the indoctrination of its students in atheism, might commit its resources to a legal battle to overturn such a requirement. Failure to alter the situation can lead to an extreme response: civil disobedience and the forgoing of public funding of any type so that the institution is not forced to cooperate with evil. It is imaginable that an institution, like a citizen, might employ force to protect its values.

"Toleration" in contrast to approval and condemnation has a very different meaning. At its root, it means to "endure". Many of us "endure" situations of which we do not approve.

Indeed, in many ways institutions, which participate in the public domain, must tolerate situations, which are, at best, incongruous, with their institutional identities. However, there are various gradations of "toleration". The first gradation of toleration, closest to approval, is to tolerate and neither approve nor disapprove. For example, a university, committed to the free expression of ideas, may tolerate speakers and groups who are intolerant. In such cases, university officials may judge that it is best simply to say nothing. One may think of a group of students within a Catholic university who form The St. Pius V Club to honor the canonized members of the Holy Inquisition or students who form a club that is "pro-choice". While the university may not endorse the club, a Catholic institution could surely tolerate such a club, within certain limits so that it could be a university and place for the debate of ideas. A hospital may tolerate spiritual healers as long as they do not interfere with the working of the hospital.

There is yet another level of toleration in which a health care or educational organization may tolerate a situation but voice concern. For example, a staff member of St. Valentine's might invite an expert to speak on in vitro fertilization. The hospital or university could tolerate the speaker yet voice its concern on all or part of the remarks or point out that there are other views on the topic that need to be represented. Or, a university might have concerns over the content of leaflets being distributed on campus and voice its concern on the topic of the material.

Another level of institutional response is that of toleration with disapproval. A religious university might tolerate a speaker defending atheism or apartheid and yet publicly disapprove of the content of the lecture. The lecture is tolerated, because the university holds other values and concerns (*e.g.*, free speech, academic inquiry) that are important to the institution and which stand at the heart of its self-identity. Alternatively, a Catholic hospital might tolerate, but disapprove of, a speaker on AIDS who endorses the use of condoms.

Yet another level on the scale of response would be toleration that emerges from active opposition. At this level, the problematic situation may be such that the institution would seek to change the state of affairs through legal action. The institution may decide to address the matter legally and live with the result. At this level, we are still a step away from "holy war", in view that the institution is willing to tolerate the results of the legal battle. For example, a group at St. Valentine's might seek to force the institution to include information about condoms in its social service counseling for HIV patients and to dispense condoms to all such patients. The hospital could oppose such demands with appropriate legal action. Similarly, one might imagine a Christian university confronted with the formation of a Young Fornicators League. It would not surprise anyone if the university decided to oppose the League through legal means. However, in both cases one could imagine the institutions living with, although condemning, the results of the court holding if such results were adverse. There are gradations even within this level. The situation could be such that an institution decided to use all possible legal appeals. However, one could well imagine that, in the course of litigation, an institution would weigh its use of resources in such litigation and decide to limit legal appeals.

In summary, for an organization the scale of approval, condemnation, and toleration has several gradations. The scale looks like this:

1. Approval
2. Toleration and silence
3. Toleration and the expression of concern
4. Toleration and explicit disapproval
5. Toleration and opposition
6. Condemnation

7. Holy War

The use of institutional resources can be understood, cautiously, as a form of organizational speech when an institution expresses toleration, approval, and condemnation through its use of resources or the resources of organizations with whom it is partnered.

The use of institutional resources is an aspect of institutional life that is best read through the lenses of this scale. Resources, especially monetary ones, come often from a mixture of public and private resources. Such a funding mixture carries with it designations and regulations that an institution may have to tolerate. This may well be described as "toleration" but not approval. Allowing a group to use its resources is not necessarily tacit approval of what the group supports. Rather, resource allocation needs to be understood as a subtle and nuanced form of institutional language—a language that has more voices than simply those for approval or condemnation.

This concern has been captured in Roman Catholic thought on the distinction of material and formal cooperation with evil. This distinction is taken up, and used more extensively, in an exploration in Chap. 10 with regard to the question of organizational partnerships, but it can be helpful at this juncture of the book as well. This distinction is grounded in the experience of a people who believe it important to live *within* the world and not apart from it. Nevertheless, it also embodies the recognition that living in the world means that people and institutions will have to work, in some way, with others, people or institutions, that hold different, and sometimes conflicting, moral values. This recognition is particularly important for organizations in both health care and education. To cooperate has meant that one concurs, in some way, with the evil act of another. Formal cooperation takes place when one shares the intention of the agent who is performing the sinful act—for example, when someone joins a friend in robbing a house. There is no justification for the robbery, yet a person helps the friend both plan and execute the robbery. Material cooperation takes place when someone contributes to the sinful/evil act without sharing in the intention. I materially cooperate when I engage in an act that supports the other or when I join in his act without sharing in the intention. For example, I have a car, pick up a friend, and give him a ride. Normally that would be a good or kind thing. However, when my friend has just robbed a house and is carrying the stolen goods, I am now driving the getaway car. Therefore, in one sense, I am cooperating with and supporting the evil act of robbery.

Material cooperation can be either *immediate or mediate*. It is immediate if it is part of the act. It is mediated if it is somehow "at a distance". Often classical writers have spoken about mediate material cooperation as being either proximate or remote.

There are clear limits to this language and this distinction. The distinction can be developed in a way that is too legalistic or Jesuitical. The distinction and language sounds as if there is some type of absolute measure that can tell one where she or he can stand in relationship to an evil act. The distinction is also limited by the view that there are discrete acts in the world that can be identified.

At the same time, however, the distinction offers an important reminder to institutions, as well as individuals, who are trying to preserve their moral identities and integrity in the world. It reminds us that there are moral evils that ought not to be supported in any way. In recent years, the distinction has taken on an important role in Catholic health care as a way to think through the range of possible relationships that Catholic institutions can have with other institutions that engage in evil practices. One view holds that cooperative arrangements were possible, insofar as they were material, and that "the object of material cooperation should be as distant as possible from the wrongdoer's act".[17]

An important, underlying assumption for this distention is that there are certain acts, relationships that are morally evil. There has been a long discussion about the nature of "intrinsically evil moral acts" in Roman Catholic moral theology.[18] However framed, this tradition sees moral evils existing in the world. If such evils exist, the question arises as to how one should approach such evils. In an ideal/perfect world, one would simply avoid them and have nothing to do with them. However, this is not a perfect world. So Catholic moral theology developed a schema for discerning the actions with which one can cooperate.

The distinction relies on an Aristotelian-Thomistic metaphysics in which a substance is composed of form and matter. The form is the essence, the core of a being. The material is the material that particularizes a particular being. So too acts can be talked about has having form and matter. The form is the essence of an act. Essential to identifying the form of an act is not only the physical action itself but the intention as well. To cooperate *formally* is to participate in the act and share the intention of the agent. *Material cooperation* is when one acts in a way that contributes to the evil/sinful act without approving of it or sharing in the intention of the agent. This occurs when A helps B by an act that is not sinful/evil and without approving of what B does. Material cooperation can be either *immediate or mediate*. Material cooperation is immediate when the object of the cooperator is the same as the object of the wrongdoer.

Immediate material cooperation is wrong except in some instances of duress. Mediate material cooperation occurs when the cooperator's action is distinguishable from the wrongdoer's and can be justified for a proportionate reason. Mediate material cooperation can be further broken down into *proximate or remote* cooperation. It is proximate when the help is intimately concerned with the act of another, and it is remote if the help given is not closely tied or sinful.

---

[17] United States Conference of Catholic Bishops, *Ethical and Religious Directives for Catholic Health Care Services, Sixth Edition*, Part Six, Introduction, (Washington, DC: 2018) p. 29. See also "The Principles Governing Cooperation and Catholic Health Care: An Overview", an excerpt from *Catholic Health Ministry in Transition: Handbook for Responsible Leadership* [Revised Edition]) (1974).

[18] "Roman Catholic Contemporary Tradition Of Moral Theology Religion Essay", November 2018. Retrieved from https://www.ukessays.com/essays/theology/roman-catholic-contemporary-tradition-of-moral-theology-theology-religion-essay.php?vref=1

Of course, using these distinctions allows us to perform a fine-tuned analysis of a decision and an act. It also allows us to perform an analysis of all of the circumstances surrounding a decision that includes an assessment of the risks an organization is facing in adopting a policy or in adapting to a set of changing circumstances. It is always worth remembering that these decisions are often less-than-exact formulas. They are, in the end, judgments about the best thing to do and the risks that are involved. One important consideration for any organization, in health care or education, is the importance of understanding the integration of particular decisions. When made, they become part of a whole, which is the organization. In addition, there is a real risk when decisions and policies are made in isolation that the organization will be at risk of disintegration or taking actions that are adverse. One can argue that a classic example of these risks is seen in the history of American involvement in the Vietnam War, where policy decisions were made in isolation from one another.[19]

6.6 Conclusions

One way to articulate a primary goal for organizational ethics in health care and educational organizations is to say that the goal is for organizations to act with moral integrity. However, to meet this goal it is important to set out a clear understanding of integrity and its complexities. The key starting point for the integrity of any organization is to begin with its identity. An organization needs to have a clear sense of its purpose and mission if it is to act with integrity. This is a necessary condition for integrity. In addition, it is important to think through how organizations can act with integrity in a morally pluralistic world that often requires compromise. In an age of pluralism, questions about institutional identity and integrity are becoming more and more important. As health care organizations with particular moral visions both compete and cooperate, moral conflicts seem inevitable. It is too simplistic to think that all cooperation is approval and that in all conflicts where an institution cannot prevail, it should condemn and withdraw. As an alternative, this chapter has sketched a *modus vivendi* for institutions with special moral commitments in a public, pluralistic world. The responses range from approval to Holy War. Between the two extremes are a number of ways that an institution can tolerate the world and the circumstances in which it finds itself. How these different responses are employed will depend on the situation and the institution's sense of integrity and self-identity. The chapter that follows examines the structures needed for building and maintaining the integrity of the organization.

[19] See David Halberstam, *The Best and the Brightest*, (New York: Random House Publishing Group, 1969).

Summary of the Main Points

1. The Moral Nature of Health Care Organizations and Educational Organizations
2. Integrity: Identity, Vision, and Mission
3. Integrity and Compromise
4. Organizational Conscience
5. Tools for Organizational Identity

Chapter 7
Building Organizations of Integrity: Tools for Living Organizational Identity

In this book we have been exploring questions about organizations that have moral identities and how they can be considered as moral agents in postmodern secular societies which are open in principle to cultural and moral pluralism. In such societies informed consent plays a crucial role in ethical justification and we can understand and assess how consent is applicable to individual agents

However, when we examine organizations as moral actors, we need to ask how the remedy of informed consent, in a secular, pluralistic society, can be applied to organizations? If we adopt the model of informed consent for moral justification in morally pluralistic, secular societies, it follows that it would be essential for organizations, in such societies, to be clear about their own identities and moral commitments, as explored and advocated in the preceding chapters. Furthermore, it seems that not only would the organization need to understand its identity and moral commitments but that such commitments should be public and known to others who work with an organization. In this second section of this book, we have begun to explore the important questions of internal steps that can be taken, and structures which can be implemented, in an organization so that it can develop and maintain its identity and moral commitments and work with others in a morally diverse society.

Earlier chapters of this book argued that the questions of organizational ethics, in the contemporary, secular world, need to be understood in the context of the moral and cultural diversity and pluralism often found in the secular world. Contemporary health care and educational organizations exist, and work, within a diverse, multicultural context in secular societies. The work of both health care and educational organizations is further complicated by the reality that views about both health care and education are always grounded in at least some basic, minimal moral assumptions which shape both the goals of the organization and the way the organization works. The cultural and moral pluralism of the postmodern condition will mean, obviously, that there can, and often will be, different judgments and views about what is or is not morally appropriate policy for individuals, governments, and

K. W. Wildes, S.J., *Organizational Ethics and Moral Integrity in Secular Societies*, Philosophical Studies in Contemporary Culture 29,
https://doi.org/10.1007/978-3-031-39097-5_7

organizations. Establishing standards for health care and education, in secular, pluralistic societies, can be challenging, given that the norms and ideals for education and health care often vary in different cultures found within such secular societies.

However, as it has been argued, here and elsewhere, many of the moral issues and controversies in postmodern, secular societies can often be resolved through the agreement or disagreement of the agents who are involved in a moral controversy.[1] When taken seriously, such moral diversity in a secular society can lead to a quasi-libertarian view about regulation and the role of government in secular societies, because moral foundations for government authority will be grounded in terms of freedom and consent.[2] The roles of consent and permission are central to the understanding and granting of moral authority in such social contexts. A fundamental question for this investigation, however, is how the role of consent can be appropriated so that it is applicable to organizations.

In education and health care, the questions of ethics and society are often interwoven with discussions about the role of government and what governments can or cannot mandate morally for moral agents. This mixture of questions about ethics, public policy, and law of course leads to further questions about the role of government in enforcing morality. In these discussions and controversies, the consent of agents serves as a foundational starting point for resolving moral controversies with moral authority in culturally and morally diverse societies.

However, organizations, particularly in education and health care, play important roles in the intermediary social space of civil society in such diverse, civil and secular societies.

Organizations in education and health care operate in the social space between individual citizens and government authority. The roles of organizations are further complicated by how we understand moral agency and the ethics of decision-making in organizations. However, the procedures of consent and approval, which are so important for individual moral agents and controversies in morally pluralistic societies, are more difficult to identify and deploy when examining organizations as moral actors; they need to be rethought. Furthermore, the questions about how we think through issues of ethics and organizations, particularly in education and health care, can be further complicated, as these organizations frequently have cooperative arrangements with other organizations and government agencies. In addition to cooperative arrangements, organizations in education and health care are often subject to government regulations, and these cooperative arrangements can raise other ethical considerations.

Understanding organizational integrity, based on the arguments in Chaps. 5 and 6 of this book, can be further complicated by such issues as regulations and expectations imposed on an organization by its sources of funding. That extends to public funding sources and the regulation and restrictions that may be imposed on an

[1] See Chap. 3. Also see K. Wildes, S.J., *Moral Acquaintances: Methodology in Bioethics,* (Notre Dame, IN: University of Notre Dame Press, 2000.

[2] H.T. Engelhardt, Jr., *Bioethics and Secular Humanism,* (Philadelphia: Trinity Press International, 1991).

organization as such. Furthermore, sources of funding and their regulations on organizations, particularly in education and health care, help to shape and create important moral assumptions for how an organization should operate and the decisions and policies that an organization will carry out. While the funding sources of these organizations often vary, organizations in education and health care are subject to oversight by different government regulatory agencies at various levels in the U.S., for example. Chaps. 5 and 6 start to explore how an organization can both structure and maintain its identity *within* the organization itself and act with integrity in the wider secular society. These policies help to ground internal structures for the organization and they can allow an organization to face some of the challenges for living and acting in the broader, diverse, secular society.

To continue this exploration of organizations, and their ethical accountability, we need to expand our investigation and examine how these organizations can interact and collaborate with other organizations, as well as individuals and society. However, there are clear risks when organizations interact with other organizations or agents in a morally diverse society. A substantial risk is that an organization may lose its identity. Organizations in health care and education are often linked to other organizations through partnerships and cooperative ventures. These organizational partnerships are common in many fields in contemporary society, but we will keep a focus on health care and educational organizations, because of the moral character of their missions and identities, to see how organizational partnerships might be created between organizations with their own identities and, perhaps, different moral views, all the while allowing for the initiating organization to maintain identity and integrity. How can an organization cooperate with other organizations in health care and education and still maintain its identity and integrity? Moreover, how can organizations assure public trust when they enter into cooperative arrangements with other health care or educational organizations?

Of course, in a secular, pluralistic society there can often be a range of options for how an organization can respond to, and work with, other organizations. At one end of the spectrum, there is an approach that might be called the "orthodox" model; under that model, an organization deals only with other organizations that share its values and commitments. One often finds examples of this model in certain religious communities, like Orthodox Jews or certain Muslim communities. This orthodox model sits at one end of the spectrum of possible responses of engagement in a secular, diverse society. At the other end of the spectrum is one model that I might label "ecumenical", since it focuses on, and accentuates, the similarities and commonalities of organizations among a host of differences. Models at this end of the spectrum favor commonality and often overlook the differences between organizations and their missions and identities, posing a real risk that particular identities are lost.

Between these two ends of the spectrum there are a number of ways in which organizations can create partnerships and engage in endeavors with other organizations. It is worth exploring ways to conceptualize such partnerships in which organizations with distinct identities, visions, and missions can cooperate, at times, with other organizations with different identities and missions. Such exploration and reflection can help an organization sharpen and deepen its own organizational identity. How might we conceptualize such a world where organizations can maintain identity and still cooperate with other organizations with different identities and missions? It will be argued that the foundation for exploring these questions is the identity of an organization. In light of that identity an organization needs to build, and utilize, internal structures that support its identity and way of proceeding. In light of these first two steps an organization can begin to explore potential relationships with other organizations in society.

7.1 Grounded in Mission and Identity

Given our discussion of integrity in Chaps. 5 and 6, it should be obvious that the identity of an organization, discussed in Chap. 6, is foundational for evaluating the integrity of the organization. Alfred North Whitehead once observed that the "obvious" is often difficult to understand.[3] It seems that keeping Whitehead's concern about "the obvious" in mind is a worthwhile reminder of the obvious at this point of exploration. At this juncture, it is worth pointing out the obvious, which has been explored more carefully in earlier Chap. 6 of Part II.[4] The obvious starting point for organizational ethics, particularly in education and health care, is the identity of the organization. The question of organizational identity is always foundational and important but is even more so in a morally pluralistic world. The identity of any organization, especially in education and health care, is foundational for ethical thought and evaluation in both what and how an organization functions. Before any organization, in education or health care, can create a partnership arrangement with another organization it should have a clear sense of who and what make up the organization and what it hopes to accomplish, as developed in Chap. 4. In Chap. 6 of this book, we examined how organizations can develop, maintain, and integrate their particular identities. However, we need to look at how the identity of an organization and its integrity can be maintained in a pluralistic, secular society. This challenge is particularly relevant for organizations in their dealings with individuals, but it is also important for how organizations deal with other organizations, particularly in cooperative arrangements in health care and education. How can organizations, particularly if they are different from one another in their identities and missions, cooperate and work with other organizations? How can we conceptualize organizations in a way that allows them to maintain identity while engaging in cooperative arrangements with other organizations?

---

[3] "It requires a very unusual mind to undertake the analysis of the obvious." A. N. Whitehead, *Science and the Modern World*, Preface.

[4] See Chaps. 4 and 5.

Just as organizations can be complex, so it is no surprise that an organization's relationship with other organizations can also be complex. Therefore, it is important that any organization, particularly those in education or in health care, should be clear about its identity and mission or purpose before establishing a relationship with another organization. A relationship with another organization must be based on not only a commonality in terms of the missions of the organizations, but the two different organizations must also find common ground in their cultures and in how the organizations operate. Next, one needs to examine how the relationship between the organizations can be structured. There is at least one tradition in moral thought, exemplified in Roman Catholic thought, which can provide us with a model and direction with the tools we need to map out such a cooperative arrangement between organizations. It is one tradition and not the only tradition. Both Judaism and Islam are rich in thought and provide examples with regard to these issues. However, the history of the Catholic Church, particularly in the United States, is rich in its significant experience with charitable organizations, particularly in education and health care. The model of the Catholic Church, including its incorporated language, is not a definitive one that should be used by all organizations. However, this model does provide a vantage point from which to initiate reflection. I want to use the conceptual language of Catholic health care to give us an example, as well as guidance as to how organizations can work with other organizations with different moral views. This example is not *the* answer, but it is one answer as to how one might think about these relationships.

7.2 Internal Structure for Organizational Identity

The exploration of the concept of integrity in Chap. 5 led to an exploration of the concept of institutional identity in Chap. 6. As we further examine the concept of organizational identity and integrity, we can identify structures that can both help to articulate the identity of an organization and maintain that identity with a level of integrity.

7.2.1 Trustees and Directors: Mission, Policy, and Evaluation

The organization's identity and mission are foundational for the organization both in what it does and how it is structured. There is no platonic form for the correct way to structure organizations. However, there are key elements, with responsibilities, which are often found within organizations, and it is worthwhile to highlight them and their respective roles.

One key element is the role of the Board of Trustees or the Board of Directors. The language that is used varies depending upon the norms of the legal jurisdiction in which an organization is established.[5] However, for our discussion, I will use the term "trustees", since it most clearly expresses the idea that the board holds the organization in trust for the larger society and the fact that the organization is different from a "for-profit" organization where the Directors can benefit from the organization and their work as Directors.

In the end the identity and mission of any organization rests with its incorporating board. Most educational and health care organizations are structured as non-profit organizations that serve a public good. The Board stands in the place of the public and the public good, unlike for- profit institutions where Boards stand for the stockholders. A key to understanding the responsibility of boards is that they act not only for the good of the health care or educational organization, but they also stand for the larger society and the services their organizations bring to society. While the legal requirements of organizations differ from jurisdiction to jurisdiction, the role of the board is to set strategic direction for the organization, in light of its mission.

The second key role for a board is to review the performance of the organization, in light of the goals, objectives, and policies that have been approved by the board. This can often be challenging for a board; a review can lead to micromanagement of the organization by causing the board to cross the fine line between thinking and working strategically toward implementation of the mission and the micromanagement of specific areas of the organization.

A key way for a board to maintain the proper balance and role is to look at the executive of the organization and how the executive is leading the organization.

There are three key roles for the board of an organization. One is to keep the organization focused on its mission and identity. A board needs to evaluate internal structures and initiatives in light of the organization's mission and identity. Any organization faces the risk of "mission creep" where, under the rubric of "mission", the work of the organization keeps expanding. A second role for a board is to work to make sure the organization has the resources needed to carry out its mission. The responsibility of ensuring appropriate resources can include making sure the organization has the appropriate internal structures. For example, does an organization need internal legal counsel, or can it rely on outside counsel? The context within which the board is to ask such questions is its view of the mission of the organization.

For an organization in general, and for a board, the language that is most appropriate is the language of policy. And, in the language of policy there will need to be regular processes of review of policy and accountability regarding its implementation.

---

[5] The two different labels, usually, reflect a difference on whom the organization and the board primarily serves. Traditionally, in non-profit organizations, trustees stand in the place of the larger society, and the organization, a health care or educational organization, is viewed as serving the larger society. While the term "Director" is most often associated with for-profit organizations where the group primarily served is comprised of the shareholders or investors.

7.2.2 Executive Responsibility and Bureaucracy

There is no platonic form for organizations that tells how they should be structured, but we do have good common practices that have been successful and which can be a guide. Of course, each organization will have to determine the structures that best fit the organization's mission and history. Moreover, the structures of an organization can change over time, depending on events within the organization or in society. Nonetheless, however an organization is structured, one of the key responsibilities of a governing Board is to choose a chief executive officer for the organization. In addition, a governing board will, minimally, be tasked with the responsibilities of supporting the executive officer and evaluating the performance of the executive officer.

Chapter 4 of this book examined the roles of organizational bureaucracies as part of an exercise in reimagining moral language and concepts. This exploration was particularly interested in recasting the moral concept of "responsibility" in light of the roles bureaucracies play in organizations. In an organization the executive function, however developed, will bear responsibility for the way the organization's bureaucracy is structured, educated, and evaluated and how it functions.

While accountability for performance will vary from organization to organization in how it is accomplished, it must be integrated within the organization and achieved in a way that is appropriate to each level of the organization.

7.2.3 Mission Officer

The complexity of an organization's mission and identity in education and health care can present risks and real challenges for an organization, particularly those in health care and education. This is so, because organizations in these fields are more complex, for example, than a manufacturing company that makes widgets. One of the arguments of this book has been that organizations in education and health care can vary significantly in their mission, purpose, history, and culture. And in these variations organizations can offer different menus of services and cultures of service. In thinking about the wide range of organizations in both education and health care there is complexity in the missions and identities of these organizations. While it is obvious that the identity and mission (purpose) of an organization is foundational to its identity we should also be clear that the mission of social organizations will vary between organizations, their histories, identities and missions.

A structure or person that can be helpful to maintain the identity of complex social organizations is a "mission" office or mission officer. While there are a variety of ways that an organization can set up internal structures that are concerned with the identity and mission of the organization, the important role for these offices would be to function, within the organization, as a voice, present in the day-to-day operations of the organization that asks questions about whether and how decisions and policies, for the organization, uphold the fundamental identity of an organization. Each organization, given its own distinct mission, identity, and culture will need to determine how best to structure such an office within the organization. Also, each organization will need to determine the appropriate *qualifications* for those who would lead and staff such offices. It would seem that one important qualification for a mission officer would be the ability to participate in the ordinary life of an organization. For example, given the specialized nature of health care and higher education it would seem appropriate that the mission office be led or staffed by those who, while familiar with the tradition of the organization, would also be qualified to participate in the primary work of the organizations either as an ordinary faculty member or as a member of the professional health care team.

Given the complexity of contemporary higher education and health care it will be important for any mission officer to have at least two qualifications. First, the officer should be familiar with and able to articulate the mission and vision of the organization. Second, it would seem important that the mission officer be professionally competent to participate in the work of the organization. So, for example, a mission officer should have some level of professional competence in some area of health care if she is to articulate the mission and vision of a health care organization. Or, a mission officer for higher education should be professionally competent to take part in the essential work of the college or university and be aware of the key issues confronting higher education.

There is a danger for organizations, particularly in the social spheres, to focus on elements that might be related to the mission but not essential to it. For example, an organization might have a relationship with an ancillary enterprise. It will be important for someone, perhaps a Mission officer or a mission committee of the Board, to review those relationships. Therefore, a question that needs to be continually asked is how a program fits with the mission and identity of the organization.

7.2.4 Building a Culture: Personnel Orientation, On-going Education, and Evaluation

It is important that the mission of an organization not simply be the work of the executive team or the trustees. Ideally, the mission ought to be part of the work of all employees, as well as volunteers in an organization. To accomplish that, an organization needs to build a culture within the organization that reflects the mission and identity of the organization. For example, a Catholic organization should aspire to build an internal culture that reflects the ethical principles and social teaching of the Catholic Church. It would, for example, ask if Saint Nowhere's hospital or university is open to the teachings of the Church on the rights of workers or on welcoming people in need no matter their immigration status.

Building this organizational culture would start with a mission-focused program of orientation. However, such a program would need to go beyond an initial orientation to include ongoing education to both reinforce and update the culture of the organization in terms of its mission and purpose.

Another structure that can play an important role in maintaining the mission of an organization is the structure of ongoing evaluation of the organization and its personnel. (See Section G below). Annual evaluations are part of the cultures of education and health care, and they take place in many ways. However, to build continually the culture of an organization, it is important to evaluate personnel, in their positions, for their work in light of the mission of the organization.

7.2.5 Planning: Budgets and Resources

We rarely think of budgets as planning documents,[6] but they are. As organizations articulate their missions or identities, one test of what they say about themselves is where they put their resources. If a health care organization says that it is committed to home health care but allocates few resources to that area, it is deceiving itself and the public. A university that says it is committed to educating first generation students but does not allocate scholarship money or academic assistance to help such students is deceiving itself and the public. One way to learn of the commitment of an organization is to read its budget.

A budget is not an audit, which informs on how an institution has used its resources.

Rather, a budget is a document that should reflect what an organization values and how it plans to realize that priority. In allocating the resources of an organization, there ought to be an alignment of the budget with the planning documents and identity of an organization.

One of the key responsibilities for any governing board is resource planning, including the use of resources. That includes making sure that the mission and identity of an organization are taken into consideration in decision-making regarding the allocation and development of the organization's resources. No matter how noble the goals of an organization, any organization needs resources to carry out its mission. It is important to remember that the allocation of resources is part of the identity and mission of an organization. If, for example, a health care organization or educational organization talks about a commitment to the poor, marginalized, or underserved in its mission statement but does not provide resources for these areas of service, the organization is deceiving itself and the public. One can see the process of developing a budget as an exercise in mission and planning for an organization. A budget ought to provide a road map that reflects what an organization values and what it hopes to become.

---

[6] I am indebted to Rev. William Byron, S.J., who often referred to budgets as "planning documents".

7.2.6 A Culture of Evaluation

Organizations are living creatures. They adapt and develop, or they fail. A key pathway to the well-being and success of an organization is through evaluation. Evaluation needs to become part of the culture of an organization. Clearly individual employees and volunteers must be evaluated on a regular basis. This is more than the good business practice of making sure people are doing their jobs; part of the evaluation should be tied to the mission of the organization and how individuals contribute to it. In building a culture of evaluation within the organization, a link to external evaluations of the entire organization is created.

7.2.7 Compliance and Audits

One of the challenges, for any organization, is the difficulty in making an account of the whole organization. This is a good reason for an organization to establish and maintain a clear, independent Audit function within the organization, as well as undergo an external audit. An audit is a systematic and independent examination of the books, accounts, statutory records, documents, and vouchers of an organization that aims to ascertain how far the financial statements, as well as non-financial disclosures, present a true and fair view of the concern. An audit also attempts to ensure that the books of accounts are properly maintained by the concern as required by law. An Audit function is often linked, in health care and education, to internal controls within the organization.

Often, when we think about the concept of "audit" we think, rightly so, about financial controls. However, in areas like education and health care, the scope of the audit function should not be limited to areas of budget and finance. Both health care and education have other regulatory concerns that need to be monitored. Both areas deal with vulnerable populations, students and sick people, for whom important legal and moral regulations exist. For example, both in education and health care, there are regulations pertaining to student and patient information. Therefore, it is not surprising or uncommon that the Audit function of an organization extends beyond areas of finance.

7.2.8 Conscience, Conflict of Interest and Whistleblower Protection

As has been pointed out, repeatedly, one of the key symptoms of the postmodern condition in secular societies is moral pluralism. This is not surprising, as secular societies frequently celebrate cultural diversity and multiculturalism.

As this book argues, it is essential for organizations, particularly in education and health care, to have a clear sense of identity and purpose and to develop structures to help them maintain that identity and purpose over time. Moreover, it is also important for them to develop methods and structures to incorporate new members into the organization; this is normally accomplished through programs like orientation and continuing education.

It is important, however, for organizations to develop other structures within to protect the consciences of employees of the organization. The Second Vatican Council defines the human conscience as "the most secret core and sanctuary of a man. There he is alone with God, whose voice echoes in his depths". It also states, "For his part, man perceives and acknowledges the imperatives of the divine law through the mediation of conscience." So, it is important, in this postmodern age, for organizations to make sure there are structures and procedures within the individual organization to allow individuals to maintain their conscience and integrity.

7.2.8.1 Conflicts of Interest

Just as human beings are complex and often have many interests, so too organizations are complex and often have many interests. That is, they want and desire material or non-material things. For example, a person may desire a new car or house or desire a good reputation among certain people. It is not uncommon that individuals experience conflicts of interest at times, as people often have many interests in common that come into conflict.

A conflict of interest is a situation in which an individual has competing interests or loyalties. Conflicts of interest involve a person who has two relationships that might compete with each other for the person's loyalties. For example, the person might have a loyalty to an employer and loyalty to a family business. Each of these businesses expects the person to put its interest first. Thus, the conflict.

A conflict of interest can exist in many different situations. The easiest way to explain the concept of conflict of interest is by using examples:

- A public official whose personal interests conflict with his or her professional position
- A person who holds a position of authority in one organization that conflicts with his or her interests in another organization
- A person who has conflicting responsibilities

One of the challenges, within an organization, is how to monitor, and prevent where possible, conflicts of interest. For example, an educational organization needs to find ways, usually through disclosure, to make sure those purchasing educational or instructional materials are not benefiting from the purchases they make. Or, in health care we need to monitor situations where health care professionals are not referring patients to clinics in which they are part owners without, at the very least, making appropriate disclosures. While the easiest way to prevent such problems is to make sure there is appropriate oversight within an organization, an alternative is to require full disclosure. For example, the physician who is part owner of an off-sight testing facility discloses this to patients who might go to the facility.

7.2.8.2 Whistleblower Protection

We know that there is no foolproof way to guarantee full oversight of an organization. While it is crucial for an organization in health care or education to have in place structures like those already discussed, it is also important for an organization to develop structures that can be used by individual members of the organization to report problems. The unfortunate term of art that has evolved for such structures and procedures is "whistleblower". However, the value of this function is to allow individuals to see and report questionable occurrences that might otherwise be overlooked or missed.

7.2.9 Evaluation

Organizations are living creatures. They adapt and develop, or they fail. As stated earlier, a key contributor to the well-being and success of an organization is evaluation. Evaluation must become part of the culture of an organization. Clearly, individual employees and volunteers need to be evaluated on a regular basis. But evaluation is more than simply a good business practice to make sure people are doing their jobs; part of the evaluation should assess how individuals contribute to the mission of the organization. The building of a culture of evaluation within an organization creates a link to external evaluations of the whole organization.

7.2.10 Mission Driven Innovation

Again, at the risk of stating the obvious, there will be change. There will be changes in society that affect what we expect from organizations in health care and education. For example, in the post-industrial information economy, many are looking for different models of what it is to be "educated". In addition, in both education and health care, new technological innovations introduce dynamics for change.

Organizations need to develop both processes and cultures that allow for change and adaptation. One structural way to approach this issue is to establish an office or team within the organization that is charged with looking for opportunities for innovation and development. This office could be freestanding or connected, in some way, to the executive team as a whole.

However, it is imperative that changes and developments in what an organization does, and how it performs, occur in line with its fundamental identity and mission. Depending on the nature of a change or development, there must be an appropriate review of the process and implementation of change so that such developments are in line with the mission of the organization.

7.3 Organizations at Work in Society: Accountability, Accreditation, and Certification

Up until this point in the chapter, we have been exploring various internal structures that help to ensure the identity and integrity of an organization. However, just as individual agents can deceive themselves about who they are, so can organizations. So, one of the challenges when thinking about organizations as moral agents is the question of how the rest of society is to know whether an organization is what it believes and says it is. The challenge, of course, in both education and health care, is particularly important for people in a secular, culturally diverse society where we need to be able to know if organizations are what they say they are. For the sake of clarity, let us use the term "accreditation" to encompass the different ways in which health care and educational organizations can be certified on behalf of the general population.

Accreditation is the process in which certification of competency, authority, or credibility is presented.

In a diverse, multicultural, secular society people will hold sometimes profoundly different moral views about what are, or are not, appropriate choices of behavior. One way to morally address such different views is through a "process" one might call "truth in advertising". That is, people, who can be moral strangers, can come to agreement on what can or should be done in a particular situation. However, organizations are more complex in that we need to find processes that will enable us to know not only what an organization claims to be but also that it is what it claims to be.

Organizations, which issue credentials such as diplomas, or certify third parties against official standards, are themselves formally accredited by accreditation bodies; hence they are sometimes known as "accredited certification bodies". The accreditation process ensures that the certification practices of accredited institutions are acceptable, meaning typically that they are competent to test and certify third parties, behave ethically, and employ suitable quality assurance.

In the United States, there is a public-private partnership for assuring the quality of educational organizations. In this partnership, the U.S. Department of Education does not accredit educational institutions or programs directly. Rather, the Department provides oversight of the postsecondary accreditation system through its review of all federally recognized accrediting agencies. The Department does this by holding the accrediting agencies accountable for enforcing their accreditation standards effectively. Since the end of World War II and the implementation of the GI Bill, the U.S. federal government has been a significant investor in postsecondary education.[7] It is public investment in education that serves as the key for justification of this oversight role of the federal government. Also, as a part of the Department's oversight role, the Secretary of Education is required by law to publish a list of nationally recognized accrediting agencies determined by the Secretary to be reliable authorities as to the quality of education or training provided by the institutions of higher education and the higher education programs those agencies accredit. The Secretary of Education also recognizes State agencies for the approval of public postsecondary vocational education and nursing education.

In the United States, the recognition of accrediting agencies by the Secretary of Education is limited by statute to accreditation activities within the United States. Although there are many recognized agencies that carry out accrediting activities outside the United States, these activities do not fall under the legal authority of the Department of Education's mandate and are not reviewed by the Department; further, the Department does not exercise any oversight over them.

The goal of accreditation is to ensure that education provided by institutions and/or programs of higher education meets acceptable levels of quality. Accrediting agencies, which are private educational associations of regional or national scope, develop evaluation criteria and conduct peer evaluations to assess whether or not those criteria are met. Institutions and/or programs that request an agency's evaluation and which meet an agency's criteria are "accredited" by that agency.

7.3.1 Regional Accreditation

There are seven regional accreditors involved in higher education accreditation in the United States. Regional accreditation is the educational accreditation of schools, colleges, and universities in the United States by one of seven regional accrediting agencies. Accreditation is a voluntary process by which colleges and universities demonstrate to each other, and sometimes to employers and licensing agencies, that the credits and degrees issued by colleges and universities meet minimum standards. It is essentially self-regulation of the higher education industry.

Each regional accreditor oversees the vast majority of public and private educational institutions, both not-for-profit and for-profit, in its region. Its primary function is accreditation of postsecondary institutions, while accreditation of primary and secondary schools is limited. Regional accreditation has been around longer than national accreditation and, with a few exceptions, is more rigorous than national

[7] The initial legislation was the Servicemen's Readjustment Act of 1944". This legislation has been reauthorized several times. One of the key benefits was an educational benefit. See, Bennett, Michael J. *When Dreams Came True: The G.I. Bill and the Making of Modern America* (New York: Brassey's Inc., 1996).

accreditation. Additionally, most non-profit institutions are regionally accredited, while most for-profit colleges and universities are nationally accredited.

Following are the seven active regional accrediting agencies for educational institutions in the United States:

1. Middle States Commission on Higher Education
2. New England Association of Schools and Colleges
3. Higher Learning Commission, (formerly part of the North Central Association of Colleges and Schools)
4. Northwest Commission on Colleges and Universities (NWCCU) for postsecondary institutions
5. Southern Association of Colleges and Schools
6. Accrediting Commission for Schools, Western Association of Schools and Colleges
7. Accrediting Commission for Community and Junior Colleges, formerly part of the Western Association of Schools and Colleges[8]

The goal of accreditation is to ensure that education provided by any institution and programs of higher education meet acceptable levels of quality. Accrediting agencies, which are private educational associations of regional or national scope, develop evaluation criteria and conduct peer evaluations to assess whether or not those criteria are met. As mentioned, institutions and/or programs that request an agency's evaluation and which meet an agency's criteria are "accredited" by that agency.

---

[8] The geographic breakdown for accreditation, in the United States, is as follows:

A. Middle States Commission on Higher Education: The Middle States Association is responsible for accrediting education institutions in New York, New Jersey, Pennsylvania, Delaware, Maryland, the District of Columbia, Puerto Rico, and the US Virgin Islands.
B. New England Association of Schools and Colleges - Educational institutions in the six New England states (Connecticut, Maine, Massachusetts, New Hampshire, Rhode Island, and Vermont).
C. Higher Learning Commission, formerly part of the North Central Association of Colleges and Schools - Educational institutions in Arkansas, Arizona, Colorado, Iowa, Illinois, Indiana, Kansas, Michigan, Minnesota, Missouri, North Dakota, Nebraska, New Mexico, Ohio, Oklahoma, South Dakota, Wisconsin, West Virginia, and Wyoming. Since 2006, the North Central Association has been part of Advanced.
D. Northwest Commission on Colleges and Universities (NWCCU) for postsecondary institutions in Alaska, Idaho, Montana, Nevada, Oregon, Utah, and Washington. Since 2012, the Northwest Accreditation Commission for primary and secondary schools has been a division of AdvancED.
E. Southern Association of Colleges and Schools - Educational institutions in Alabama, Florida, Georgia, Kentucky, Louisiana, Mississippi, North Carolina, South Carolina, Tennessee, Texas, and Virginia.
F. Accrediting Commission for Schools, Western Association of Schools and Colleges - 4-year educational institutions in California, Hawaii, Guam, American Samoa, Micronesia, Palau, and Northern Marianas Islands, as well as schools for American children in Asia.
G. Accrediting Commission for Community and Junior Colleges, formerly part of the Western Association of Schools and Colleges – 2-year educational institutions in California, Hawaii, Guam, American Samoa, Micronesia, Palau, and Northern Marianas Islands, as well as schools for American children in Asia.

In the United States, for example, there are also a number of accrediting associations that are more specialized in that they focus on particular areas of professional skills and knowledge such as Law, Medicine, Counseling, and Music. These are specialized areas of knowledge that have grown with the development of specialized educational areas; they also play roles in public certification of specialized knowledge.

One of the most profound criticisms of this method and model of accreditation is that it relies on people, within an organization, who are free to be honest with accreditation visitors and evaluators when they make their site visits. Some have argued there is a risk that accreditors cannot truly make informed decisions because of the inherent incentive to present information about an institution only in a favorable light. One suggestion posits that accrediting organizations should allow the submission of anonymous observations and complaints.[9]

7.3.2 Health Care

Health Care also has a complex history of certification and accreditation. This complex history is the history of the development of Medicine and its institutions over time. Part of the complexity has to do with the legal structures governing Medicine where medical professionals, like physicians, are governed as much by State law and the governance of professional licensure by the Sates, as by Federal law. In the early 1950s the American College of Physicians, the American Hospital Association, the American Medical Association, and the Canadian Medical Association joined together to create the Joint Commission on Accreditation of Healthcare Organizations to reflect an expanded scope of activities dealing with patients.

The area of accreditation and certification, which continues to grow and develop, is very important for organizational identity and integrity. The processes of accreditation and certification are both public and specialized. They provide specialized, professional evaluation of organizations and programs, and through the public nature of their findings, they provide a basic level of assurance for the diverse society in which organizations function.

7.4 Organizations at Work in Society: Cooperation with Other Organizations

In this part of the book, we have been exploring the elements of organizational integrity and the internal structures that can help to ensure the integrity of an organization. However, as it was argued earlier in this chapter, organizations rarely exist

[9] Joshua Wolff, "The Fatal Flaw in Accreditation", *The Chronicle of Higher Education*, December 1, 2019.

by themselves. They do not exist in isolation. They often have cooperative arrangements with other organizations. Because, in a secular society, they exist in a morally, culturally diverse world we need to think through how organizations can cooperate with other organizations with different identities but retain moral identity. Following our analysis of how particular people can exist and cooperate peacefully in such a diverse world, we need to think through how organizations can both maintain identity and still cooperate with other organizations in this diverse, secular setting.

In exploring the area of "cooperation" between organizations, whether private organizations or government organizations, I am borrowing from the Roman Catholic moral tradition as one example of how one might think about these issues. The reasons for borrowing from this tradition are simple. First, this particular tradition involves a community that has a moral code, as well as a tradition of living and working in the secular world and not separate from it. Second, this is a community that has had a long history of institutions, particularly in health care and education, which are involved in and serve the secular world. These organizations have existed in a wide variety of cultures and legal and financial systems. So, we have here an example of a community that is both committed to institutions in health care and education and which has a long history of thought about how such organizations can operate in a diverse, and sometimes hostile, society. This conceptual framework of "cooperation" is not the only answer to these questions, but it does offer one systematic model of one coherent way to think through these issues.

To understand how this particular conceptual framework might be used as an example, it is important to start by articulating the basic assumptions that are foundational for this particular moral tradition in terms of its content and method of thinking. The Catholic moral tradition starts with the most basic assumptions of the Scripture and the tradition of Natural Law ethics: one should do good and avoid evil. However, the tradition moves on to try to fill in and articulate the most basic premise and address the evils to be avoided and the goods to be done. There is a realism and coherence in this line of moral thought. It is based, in part, on the fundamental convictions that (1) there is an objective moral order, which can be known by the intellect, and it assumes that (2) there are some actions, in this order, which are "intrinsically evil," that is, they are never morally justifiable regardless of the circumstances of the act.

Three theological principles have been developed to deal with the ethical permissibility of actions, which relate to either physical evil or the moral evil of other agents. A "moral evil" is any morally negative event that is caused by the intentional action or inaction of an agent, such as a person. An example of a moral evil might be murder, or any other evil event for which someone can be held responsible or culpable. This concept of a moral evil can be contrasted with natural evil, in which a bad event occurs naturally, without the intervention of an agent. The dividing line between natural and moral evil is not clear, however, as some behavior can be unintentional yet morally significant, and some natural events (for example, global warming) can be caused by intentional actions.

The distinction of evil from "bad" can be complex and will depend on the language game in which the terms are used. In the Catholic tradition, from which I am borrowing, the term evil is a term that connotes an action or situation that is more than simply "negative" or "bad".

Something is "bad" when it is either undesired or inhibits a good. The term evil can be used on its own, and without reference to any other event that is morally incorrect. The validity of "moral evil" as a term, therefore, rests on the validity of one's moral or ethical assumptions.

Nevertheless, human or organizational actions do not happen in isolation, given that actions, particularly those of organizations, are often interrelated. Therefore, there we can discover other principles, regarding actions, such as the principles of cooperation.[10] They are used here simply as one example of how one might think about how an organization, with a particular moral identity, might work with other organizations in the postmodern world.

7.4.1 Historical Origins of the Distinction[11]

Again, I remind the reader of what I have said before. The examples are drawn from the Catholic tradition, because, in both education and health care, it is a tradition rich in thinking about these questions surrounding organizations. As noted, this tradition is being used here as an example. There are a number of excellent explorations of this distinction, and its use in Catholic health care, which should be explored and which have been cited in the endnotes of this chapter.[12]

One reason for this organizational history of thought is the long tradition in the Catholic Community of institutional development in both heath care and education. As Catholic health care and educational institutions have faced issues and questions in dealing with the broader secular society, the Church has been given a way to think through issues surrounding questions of how Catholic organizations can participate in secular, pluralistic societies and work with governmental and other organizations in education and health care.

---

[10] *Ethics & Medics* March 1995 – The Principle of the Double-Effect.

[11] Kevin L. Flannery, *Cooperation with Evil: Thomistic Tools of Analysis*. Washington, D.C.: Catholic University of America Press, 2019. doi:10.2307/j.ctvr7fd64.

[12] See, for example, James Keenan, "Prophylactics, Toleration, and Cooperation: Contemporary Problems and Traditional Principles", *International Philosophical* Quarterly, June 1989, pp. 205–220. M. Cathleen Kaveny and James F, Keenan, Ethical Issues in Health Care Restructuring", *Theological Studies*, June 1995.

St. Alphonsus Liguori (d. 1787)[13] developed a way to think about how organizations could participate and work with other organizations and society in general. He developed what have become known as principles of "cooperation". He did so by introducing the distinction between formal and material cooperation and by considering scandal as a serious invitation to sin. Cooperation in the ethically significant sense is defined as the participation of one agent in the activity of another agent to produce a particular effect or share in a joint activity. This becomes ethically problematical when the action of the primary agent is morally wrong.

In this distinction, as traditionally developed, there are three basic examples that have been used in cooperation on the part of individuals: the hostage, the taxpayer, and the accomplice. In these examples, which are often used in cases, the participation or cooperation of the cooperating individual in the morally questionable acts of the principal agent is quite distinct one from another. Often the freedom of the cooperator is compromised. For example, a hostage is forced with threats to comply with the evil act of another person. In such an example, fear more or less compels the hostage to cooperate. This situation diminishes his culpability and, in some cases, eliminates it completely. In contrast, the accomplice may perform the same act as the hostage, but culpability is imputed fully, because cooperation in this instance is free and willed (directly intended). The taxpayer is an example of one who cooperates with a principal agent such as the government in an important – in fact, essential – mission (*i.e.,* the governance of society). Nevertheless, the government may sponsor activities that are viewed as immoral, such as the judgment on whether to wage war. The taxpayer then contributes in some degree to this immoral activity. However, contributing to the stability of society is not an intrinsic evil but a good.

7.4.2 *The Different Kinds of Cooperation*

The principles governing cooperation help to identify morally licit and illicit types of cooperation through several basic distinctions.

---

[13] The distinction, used by the Pope, was born of Alphonsus' pastoral experience, his ability to respond to the practical questions posed by the faithful and his contact with their everyday problems. He opposed sterile legalism and strict rigorism. According to him, those were paths closed to the Gospel because "such rigor has never been taught nor practiced by the Church". His system of moral theology is noted for its prudence, avoiding both laxism and excessive rigor. He is credited with the position of "equiprobabilism", which avoided Jansenist rigorism as well as laxism and simple probabilism. Since its publication it has remained in Latin, often in 10 volumes or in the combined 4-volume version of Gaudé. It saw only recently its first publication in translation, in an English translation made by Ryan Grant and published in 2017 by Mediatrix Press. The English translation of the work is projected to be around 5 volumes.

7.4.2.1 Formal and Material Cooperation

The first distinction that is often used is the distinction between formal and material cooperation. Cooperation is formal when the one who is cooperating "concurs in the bad will of the other [the principal agent]." Such cooperation occurs when the cooperator intends the evil action of the principal agent either for its own sake or as a means. In terms of the traditional distinction between object, intention, and circumstances as sources of the morality of human acts, in formal cooperation the cooperator agrees either with the evil moral object of the act (*finis operis*) or with the evil intention (*finis operantis*) of the principal agent.

If the cooperator neither intends the object of the act nor agrees with the intention of the principal agent, yet nevertheless contributes in some way to the principal agent's performance of the act, the cooperation is material. With regard to the degree of material cooperation in the performance of the immoral activity, moral theologians have developed a second major distinction, that between immediate and mediate material cooperation.

Material cooperation can be defined as immediate when it is cooperation in the evil act itself and mediate when it is cooperation in an action that in some manner contributes to or prepares the way for the evil act or aids in its execution. In addition, mediate material cooperation is called proximate if the cooperator's act is close in causal terms to the act of the principal agent and remote if causally distant from the principal agent's act. For example, a nurse may work in a hospital where abortions are performed. Different actions on her part would aid in different ways in the principal agent's performance of the abortion. The nature of her cooperation can be analyzed using the following questions.

In the Catholic tradition of moral thought, the *intention* of the agent is crucial to understanding and assessing the moral character of the action. This means that moral analysis should look beyond the mere physical description of an action to the surrounding circumstances and the intention of an agent. So, for example, when a person is killed the moral analysis needs to go beyond the mere physical description that Joe was killed. The moral analysis needs to consider first whether the action was intentional or accidental. Did I accidentally hit Joe when he was crossing the street, or did I take aim for him and accelerate my car to hit him? Therefore, in looking at questions of cooperation it is important to ask if the cooperating agent shared the intention to do the immoral action. If yes, then the cooperation is formal. If no, then the cooperation is material.

Another important question asks if there is cooperation in the evil act itself. If yes, then the material cooperation is immediate. For example, the nurse does not want the woman to have an abortion. Nevertheless, she assists in the procedure itself, handing the doctor each item as needed. If no, the material cooperation is mediate. The nurse does not want the woman to have an abortion. Nevertheless, she attends to the patient during the preparation for or follow-up to the procedure itself.

7.4.2.2 Assessing the Permissibility of Different Kinds of Cooperation

In this tradition of thought, formal cooperation with an evil act is always morally wrong. Immediate material cooperation is also morally wrong. For example, I may assist a friend as he or she commits a murder. The act is evil, and while I may not commit the murder myself, my participation (cooperation) makes the act possible. Mediate material cooperation can be morally licit in some cases. While everyone has a moral duty to avoid cooperating in evil as much as possible, sometimes there are situations in which it is permissible to cooperate in a mediate material way in order either to gain some good or to prevent the loss of some good.

St. Alphonsus[14] summarized the basic conditions for acceptable mediate, material cooperation in the following manner:

(a) The act of the cooperator must be "in itself either good or indifferent." That means that what the cooperator does cannot be morally evil in itself. While on one level this might seem self-evident, it also serves as a reminder that one may never perform an intrinsically immoral action, even if one hopes by means of this action to obtain some good result.
(b) Second, if there is cooperation, the agent, whether an individual or organization, must have a reason for cooperating that is "just and proportionate to the gravity of the sin of the other and to the proximity of the contribution that is provided to the performance of the sin." In other words, any licit act of mediate material cooperation requires a good to be gained or an evil to be avoided that is proportionate both to the gravity of the principal agent's wrongdoing and to the causal proximity of the cooperator's act to the act of the principal agent.

Assuming that the cooperator's act in itself is either good or indifferent, the acceptability of mediate material cooperation thus depends on its evaluation in terms of whether or not the reason for cooperating is proportionate. The greater the gravity of the wrongdoing, the more serious must be the reason for the material cooperation to be licit. Likewise, the greater the gravity of the wrongdoing, the more causally remote must be any cooperation if it is to be morally permissible.

7.4.2.3 Scandal

However, a further issue must be taken into consideration in cases of material cooperation; that is the topic of scandal. "Scandal is an attitude or behavior which leads another to do evil."[15] While it is obviously wrong to perform an evil act with the intention of inducing another person to perform some evil act, it sometimes happens that one's act can be a source of scandal to another person, even if that act is morally

---

[14] St. Alphonsus Liguori, *Theologia moralis*, I, II, tract.III, cap. 2, dub. V, art. III, n. 63.

[15] *Catechism of the Catholic Church*, Section Two on The Ten Commandments, Chapter Two, You Shall Love Your Neighbor as Yourself, Article 5, The Fifth Commandment, Respect for the Dignity of Persons, #2284.

permissible in itself and one does not intend to cause scandal. Such situations require careful judgment. One is not obligated to refrain from every action that might possibly be taken as scandalous by someone. Nevertheless, charity does require that one avoid giving rise to scandal when this is possible without causing grave inconvenience. The Ethical and Religious Directives state: "Cooperation, which in all other respects is morally licit, may need to be refused because of the scandal that might be caused."[16]

Observation

This set of distinctions about the types of action and an agent's participation in action may seem to represent a lot of needless speculation, like theologians who debated the question of how many angles can dance on the head of a pin. However, I think they offer something far richer. That is they examine and reflect on the complex relationships that organizations can and often do have with one another, persons, and society. In addition, in that reflection they help us to think through how we might think about the moral agency, accountability, and responsibility of organizations.

7.4.3 Application to Contemporary Corporate Partnerships

In this tradition of "cooperation", taken from Roman Catholic thought on casuistry, the tradition developed and was used for the actions individuals who cooperate with the actions of others.

However, in recent years, with changes in health care and education, we have had to look beyond a focus on individual agents and actors to organizations as the principal actors And, furthermore, we have needed to broaden the scope of our conversation to include partnerships with other organizations.

There are important areas of exploration when considering the questions about "corporate actions" of cooperation, such as joint ventures between health care institutions that may be morally questionable, because some actions of one of the partner institutions may be ethically unacceptable to the other cooperative institution.

A complicating factor here is the fact that "cooperation" between institutions or systems is an arrangement made on the level of a legal corporation. The cooperative venture ought to have a very precise and clearly defined identity and purpose, which may not be evident in the public forum. The partnership is a legal and/or corporate structuring intended to perform only functions (1) when conditions are mutually agreeable to all partners, (2) which do not include any procedures with which any

[16] National Conference of Catholic Bishops, *Ethical and Religious Directives for Catholic Health Care Services,* 4th ed., Washington, DC, 2001.

partner disagrees on moral grounds, and (3) which explicitly separate the partnership from activities in which an individual partner may continue to engage.

It is important to ask, and to be clear about, why this sort of partnering is necessary.

There are several reasons. First, clinical medicine has reduced the need for the present number of hospital beds. Many procedures are handled on an outpatient basis; procedures that are more complicated require a shorter hospital recovery period; and, in the health care market, competition is driving cost, not containing cost. The need to downsize acute care settings and to create state of the art diagnostic and day treatment centers has led to the realization that health care must be cast in another form, which is often referred to as "rationalizing" care.

The practical conclusion to the reconfiguration of an organization is that a "stand-alone" position is not always a viable option for an organization. In most cases, the reason for developing a cooperative is that, as foreseen, isolation would entail eventual closure. There are often "market pressures", particularly in health care, that cause an organization to consider cooperative, collaborative ventures. Market pressure can be considered the "sufficient reason", which is one of the "ingredients" necessary to justify material cooperation. Scandal must also be overcome. Scandal is not the same as a public relations problem. Scandal is the serious suggestion that evil is attractive or permissible. Any collaboration between Catholic and non-Catholic health services must avoid the impression that Catholic moral doctrine is not being observed.

7.4.3.1 Contractual Arrangements of Organizations

Organizations rarely exist in isolation and they often have agreements or various types of arrangements with other organizations. In these more complex arrangements it will be important, for an ethical analysis, to identify which organization has moral responsibility for decisions and actions.

A moral person can be a group of natural persons such as an organization. Furthermore, with regard to the question of scandal, because the organization is a moral agent, and because it is public, there is a risk of the danger of scandal not only in what it does but also in how it accomplishes its goals and collaborates with other organizations.

In this tradition of thought, an organization can be considered as a moral person. The organization would need to be "a group or succession of natural persons who are united by a common purpose and, hence, who have a particular relationship to each other. As the *Ethical and Religious Directives* observes there may be significant challenges to imagine partnerships as a single entity."[17] Nonetheless, the Directives go on to argue that such partnerships do not necessarily preclude their

[17] "The Principles Governing Cooperation and Catholic Health Care: An Overview", *Health Progress*. Catholic Health Association, 2013.

possibility on moral grounds. Nevertheless, all such collaborative arrangements must be thoroughly scrutinized in terms of their moral implications. Only by a careful application of the principles governing cooperation in evil will Catholic health care organizations be able both to meet the challenges and take advantage of the opportunities presented by the contemporary context for health care in this country.

Among the principles of cooperation, the primary distinction is between formal and material cooperation. Formal cooperation is a willing participation on the part of the cooperative agent in the sinful act of the principal agent. This formal cooperation can either be explicit ("Yes, I'm happy to drive the getaway car, because I want to be an accomplice") or implicit.

"Implicit formal cooperation is attributed when, even though the cooperator denies intending the wrongdoer's object, no other explanation can distinguish the cooperator's object from the wrongdoer's object."[18]

The category of the implicit formal cooperator is demonstrated by this way of thinking: "I am personally opposed, but..." This type of cooperation is as immoral as explicit formal cooperation. Material cooperation has several inherent distinctions, the most basic being that of immediate and mediate material cooperation. Theologians maintain that in the objective order, immediate material cooperation is equivalent to implicit formal cooperation, because the object of the moral act of the cooperator is indistinguishable from that of the principal agent. Those who use the term "immediate material cooperation" have understood this as ethically unacceptable behavior. An example of this is any form of employment in an abortion clinic.

Immediate material cooperation is set in contrast with mediate cooperation. Here the moral object of the cooperator's act is not that of the wrongdoer. (An example of this is a health care worker employed in a secular hospital that provides morally prohibited procedures but does not require the conscientious objector to such procedures to participate.) This kind of cooperation can be justified (1) for a sufficient reason and (2) if scandal can be avoided. It is a form of cooperating with the circumstances surrounding the wrongdoer's act. Depending on how closely these circumstances impinge upon the act, there is a distinction between proximate and remote material cooperation. Proximate material cooperation is the recovery room nurse who cares for all post-surgical patients, including those who may have undergone morally illicit procedures. This form of routine care is not intrinsically evil.

Further, necessary material cooperation is that without which the sinful act could not occur. Contingent cooperation (also called free cooperation) is that without which the evil act would still take place. An example of necessary material cooperation is being the only anesthesiologist available to assist with a woman undergoing a combination C-section and tubal ligation. Contingent material cooperation would exist if one were not the only such professional available.

---

[18] James F. Keenan, S.J., and Thomas P. Kopfensteiner, "The Principle of Cooperation: Theologians Explain Material and Forma Cooperation", *Health Progress*, April 1995, pp 23–27.

7.4.3.2 Summary: Five Basic Principles for Understanding Cooperation

There are five basic principles the Pope John Center is using to evaluate partnerships.

(1) Cooperation must be mediate material, never formal or immediate material.
(2) We can only do together what all partners agree to be appropriate. This means that while the partnership need not be Catholic, it must nevertheless observe the Ethical and Religious Directives as respecting the "corporate conscience" of the Catholic partner.
(3) Morally illicit procedures cannot be provided on the Catholic campus.
(4) Any morally illicit procedure(s) provided on the campuses of non-Catholic alliance partners must be excluded from the new alliance corporation through separate incorporation (governance, administration, and finance).
(5) All publicity should be straightforward. That is, the publicity should highlight the need to form an alliance for the survival of a worthy apostolate, and it should be made known that the good achieved by rationalizing health care must be to the patients' benefit; immoral procedures must be excluded from the partnership (while these services may still be available on the campuses of some partner[s]). Furthermore, this publicity should also appear in the promotional literature of the Catholic hospital.

7.5 Conclusions

It is worth pointing out what can be easily forgotten in these explorations. First, it is worth remembering that, even in a secular, morally diverse society, both health care and educational organizations inevitably embody some level of moral values, even if minimal. Second, it is important to recognize and understand those values in a society that is both secular and morally pluralistic. Furthermore, it is important for educational and health care organizations to articulate their moral commitments if they are to function, ethically, in such societies. An organization needs to be aware of its mission and moral identity, and an organization needs to be clear about its identity with others, people and organizations, in the secular society in which it works. Of course, a risk for any organization with a moral identity is that the organization can lose, overtime, the awareness of the identity and the culture which supports it. This corporate "self-awareness" is the basis for "truth in advertising" in the secular, morally pluralistic society. Beyond this basic level of corporate self-awareness, the organization needs to keep this sense of itself, and its moral identity, in mind when and if it enters into cooperative arrangements with other health care and educational organizations, whether private or public organizations.

Summary of the Main Points

1. Grounded in Mission and Identity
2. Internal Structures for Organizational Identity
    (a) Trustees and Directors

        Policy
        Review and Accountability

    (b) Executive Responsibility, Organizational Bureaucracy, and Accountability
    (c) Mission Office
    (d) Building a Culture: Personnel Orientation, On-going Education, and Evaluation
    (e) Planning: Budgets and Resources
    (f) A Culture of Evaluation
    (g) Compliance and Audits

        Conflicts of Interest
        Whistle-Blower Protection

3. Organizations at Work in Society: Accountability, Accreditation and Certification
4. Organizations at Work in Society: Cooperation with Other Organizations
    (a) Different Kinds of Cooperation
    (b) Application to contemporary corporate partnerships
    (c) Arrangements with other organization

Part III
Working with Others: Organizations in a Post-modern Secular Society

Chapter 8
Truth in Advertising: Organizational Identity, Accountability, and Accreditation

Throughout this book, it has been argued that one of the characteristics of postmodern, secular societies is that they are, in principle, open to cultural and moral diversity. These societies are open to diversity precisely because of their secular character, as argued particularly in Chap. 3. Cultural diversity can often be a source of moral diversity and moral pluralism, given the relationship that exists between morality and culture. Even thinkers who have been traditionally committed to some form of Natural Law ethics have recognized that natural law is instantiated within a culture and may vary in its stipulations in different cultures. Contemporary national, secular societies often celebrate some level of freedom given their secular character and freedom, in a secular society opens the door for cultural diversity; as stated, cultural diversity brings with it the possibility of moral pluralism. Such cultural and moral pluralism leads to questions about how moral agents, with different moral views, can live and work together in the context of a diverse secular society. Such moral pluralism and diversity lead to questions about what a notion of "common morality" could possibly mean in a secular society. In light of the questions about common morality, one needs to ask about the foundation for government authority in the areas of morality, and its limits, in enforcing morality in a secular, morally diverse society.[1]

We know that we can examine the justification and limits of moral authority of individuals, professions, and government agencies through an analysis of procedures like those of free and informed consent. However, when we turn to organizations, we need to reimagine the procedural tools that can be used to resolve moral controversies involving moral agents and concepts and tools that can help us to think about organizations as moral agents. How can organizations make moral

[1] H. T. Engelhardt, Jr., has developed a clear analysis for the relationship of secular societies and common morality. See, H.T. Engelhardt, Jr., *Bioethics and Secular Humanism* (Philadelphia: Trinity Press International, 1991), and H.T. Engelhardt, Jr., *Foundations of Bioethics*, Second Edition, (New York: Oxford University Press, 1996).

K. W. Wildes, S.J., *Organizational Ethics and Moral Integrity in Secular Societies*, Philosophical Studies in Contemporary Culture 29,
https://doi.org/10.1007/978-3-031-39097-5_8

commitments? How can we know the moral values to which an organization is committed? That question is important for those who are members of an organization as well as those outside the organization. Organizations, unlike persons, are not singular moral agents. Legally, organizations have been treated like persons. However, unlike persons they are often complex and composite both as organizations and as moral agents. In moving to analyze organizations as moral agents, one needs to face the immediate question of how we can know the ethical values to which an organization is committed. The second part of this book, Chaps. 5, 6 and 7, explored and articulated some of the ways that an organization can articulate, monitor, and maintain its organizational identity and the moral commitments of its identity and mission.

We have been exploring and laying the groundwork for how we can ask and answer some of these questions in the second part of this book—in Chaps. 5, 6 and 7—and how an organization can both develop and live with integrity. Now, we need to push our exploration further and examine more carefully how organizations can operate ethically, as organizations, in secular societies that are morally and culturally diverse. How can they interact with other organizations, society, government regulators, and individual persons? This is an important question, particularly in terms of organizations and their moral identities. As we examine how health care and educational organizations can function, ethically, in a postmodern, morally pluralistic secular society, we can assume that any organization has, at least, some minimal set of moral values. In a diverse, secular society those values can range from a full set of religious moral commitments to a set of moral commitments where making a profit is the only values.

The Second Section of this book explored some of the important questions, and steps that can be taken, within an organization, so that any organization can develop and maintain its identity and moral commitments. That section of the book explored questions of organizational identity, as well as some of the possible building blocks needed for organizations to operate, with integrity, in a secular society. These building blocks are important for the internal life of an organization, but they are also important in supporting how an organization interacts with the wider, secular society in which it lives and works.

In exploring postmodern ethics in secular societies, we most often focus on the nature of the relationship that exists between individual moral agents, other moral agents, or the rest of society. In particular, the focus often falls on the role of law and its authority in regulating the behaviors and actions of individual agents and morality in a secular, morally pluralistic society. In these different relationships and situations, the focus has usually centered on the role of consent, by moral agents, as a key for understanding justification in a secular society. If we are to use, and build, on the idea of informed consent as a key to moral justification in a secular society, we now need to ask how moral strangers can think about consent in relation to an organization.

One of the first elements necessary for consent is that the identities and moral commitments of those involved in the consenting agreement be known. Therefore, a first question to ask in exploring the practice of consent between agents and organizations will turn on the question of how one can know, and trust, the identities of organizations. Then, it would seem to follow that we also need to ask how organizations can work with other organizations with moral integrity. How can moral strangers gain confidence in the truthfulness of the identity an organization proclaims about itself? Organizations present a more complex set of questions and circumstances than individual persons do, making it necessary to rethink and reimagine the model of consent, so important for individual agents. Simply put, it can be more difficult to both understand and verify the moral identity of an organization.

In earlier chapters of this book, it was argued that the questions of organizational ethics, in the contemporary, secular world, cannot be separated from the reality of the moral and cultural pluralism that is possible in secular societies. The work of health care and educational organizations is further complicated by the reality that any particular view about both health care and education will make basic moral assumptions, even if minimal, that shape the way organizations work. Health care seeks the good of patients, and education seeks the good of students. However, the notion of "good" needs to be specified, and this is where, in a culturally pluralistic society, differences will become evident. The introduction of the concept of "good" automatically casts these organizations into moral frameworks and necessitates their use of moral language. The cultural and moral pluralism will mean, obviously, that there can, and often will, be different judgments and views about what is or is not morally appropriate policy for individuals, governments, and organizations. Establishing standards for health care and education, in such pluralistic environments, can often be challenging, depending on the cultural pluralism of the societies in which they are found.

However, as it has been argued, in Chap. 3 and elsewhere,[2] many moral issues and controversies in postmodern, secular societies can often be resolved through processes of agreement, or disagreement and the consent of agents involved in any type of moral controversy.[3] When taken seriously such moral diversity and agreement will lead to a more libertarian view about the role of government regulation of the activity of moral agents in secular, pluralistic societies, given that moral foundations will be couched in terms of freedom and consent.[4] The roles of consent and permission are central to the granting of moral authority in such social contexts. In many secular societies the questions of ethics are raised in the context of discussions about governmental authority, the role of government, and what government can or cannot mandate morally. This set of questions involving ethics, public policy, and law leads to further questions about the role of government in relationship to

[2] H. T. Engelhardt, Jr. *Foundations of Bioethics*, Second Edition (New York: Oxford University Press, 1996).

[3] See Chap. 3. Also see K. Wildes, S.J., *Moral Acquaintances: Methodology in Bioethics* (Notre Dame, IN: University of Notre Dame Press, 2000.

[4] H.T. Engelhardt, Jr., *Bioethics and Secular Humanism* (Philadelphia: Trinity Press International, 1991). Also see, *Moral Acquaintances: Methodology in Bioethics*, (Notre Dame, IN: University of Notre Dame Press, 2000).

morality. In these discussions and controversies of ethics, the consent of agents has served as a foundational starting point for resolving moral controversies with moral authority in culturally and morally diverse societies.

However, when we move to moral questions involving organizations, we need to rethink the model of the individual agent and consider how organizations can be understood as moral agents. Earlier, this book, in Chaps. 5 and 6, attempted to establish the language and conceptual framework for a model of consent in ethics that it might be used, analogously, for organizations.

8.1 Civil Society

It is worth pointing out, for sake of conceptual clarity, that our analysis and discussion of organizations is focused on organizations in the context of *civil* society.[5] When we think about postmodern society we often think, primarily, about the relationship of individual agents and government or governmental authority. However, it is worth pointing out that organizations are also actors in secular societies. Organizations, as moral agents in education and health care, play important roles in the intermediary social space of civil society in such diverse, civil, and secular societies. It is important to point out the role of civil society in order to undertake a more complete ethical analysis. The social space of civil society lies between individual moral agents and the government. It is worth explicitly pointing out this space of society, as all too often discussions about ethics become focused on individual agents and the role of government. The roles of organizations are further complicated by how we understand moral agency and the ethics of decision-making in organizations. However, when one moves beyond individual agents and looks at organizations, the procedures of consent and approval, which are so important for individual moral agents, and the role they play in controversies can be more difficult to identify and must be rethought. Furthermore, the questions about how we think through issues of ethics and organizations, particularly in education and health care, can be further complicated, as these organizations frequently have cooperative arrangements with other organizations. In addition to cooperative arrangements, which can raise other ethical considerations, organizations in education and health care are often subject to government regulations.

In considering these arrangements with other organizations, the identity and mission of a particular organization should serve as a fundamental starting point and a key element in assessing how the organizations should move forward, if at all, in building relationships with other organizations. If an organization, in education or health care, has a particular moral identity, it will need to think carefully about how it can structure a relationship with another organization with a different moral identity and mission.

---

[5] See Chap. 7.

Attempts to understand organizational integrity can also be complicated further by issues that may surround the sources of funding for an organization, including issues related to the expectations of the funders of the organization and questions of public disclosure about, and the regulation of, funding. Furthermore, the sources of funding for and regulation of organizations, particularly in education and health care, can help to shape and create important moral assumptions for how organizations operate and the goals they set for themselves and need to achieve, along with the decisions and policies they live out. While the funding sources for organizations vary, they are often a mixture of public and private sources. Organizations in education and health care are subject to oversight by different government regulatory agencies at various levels in the United States. Chapters 5 and 6 explored both how an organization can structure and maintain its identity *within* the organization and so act with integrity. The structures of an organizations can allow an organization to face some of the challenges of living and acting in the broader, diverse, secular society.

To continue this exploration of organizations, and their ethical accountability in secular, postmodern societies, we need to expand this investigation further and examine how organizations, in education and health care, can interact and collaborate with other organizations, as well as with individuals, in society. Often when we address questions of ethics in postmodern societies we focus on individual moral agents and the role of government. However, organizations in health care and education are often linked to other organizations through partnerships and cooperative ventures. Health care organizations, for example, often have relationships with entire networks of providers such as multiple hospitals, clinics, and diagnostic and testing facilities, as well as physician networks. Educational organizations often have relationships with other institutions to facilitate the transfer of credits for students or study abroad programs, or work-study and internship programs for students. These organizational partnerships are a common part of contemporary society in many fields. We will keep a focus on health care and educational organizations because of the moral character of their missions and identities to see how organizational partnerships can be created with other organizations that have different identities and, perhaps, different moral views—partnerships that allow the organizations to still maintain their identities and integrity. If an organization has a moral identity it will be important for the organization to ask how can it cooperate with other organizations in health care and education and still maintain its identity and integrity? Moreover, how can organizations assure public trust in themselves when they enter into cooperative arrangements with other health care or educational organizations?

Of course, in a secular, pluralistic society there is often a range of options for how an organization can work with, and respond to, other organizations. If we imagine different organizations as located on a spectrum, in terms of how they are related to one another, we can label the farthest point of the range on one end as the "orthodox" model. This orthodox organization deals only with other organizations that share its values and commitments. For example, one finds this model in certain religious communities like Orthodox Jews or certain Muslim communities. The orthodox model at one end of the spectrum is one response and possible method of engagement in a secular, diverse society. At the other end of the spectrum is what one might label the "ecumenical" model; it focuses on, and accentuates, the similarities and commonalities of organizations amidst their differences. At this end of the spectrum, however, the differences between organizations, and their missions and identities, are often overlooked.

This model carries the real risk that particular identities can be lost.

However, it is worth exploring ways to conceptualize such arrangements where organizations with distinct identities, visions, and missions can cooperate, at times, with other organizations with different identities and missions. Such exploration and reflection can help an organization sharpen and deepen its own organizational identity. How might we conceptualize such a world where organizations can maintain identity and still cooperate with other organizations with different identities and missions?

8.2 Organizational Identity[6]

As has been argued in this book the identity of any moral agent, including organizations, is foundational to understanding and assessing the integrity of an agent. This is particularly important in a pluralistic, postmodern society. Therefore, it is not surprising that we should focus on identity and integrity when we turn our attention to organizations. If we build on our discussion of integrity throughout this book, and particularly in Section Two, it should be obvious that the identity of an organization, discussed in Chap. 6, is foundational for the integrity of an organization, particularly in a secular, postmodern society. I have often quoted Alfred North Whitehead's observation that it is often difficult to understand the obvious.[7] It seems that keeping Whitehead's concern about "the obvious" in mind is a worthwhile reminder at this point in our exploration. It is worth pointing out the obvious, which has been explored more carefully in earlier chapters in Part Two.[8] The obvious starting point for organizational ethics, particularly in education and health care, is the identity of the organization.

Organizational identity is always a key foundational starting point and important for the analysis of any organization. The questions of identity take on an added level of importance in a morally pluralistic world, particularly regarding how an organization can operate in a pluralistic, secular society. The identity of any organization, especially in education and health care, is the starting point and foundation for ethical thought and evaluation of what an organization is, how an organization functions, and what it does in a secular, diverse society.

---

[6] Kevin W. Wildes, S.J. "Institutional Identity, Integrity, and Conscience", *Kennedy Institute of Ethics Journal* 7, (1997), 413–419.

[7] "It requires a very unusual mind to undertake the analysis of the obvious", A. N. Whitehead, *Science and the Modern World*, Preface.

[8] See Chaps. 4 and 5.

The identity of an organization is foundational for understanding and assessing the organization and what it does. However, the identity of an organization should also be foundational for any relationships it might forge with other organizations and for its moral identity. Before any organization, particularly in education or health care, can create a partnership arrangement with other organizations it should have a clear sense of who and what it is and what it hopes to accomplish, as developed in Chap. 4. Earlier in this book, we examined how organizations can develop, maintain, and integrate their particular identities. However, organizations do not exist by themselves. They exist with others, whether organizations, people, government agencies, or all. However, we need to look at how the identity and integrity can be known and maintained in a pluralistic, secular society. This challenge is particularly relevant for organizations in their dealings with individuals, but it is also important for how organizations deal with other organizations, particularly in cooperative arrangements in health care and education. How can organizations, particularly if they are different in their identities and missions, cooperate and work with other organizations? How can we conceptualize organizations in a way that allows them to maintain their identities while engaging in cooperative arrangements with other organizations?

Just as organizations, by themselves, are often complex in trying to understand the questions of organizational identity, so it is no surprise that the questions of identity can become even more complex when an organization develops a relationship with other organizations.

Therefore, it is important that an organization, not only those in education or in health care, be clear about its identity and its mission or purpose before establishing a relationship with another organization. A relationship with another organization entails finding not only a commonality in terms of the missions of the organizations but finding common ground with regard to the cultures of the different organizations and how they operate. The organizations should have a common way of proceeding. After establishing this common ground, the organizations can begin to explore how to structure their relationship.

There is at least one tradition in moral thought that provides a helpful example for thinking about these questions. That is Roman Catholic moral thought, which presents one model as well as direction regarding the tools we need to map out cooperative arrangements between organizations. The tradition of Roman Catholic thought is one tradition but not the only tradition. Both Judaism and Islam are rich in thought and excellent examples for these questions as well.

However, the history of the Catholic Church, particularly in the United States, is a rich history of charitable organizations, particularly in education and health care. The language and model of Roman Catholic moral thought is not a definitive one that should be used by all organizations.

However, it does provide one model from which to initiate organizational reflection. I will use the conceptual language of Catholic health care to provide one example, and guidance, as to how organizations can work with other organizations with different moral views. This example is not *the* answer but one answer to how one might think about these relationships.

8.3 Organizational Identity: Accountability, Accreditation, Certification, Regional Accreditation

In diverse, secular societies, the procedure of informed consent is crucial for conveying moral authority in health care and education. We need to think through how the procedure of informed consent can become part of health care procedures or aid in the decision to enroll in an educational program. However, the procedures and processes of informed consent raise a new set of important questions when we examine the actions of organizations. How are people to know not only what organizations say they are but also how to verify such claims? How are consumers, or those who use the services offered by such organizations, to have confidence in knowing organizations are what they say they are?

If we start with particular organizations, how do those of us outside the organization in the wider society know that they are what they claim to be? This question is a particular challenge in health care and education in secular, morally diverse societies, as people will need to be able to know if organizations are what they say they are.

In some ways this question evolves from a basic concern about "truth in advertising", which is part of an exchange between moral agents, particularly when they are moral strangers. It is relatively easy to make these judgments and assessments when dealing with individual moral agents. But how are moral strangers to know if an organization in education or health care is what it says it is?

We need to find procedures to certify that organizations are what they say they are in diverse, pluralistic secular societies. For the sake of clarity, I will use the term "accreditation" to encompass the different ways in which health care and educational organizations can be certified for the general population. Accreditation is the process by which certification of competency, authority, or credibility is established.

In a diverse, multicultural, secular society people will hold sometimes significantly different moral views about what are, or are not, appropriate choices for behavior. One way morally to address such different views is through processes and procedures that one might label as "truth in advertising". Under these processes, individuals who are moral strangers can reach agreement on what can or should be done. However, organizations are more complex in that we need to find processes that will enable us to know not only what an organization claims to be but also that it *is* what it claims to be.

Organizations, which issue credentials or certify those who complete programs, as measured against official standards, are themselves formally accredited by accreditation bodies; hence, they are sometimes known as "accredited certification bodies". The accreditation processes ensures that the certification practices of accredited institutions are acceptable, typically meaning that they are competent to test and certify third parties, behave ethically, and employ suitable quality assurance.

The certification of organizations, in health care and education, is important in contemporary secular societies. The certification by accrediting associations, explored in Chap. 7, is one way for the general population, and people who may potentially use the services of the organization to verify the ability of the organization to deliver the services it offers. At the same time, the certification process, through accreditation processes is an important step in the process of Federal investment in higher education through financial aid.

Accrediting agencies, which are private educational associations of regional or national scope, develop evaluation criteria and conduct peer evaluations to assess whether or not those criteria are met. Institutions and/or programs that request an agency's evaluation and that meet an agency's criteria are then "accredited" by that agency. The goal of accreditation is to ensure that education provided by institutions and/or programs of higher education meet acceptable levels of quality. Accrediting agencies, which are private educational associations of regional or national scope, develop evaluation criteria and conduct peer evaluations to assess whether or not those criteria are met. Institutions and/or programs that request an agency's evaluation and that meet an agency's criteria are then "accredited" by that agency.

Because of the nation's secular nature, and its mixture of public and private educational organizations we have noted, already, in Chap. 7, that there are several regional accrediting associations in the United States. In the United States, accreditation is a voluntary process and is essentially a self-regulating process.

Each regional accreditor oversees the vast majority of public and private educational institutions, both not-for-profit and for-profit, in its region. Its primary function is accreditation of post-secondary institutions, though there is a limited amount of accreditation of primary and secondary schools. Regional accreditation is older than national accreditation and, with a few exceptions, more rigorous than national accreditation. Additionally, most non-profit institutions are regionally accredited, while most for-profit colleges and universities are nationally accredited.

8.3.1 Specialized Accountability and Certification

In addition to the regional accrediting associations in the United States for colleges and universities there are a number of specialized accrediting groups and professional associations that focus on certifying particular areas of professional skills and knowledge. For example, the Association to Advance Collegiate Schools of Business (AACSB) offers both standards for schools and a process of evaluation for schools of Business in the United States.[9]

One can also find accreditation standards and processes in other fields such as Counseling or Music, for example, specialized areas that have grown with the development of specialized educational areas. The areas of Law and Medicine provide two of the best known, most common, and clear examples of professional accreditation and certification. Law schools, for example, are nationally accredited

[9] https://www.aacsb.edu/accreditation/accredited-schools?gclid=EAIaIQobChMI3-m5nvKf6QIVqdSzCh1h1QjkEAAYBCAAEgIxsfD_BwE

by the American Bar Association (ABA), and graduates of these schools may generally sit for the bar exam in any state. There are 201 ABA-accredited law schools—200 with full accreditation and one with provisional accreditation.[10]

At this point, one can strengthen this argument by pointing out a particularly illustrative example and model in higher education. As mentioned, the idea of higher education has expanded in the last sixty years, resulting in a wide variety of colleges and universities in the United States today. Moreover, they are not all the same. One cannot assume that the content and curriculum at State University is the same as the curriculum and model of education at Saint Nowhere's College. The various accrediting associations provide a basic guarantee for the programs and credits of an institution of higher education. However, that guarantee provides a minimal framework for a college or university.

In the last decade, the Association of Jesuit Colleges and Universities, along with the Jesuit Conference and the Superior General of the Society of Jesus, developed a document on the "*Characteristics*" of Jesuit education. The document is included in an appendix of this book. The document serves a number of purposes. In part, it was a response by American Jesuits to issues raised by Pope St. John Paul II in *Ex Corde Ecclesiae.* In that document the Pope raised issues pertaining to, and attempted to articulate, the different aspects of the relationships of colleges and universities to the Roman Catholic Church. In the midst of a changing educational environment, along with changes in the Church, the *Characteristics* document attempted to articulate the fundamental qualities that define a "Jesuit" college or university and the educational experience it offers. The document has also served as a way to evaluate and measure the nature of an education offered at any college or university that identities itself as Jesuit. Along with the *Characteristics* document, a process referred to as the "Mission Priority Examen" for the evaluation of colleges and universities that identify themselves as Jesuit, was also developed.

The "Mission Priority" process is an evaluative tool, supported by the *Characteristics* document, to document how a particular college or university is living out its Jesuit mission and identity.

These two documents, the *Characteristics* document and the "Mission Priority Examen" document, are included in the appendices of this book as examples of how organizations, with particular missions and identities, can monitor their identities.

8.3.2 Health Care

Health Care also has a complex history of licensure, certification, and accreditation, which continues to this day. In light of that history, the present reality is that health care organizations, today, must meet a number of requirements for professional certification. In addition, the legal and regulatory structures of health care in the

[10] https://www.americanbar.org/groups/legal_education/accreditation

United States are not defined solely at the federal level but are also shaped at the state level. This complex history of certification is reflective of the history of the development of medicine and its institutions over time. Part of that complexity has to do with the legal structures governing the oversight of medicine: medical professionals, like physicians and nurses, are governed as much by the laws of states, in the United States, or regions as by U.S. authorities. Medical professionals, particularly physicians and nurses, are governed by professional licensure, which is governed by the laws of different states.

Hospitals, as the primary delivery organizations in health care, are accredited by the Joint Commission on Accreditation of Healthcare Organizations. In the early 1950s the American College of Physicians, the American Hospital Association, the American Medical Association, and the Canadian Medical Association joined together to create the Joint Commission on Accreditation of Healthcare Organizations as a reflection of the expanded scope of activities dealing with patients.

While health care is an area that continues to grow and develop, the entire area of accreditation and certification is very important for organizational identity and integrity. These processes are both public and specialized. They provide specialized, professional evaluation of organizations and programs, and through the public nature of their findings, they provide a basic level of assurance for the diverse society in which organizations function.

8.4 Conclusion

It is worth pointing out what can easily be forgotten in these explorations. First, no matter what form it may take, the processes of accreditation are a way of building trust in organizations in education and health care. The processes of accreditation and certification provide an assurance to individual agents and society in general that organizations are what they say they are.

One way we can justify moral authority in a pluralistic, secular society is through the process of free and informed consent. The processes of accreditation and certification enable individuals, in a complex society, to have confidence in knowing that an organization is what it says it is.

The processes of accreditation and certification are important in two ways. First, they give a level of assurance, in a secular, pluralistic society, that an organization is what it claims to be. Second, these processes help organizations to stay true to their self-identities and missions as organizations. The processes set into motion a regular cycle of internal, as well as external, review that can help organizations to better articulate the moral values they hold, no matter what those values might be, and assess how they are meeting their values and commitments. This process should lead an organization to an ongoing awareness of its mission, its moral identity, and the needs of society. This organizational or corporate "self-awareness" is the foundation for "truth in advertising" in a secular, morally pluralistic society. Beyond this basic level of corporate self-awareness, an organization needs to keep this sense of itself, and its moral identity, in mind when and if it enters into cooperative arrangements with other health care and educational organizations, whether private or public organizations.

Summary of the Main Points

1. Civil Society
2. Organizational Identity
3. Organizational Identity: Accountability, Accreditation, Certification, Regional Accreditation

Chapter 9
Living With Limits: Justice, Organizations, and Post-modern Societies

In many ways this book has been a further exploration of the different aspects of postmodern, secular societies. Often, such explorations focus on questions concerning the liberty of individual moral agents and the limits of government authority. However, this book has moved beyond the questions that we often confront in postmodern secular societies.

While asking about how individual persons and the limits of government authority are important for these societies, this book has focused on organizations as moral actors (Chap. 4) in morally pluralistic, postmodern, secular societies. The argument has been made that in examining the moral landscape of postmodern, secular societies, one needs to include organizations, as well as individual agents and government, as moral actors. Specifically, the book has focused on organizations in education and health care, because those entities deliver goods that have some level of commitment to moral values. So, the questions that need to be asked concern how organizations which have moral commitments operate in a secular, morally diverse society.

Until this point in our exploration, this book has been examining how organizations can be understood and function with integrity in secular, postmodern societies. Also, the book has argued for steps that can be taken by an organization to help it both articulate and sustain its mission and identity in a postmodern, secular society. Because organizations are, at best, analogous to individual moral agents, this book also has argued, in Chap. 8, for the importance of a standard of "truth in advertising" as a necessary condition to morally evaluate an organization and for an organization to participate with other agents, ethically, in a secular society outside of the organization. This necessary condition of truth in advertising is particularly important for organizations in diverse, morally pluralistic, secular societies where moral agents, with different moral visions and values, seek to find ways to live and work together peacefully.

By using a truth in advertising standard, other moral agents, both individual agents and other organizations, can know what the moral commitments and values of an organization are; this is an important condition for free and informed engagement between agents in such societies.

K. W. Wildes, S.J., *Organizational Ethics and Moral Integrity in Secular Societies*, Philosophical Studies in Contemporary Culture 29,
https://doi.org/10.1007/978-3-031-39097-5_9

The focus of this exploration into organizational ethics, thus far, has centered on the possible range of internal structures that can be utilized within an organization to help maintain the mission, identity, and moral commitments of the organization. However, there is another set of relationships that needs to be explored for organizations, as they function in a morally diverse, secular society; the identity of an organization plays a key role in establishing these relationships and their limits.

Most organizations, particularly in education and health care, rarely exist or function by themselves as solipsistic, self-contained entities. They often work, in some way, with other organizations to accomplish their missions and work. Often, organizations in education and health care decide to collaborate with governmental programs that help to facilitate the work of the organization. And, in most cases, organizations that have established partnerships with government agencies do not act as "silent" partners but bring sets of demands and expectations to the relationship. These types of collaboration by organizations, either with other organizations or in partnership with government, means that we need to explore how organizations can both maintain their identities and integrity while working with other organizations or agencies which have different moral commitments. So, part of this investigation into organizations and ethics needs to examine how organizations, with particular moral identities, can work with other organizations that may have different moral identities or commitments.

To move our investigation beyond particular organizations we need to consider the broader social context and setting for organizations. There are two important, but different questions that need to be addressed. First, we need to consider how organizations, with their own particular identities, can partner with other organizations. It is important to think about how organizations, in health care and education, can function ethically in a morally pluralistic, secular society. Those boundaries and thoughts will help to shape the geography for how organizations can create partnerships. We have been examining common internal structures often found in the lives of organizations with an eye to how these structures can help to support the particular mission and identity of an organization.

There are at least two very different approaches an organization can take when it moves beyond its own boundaries and into the context of a larger, diverse, secular society in order to work with other moral agents, individuals, or organizations that may have different moral commitments. One approach mandates that an organization not engage with the larger, secular society and deal only with its own kind. This approach can be seen in religious traditions which limit their dealings with those outside the tradition and limit dealings, as much as possible, to those within the community. Most organizations, however, do not choose to exist as isolated or solipsistic enterprises. Most organizations, particularly those in health care and education, engage people and communities from a wide variety of traditions. It is important therefore that we explore how they can work with societies, other organizations, and enterprises with integrity. We need to shift our focus and begin to examine how organizations can participate, ethically, in the society around them and still maintain their identities.

In a sense, the first part of the book outlined the possibilities for the second part of the book. If organizations can exemplify moral failure in contemporary, post-modern societies, as highlighted in the first chapters, it is possible that organizations can succeed as moral agents. The second section of the book explored and attempted to flesh out the idea of organizational integrity and some of the ways it can be implemented. The concepts of identity and integrity are essential in postmodern, secular societies, given the potential cultural and moral pluralism of these societies. We have explored how an organization can structure itself to maintain the integrity of the organization through the anchors of mission and identity. While the particular structures identified in the second part of the book may vary from organization to organization, many of these internal structures can be used to maintain and support the identity of an organization. Now, in the third part of this exploration, we are examining possible ways that an organization, with a particular moral identity, can participate in a postmodern, morally diverse, secular society and work with other individuals and organizations, particularly when there are moral commitments involved.

When examining ethical issues in postmodern, secular societies it is important to remember, as has been argued elsewhere, that free and informed consent is the foundational starting point for moral justification for individuals and their actions in contemporary, postmodern, secular societies.[1] Using the ethical starting point of free, informed consent, however, means that organizations can only be thought of as analogous, at best, to individual moral agents. So, we need to think through how we can use the insights about contemporary secular societies, moral pluralism, and moral strangers living and working together to find what can be applied to thinking about the decisions and actions of organizations in a secular, morally pluralistic society. If we think analogously about organizations as moral agents, one needs to explore how important elements of procedural morality, like informed consent and its elements, can be reimagined when examining ethical questions for organizations and their actions in secular, postmodern societies.

Because contemporary secular societies are finite and limited, few organizations, if any, are completely self-sustaining. In the nineteenth and early twentieth centuries, in the United States, for example, there were a number of corporations, like Standard Oil, which sought to control all aspects of their production and marketing. However, social pressures and political leaders, like Theodore Roosevelt and Republicans of the Progressive Era, fought these monopolistic practices and created legislation that sought to control monopolies and trusts.[2] Still, it is not uncommon for organizations to try and meet their needs within themselves; these attempts can lead to significant expansion of the size and scope of any organization. Historically

---

[1] H.T. Engelhardt Jr, *Foundations of Bioethics* et al, Wildes.

[2] The Sherman Anti-Trust Act of 1890, U.S. Code Title 15. COMMERCE AND TRADE Chapter 1. MONOPOLIES AND COMBINATIONS IN RESTRAINT OF TRADE Section 1. Trusts, etc., in restraint of trade illegal; penalty 15 U.S. Code § 1.Trusts, etc., in restraint of trade illegal; penalty.

this type of organizational expansion was certainly the case in late nineteenth and early twentieth century capitalism in the United States with the development of large scale, comprehensive business organizations. On the other hand, particularly in the late twentieth and early twenty-first centuries, there were substantial efforts by for-profit business organizations to "outsource" many non-essential aspects of their businesses as a way to reduce the size of the organization and to control costs and quality.

Nonetheless, almost any contemporary organization will need to have relationships with other organizations that are vital for its mission. We need to think through how an organization can act, as an organization, in relationship to other organizations, in light of its own mission and identity and still maintain a level of integrity. How can an organization act with other organizations and still maintain its moral commitments? This chapter, in the third part of the book, continues our exploration of organizational ethics insofar as it seeks to examine questions about how organizations can act and work with other organizations and government agencies and regulators and still maintain identity and moral integrity.

At this point, the investigation into organizational ethics in health care and education needs to investigate how organizations can engage and work with other organizations, or with individual agents, that will likely have different identities, missions, and moral views. Is it possible to create partnerships or different types of work agreements with other organizations that hold different moral views? The topic of partnerships, with other organizations, will be explored more carefully in Chap. 11 of this book. At this point in the book, after examining possible internal structures of an organization concerning its identity and purpose, we now need to refocus our exploration to questions of how an organization can engage with other organizations and a secular, morally pluralistic society in which it finds itself and retain its identity as an organization.

9.1 Organizational Mission and Limits for an Organization

We need to take up, explicitly, one of the most stubborn and "obvious" realities that is often a part of any discussion about practical ethics. That is the *reality of limits*. No matter our cultural mythology or rhetoric human beings are finite creatures in a finite world, and this reality of finitude is certainly a part of decision-making that organizations, particularly those in education and health care, must confront. Moreover, the discussion of limits is a practical reality that is often avoided, or at least left unspoken, both by individual agents and organizations, and it can be one the most difficult topics to address. Indeed, some of the great existentialist thinkers, like J. P. Sartre and Martin Heidegger, reflected on the limits of human existence and how those limits, particularly death, raise fundamental questions about the meaning of human life.[3]

[3] Sartre, J.-P., 1943 [1992]. *Being and Nothingness*, Hazel Barnes (trans.), New York: Washington Square Press, 1992. Heidegger, M., 1927 [1962]. *Being and Time,* John Macquarrie and Edward Robinson (trans.), New York: Harper and Row.

The reality of limits is not only something that organizations in education or health care must confront, as limits are fundamental to the human condition in general. Human beings are finite creatures; human finitude and the limits we face are part of the human experience and part of nearlyt every moral decision. We need to make choices, in real time, with the resources that are available. Theodore Roosevelt summarized this reality in his autobiography: "Do what you can, with what you've got, where you are."[4]

Human beings are finite creatures, and living with limits is an important part of human life. However, limitation is not a natural state of mind for many westerners, particularly Americans, who live under the myth of unlimited resources and the dream of the frontier. The reality of human limits is most often a factor in ethical questions. We are confronted with making judgments about what is the best thing to do when we cannot do everything. And, we are confronted with our finitude when our knowledge is limited and our knowledge about what will happen is limited, especially in education and health care.

In both health care and education, we often forget, or avoid confronting, the fact that as finite human beings we do not have unlimited resources to do everything for everyone. The reality is that, in a finite world, we cannot do everything for everyone in the areas of health care or education. Furthermore, the reality of our limits, both as a society and as individuals, is an obvious factor that ought to be part of any ethical reflections about how we use the resources that we have.

This means, of course, that organizations, like other moral agents, are limited both in their knowledge and in their resources, and they will have to make decisions in light of these limits. The reality of limits for organizations poses important ethical questions, for individuals, organizations, and society. These ethical questions involve more than simply deciding what to do with our resources; ethical questions concerning the use of resources also involve how an organization makes decisions about the allocation and use of the organization's resources. To be ethical, an organization ought to have a clear process for how the organization allocates resources and makes investments. The criteria that can be used for making such decisions should be known in an organization. It should also be known within an organization who the persons are who wield the appropriate authority to make these decisions. And, the internal processes for making decisions regarding resource allocation should be known and understood within the entity. At the same time, human knowledge and the advances in technology that allow the use of such knowledge, though also limited, will continue to increase. This means the ability for society and organizations to do "more" than we can do now will grow. The expanding universe of knowledge and technology poses an important background factor and a potential set of tensions for organizations in education and health care.

However, the growth in knowledge and the expansion of technological capabilities can lead people to forget that humans are limited, finite beings. While the

[4] *Theodore Roosevelt, Theodore Roosevelt; An Autobiography*, Bill Widener quoted by Theodore Roosevelt Chapter IX, to Squire Bill Widener of Widener's Valley, Virginia. (New York: MacMillian Publishing, 1913).

possibilities for what we know, and what we can do, will increase, at the same time, human beings will not have unlimited resources; so, in both education and health care, we will not be able to do "everything for everyone." This reality is particularly challenging for organizations in health care and education because of the continued growth in those fields of what is known and what can be done for individuals. The moral tension will revolve around how to balance continued technological innovations that benefit society against the reality of limited resources.

The reality of limits, in human knowledge, understanding, and decision-making, is contrary to the cultures found in many contemporary societies. American society, for example, is rooted in the history and vision of progress and endless frontiers. One has only to recall the history of the westward expansion of the United States and the aspiration of the "new frontier"— space exploration—to see how deeply the idea of unlimited possibility is rooted in American culture.

However, human beings are *not* unlimited. Confronting the reality of human finitude should sharpen the choices that are made about human identity, whether as individuals or as organizations. Moreover, in light of the reality of limited resources, the questions of how people decide to use the resources becomes a central ethical question both for individuals and for organizations. The reality of limits for organizations in education and health care should not be surprising. We have limited resources in all aspects of human life. Therefore, one ethical question, which becomes paramount, is whether there is a way to articulate the ethical criteria and procedures used in allocating resources, which would help to explain and justify why we allocate common resources the way we do.

In everyday life, the issues of how to address limits are left to individual moral agents and consumers who, in turn, make decisions on how to use their own resources. Those choices are treated as matters of personal choice and stewardship. However, the scope of the question about how resources are used changes when the resources that are allocated and used are shared resources. This is the case with partnerships or when organizations work with other organizations. No matter what principles of allocation are used, common, public procedures, which shape the allocation decisions for the organization's resources, must exist for an organization to follow in any matter.

An important first step in resolving ethical questions pertaining to the use of resources is to recognize the importance of limits in the allocation of resources within and by an organization. Another important step is to articulate the limits on the use of resources. In a diverse, secular society it is ethically important that the articulation of limits on common resources be carried out in a way that is both clear and public. These two steps are important for integrating our understanding of a particular organization and our understanding of how it acts. In attempting to live out its mission or identity, every organization must make decisions about how it allocates the resources it possesses and can use. And these decisions will shape other decisions about future planning and about efforts to increase resources, two areas of particular importance for traditional non-profit organizations in education and health care.

The human experience of living with limits and the reality that human beings exist as finite creatures, living with limits, is an important, necessary condition for exploring the questions of justice in a postmodern society. In confronting our limits, we need to think about how we use the resources that we have and how we can justify our decisions about the use of those resources. The allocation and use of resources are a concern at every level—not only for individual moral agents but for society as a whole. The concern over allocation and use of resources must be addressed by every organization and particularly by those in health care and education.

Understanding how these decisions are made by an organization should be grounded in an understanding and assessment of the moral identity of the organization. What are both the values and processes an organization uses in making such policy decisions? In addition, and obviously, decisions on resource allocation will vary according to the organization and its mission and identity, in view that these decisions ought to be rooted in the identity and mission of the organization if it hopes to maintain a level of integrity. Nevertheless, in understanding an organization one needs to grasp its mission and identity and verify the roles played by mission and identity in the decisions made by the organization, such as how to allocate resources. The questions surrounding the use of resources is rooted in the realities of limited resources available to the organization. This reality lays the groundwork for two other ethical considerations for an organization: the questions of stewardship and justice.

9.2 Social Sin and the Language of Justice

At this point, before moving to a more explicit exploration of justice, it is worth identifying, in a brief manner, the topic of social "sin" or wrongdoing and its relationship to organizations in postmodern, secular societies. This book has argues that, in light of the limits of moral epistemology and the realities of moral pluralism in a secular society we need to be cautious, or perhaps skeptical, about moral language that is used across the whole of a diverse, secular society. However, one can still argue that it is possible for a society, not just individuals or organizations, to act badly even in the context of a morally pluralistic, secular society. Given the moral pluralism of secular societies, the key element for social sin or wrongdoing concerns how a society is organized and how it structures itself. So, in general, one can argue that a secular society begins with a moral foundation: the value of the human person and the importance of the person as a moral agent. It follows that in such a society one needs to attend to the role of consent by persons as a foundation for moral justification. It also follows that social authority proceeds from the consent of the governed. In a secular society, if a class of people were to be excluded, against their will, from the processes of government by arbitrary criteria, such as race or gender, which would be an example of a secular, social sin or evil. Therefore, it would be morally inappropriate in a secular society for its structures to be built on such exclusions as race, creed, or gender, as has occurred historically in some societies. In the United States, one can highlight historical examples such as the existence of certain prejudicies led to the creation of laws that allowed for the enactment and enforcement of racially discriminatory laws.[5]

In the context of a secular society, one needs to think about rules, procedures, or laws in a secular society that excluded people from participation in the society. Historically, examples of this type of socially inappropriate ethical behavior include the exclusion of individuals from participation in the life of society through involuntary, hereditary slavery and exclusion on the basis of race or gender. While this book has argued for skepticism with regard to generalizing the terms or content of particular moral views, the book has also argued for the importance of assuring opportunities for members of a society to participate in the life of that society. It would be impossible for a postmodern, secular society to exclude moral agents as citizens, for particular, content-full reasons. Specific moral communities within a secular society may well have their own rules governing inclusion in and exclusion from a community or roles within the community.

9.3 Organizational Keys to Stewardship: Mission and Social Justice

The recognition that human beings live in a world of limited resources is often difficult for many to truly comprehend in their day-to-day lives. This lack of appreciation for limits is particularly noticeable in those who live in the most economically developed countries and particularly evident in the practices of both the health care and education industries. However, raising awareness of the limits on resources not only brings human beings face to face with their finitude but also raises ethical questions about how we use our resources. Confronting human limits raises important moral questions for any moral agent, whether an individual or organization. The reality of limits leads to further questions about how an agent will choose to use the resources available to the agent. It is worth noting that how moral agents respond to the questions and challenges regarding the use of resources ought to be grounded in the moral commitments of the agent or organization which makes the decisions about allocation.

A simple, non-organizational example can help to illustrate this point about the use of resources. An individual agent, a person, has resources, and one of those resources is time. Each day, a person has a limited resource, twenty-four hours, meaning that the person must make decisions about how to utilize and allocate the resource of time. Normally, the person will make choices about allocating the resource of time according to the needs, demands, priorities, and requirements of the demands the agent wants to meet. Of course, these decisions about allocation become more complex if there are competing needs and demands on the person.

[5] *Plessy v. Ferguson*, 163 U.S. 537 (1896). The case became foundational for the practices of "separate but equal" racial segregation.

Organizations face similar types of questions with regard to the use of resources, but these questions become more complex when taking into account the nature of the organization, its structure, and the demands made on it and the commitments it has made. The concerns for organizations, facing limits on the use of resources, also raises other, related ethical questions about the stewardship of resources. Any agent, individual person, or organization, needs to think about how resources are to be used and why. Because moral agents, as individuals or organizations, have limited resources and commitments to particular missions and identities, they should be held accountable for the stewardship of the resources at their disposal and how they are utilized. These questions of resource utilization, or stewardship, are particularly complex if the resources are not simply those of an individual but shared, as in health care and educational organizations. In addition, ethical questions of stewardship can be even more complicated if the resources are common to, or shared by, others, such as a society or another organization or group.

In addressing the questions surrounding the stewardship of resources, the concept of *social justice* can become an important concept to investigate, in terms of how a *society* is structured, while the consideration of social justice can be helpful in how we respond to questions involving resources that are shared by several organizations or society as a whole. It should be noted that the term and questions of social justice are distinct from the questions of *distributive justice,* which are concerned with how resources are distributed. The distinction between the terms of social and distributive justice is important for conceptual and analytic clarity, but the distinction is also important for understanding the interrelationship of the two concepts. They are, one can argue, interrelated but distinct, and confusion can result when social justice and distributive justice are confused, which happens often. There is a relationship between the two terms, given that the way a society is organized, which is investigated under the rubric of social justice, influences how goods are distributed within the society. At his point, it is important to mention the distinction between the terms, even though the two types of justice are related, so that they are not conflated with one another. The question of the use of resources, or what many would label as "stewardship" of resources, is an essential ethical question for any agent, whether an individual agent or an organization.

One can argue that there is no precise formula, in most cases, for how a society's resources should be allocated and used for the benefit of a society or an organization. Such determinations need to be made by an organization individually and in light of the organization's mission, identity, and planning apparatus. In addition, one can argue that those questions will also be answered, in part, by the moral commitments of a society. However, we can argue that to evaluate and answer the questions of how resources are to be used by a moral agent is a pursuit best addressed by starting from the basic identity and mission of an organization to act ethically and with integrity. An organization needs to ask how its resources are being used internally in light of its identity and purpose. Next, an organization needs to look to society and ask what the society expects from the organization, how the society is organized, and whether the society is deploying resources according to its identity and social policy.

The realization that moral agents need to confront and address the realities of limited resources and opportunities leads to further questions about how any moral agent, whether an individual or organization, can resolve by questions about what is an ethically appropriate use of resources. To answer questions about the use of resources by an organization, one needs to turn internally first and be sure that the allocation and use of resources is aligned with the mission and identity of an organization. However, ethical questions about the use of resources go beyond the internal structures of an organization and are often related to the larger questions and policies of a society. This means the second place to turn when examining these questions is toward the society itself and ask how a society is organized, and how a society sets its priorities, and be sure its priorities and organization are aligned with its identity as a society.

We often discuss and argue about ethical issues as if they exist in isolation. For example, we may argue about treatment decisions for a patient or the application of policies to a student. However, many moral controversies go beyond the boundaries of the immediate moral agents who are immediately involved and turn on issues involving organizational policy and the use of resources. They transcend the boundaries of the particular relationships of the agents involved, and the way a society is organized will reflect the assumptions and values of a society. For example, health insurance programs will often dictate the treatment choices for patients, or public educational policy will set standards for educational organizations. In such instances, there is a need for an additional layer of ethical investigation and argument in addition to the primary issue being considered. In the wake of a pandemic, for example, there may be a need for respirators for people, but the need far exceeds the current number of available respirators. Such moral controversies go beyond the particular patient, physician, or hospital in the same way that educating a pool of students goes beyond particular students or teachers directly involved.

Because many ethical issues go beyond particular patients, students, or even organizations for that matter, these issues about the allocation and use of resources often become part of much broader discussions about who makes these decisions, how they are made, and how a society is structured. Because these conversations about the allocation and use of resources move to a broader social arena, we often start to use the term "justice" in the discussion of resources. The questions of justice often become part of a moral discourse in such instances, and this language requires discipline, as it can be used when performing an ethical analysis of society or organizations or both at the same time!

The term "justice" is a philosophical, legal, and moral term with an ancient history and a variety of different uses, applications, and specifications. These variations can often lead to confusion in general use, particularly in contemporary, secular, postmodern societies.[6] Of course, the different ways the term can be used is precisely why the term "justice" can be so problematic: many people may be using

[6] I believe that one of the best, comprehensive treatments of this question is Alasdair McIntyre, Whose *Justice? Which Rationality?* (Notre Dame: University of Notre Dame Press, 1988).

the same term, but in reality, they are speaking different languages. Justice is a term that has numerous stipulations and ways of formulating the specification of the term. Furthermore, the term can be applied, appropriately, to very different types of situations. One can speak, for example, of criminal justice, distributive justice, or commutative justice.[7]

How can the term justice be deployed and applied to organizations? The turn to the language of justice reminds us that the word "justice" has been used extensively in western philosophical thought and in popular rhetoric.[8] To sort out the different possible uses and stipulations of the term, it is worthwhile to note that there are different types of "justice" that relate to the different applications of the concept to different aspects of human life. For example, one of the best-known uses of the term is when we address criminal matters in a society. At the same time, we can and do use the term justice to refer to matters of distribution in a society. So, to prevent confusion, one must be mindful about which type of language to use when employing the term "justice".

In a sense, this exploration has added an additional layer of analysis to the questions we have been examining thus far. So far, the analysis of this book has focused on people within organizations and how organizations may be potentially structured internally so that they can act ethically and with a procedural justice. Now, the investigation needs to move outside the model of a particular organization and start to investigate questions about how a society can engage in the questions of justice, as well as how a society organizes itself. We are moving from the questions of justice that ask how an organization is structured and acts internally to questions pertaining to how an organization acts in the broader society.

9.4 Justice Within an Organization

Every organization has the resources of time, talent, and opportunity, most of which can be monetized in some way. Some internal resources can also be budgeted, in many ways, and accounted for in an organization's budget. As I have argued elsewhere, a budget is in essence a planning document that speaks of how a person, or organization, will allocate its resources. This, for example, may be done with the allocation of space, money of course, and talent.

For any organization, the allocation of resources, monetary and non-monetary, is a question of justice, within the organization, and these decisions on allocating resources ought to be tied to the mission and identity of the organization. Given that organizations in health care and education, while similar, vary, it is important for the

[7] Robert Nozick, *Anarchy, State, and Utopia* (Oxford: Blackwell, 1974); John Rawls, *A Theory of Justice* (revised edition, Oxford: Oxford University Press, 1999); Plato, *Republi*c trans. Robin Waterfield (Oxford: Oxford University Press, 1994).

[8] John Rawls, *A Theory of Justice*, Cambridge, MA: Harvard College, 1971; Robert Nozick, *A Theory of Justice*, (New York: Basic Books, 1974).

allocation of resources within an organization to be tied to the fundamental mission and identity of the organization (see Chaps. 5 and 6). In addition, the internal processes for allocating resources within an organization should be understood within an organization. Now, these internal processes can vary significantly from organization to organization. What seems to be morally important is that the processes be known and honored within the identity and culture of an organization. The more difficult and intellectually challenging issue is how to understand and morally justify the allocation of resources in a secular, postmodern culture.

9.5 Social Justice and the Language of Justice in a Postmodern Society

At this point, it is worth exploring, even briefly, the use of the term "social justice"—both how and why it might be used in examining organizations in education and health care. However, I do so with caution. If one looks up, or conducts an Internet search for the term "social justice", one is likely to find a variety of definitions and stipulations for the term. Part of the challenge when this term is used lies in the reality that the term "justice" itself can be defined or stipulated in a number of ways and as such is shaped by the relationship being described. For example, the term "legal justice" is used to define the legal relationship that exists between people. The term "criminal justice" seeks to characterize the relationship of individuals to the whole society with regard to certain actions that are defined by the society as "criminal". The term "distributive justice" is used to examine how goods are distributed in a society or among individuals.

Some of the potential confusion around the use of the term justice is that the formal concept of justice itself can be developed in different ways. For example, justice can be used to mean that one should treat equals equally. Alternatively, it can be used to indicate that we should render to each agent what is due. Of course, in this use, we need a principle to enable us to determine what is due to each, as well as what is the sense of obligation and who owes the obligation that is due. Therefore, a first, and important step, in using the term justice, is to determine which notion of formal justice is to be deployed.

Beyond the notion of formal justice, other types of justice reflect the different types of relationships and situations to which the term justice can be applied. One can think, for example, of retributive or criminal justice, which is not only about an individual who has been harmed by, say, a robbery or an injury but the whole of society that is threatened or harmed by such an act. Another type of justice is communitive justice, which is, primarily, about relationships between individuals who have agreements (e.g. contracts). One can argue here that the social concern is concerned with the value of promises and contracts. There is also distributive justice, which is focused on the distribution of common goods in a group or a society. In questions of distributive justice, we immediately develop questions of what principles will be used in the distribution of what is held in common. In a socialist society, there exists an underlying commitment to social equality, and positive rights limit liberty rights. By contrast, in a more libertarian society, the goal is to protect the life, liberty, and property of members. In classical liberal theory, it is assumed that those who have more than enough must help those in need; the political arguments typically center on how best to accomplish this.

9.5.1 Social Justice and Society

The term social justice is applied, appropriately, to social structures within a society. Links between social structures, such as modern governmental structures and practices, can be seen through the historical roots of religion and its emphasis on social justice. The language of justice in the Catholic tradition is founded on the notion of dignity of the human person. The concept of human dignity is a fundamental object of concern in the tradition of Catholic social thought. In this tradition, the language of human dignity is tied to the idea of community; in essence, the language of justice is inextricably bound to the language of community and the dignity of the person. This tradition of justice is distinct from atomistic accounts of many modern philosophers, which begin with assumptions about the human person existing separately, like an atom, and subsequently making the decision to join a society. In the Catholic tradition the person cannot be conceived of without a community of persons.

The fundamental assumption in the Roman Catholic tradition is that the human person is made in the image of God (*imago dei*).[9] Theologians and philosophers in the early church, throughout the Middle Ages, developed this language, based on the Hebrew and Christian scriptures.[10]

In the early church and during the Middle Ages, the language of the image of God carried with it a Trinitarian understanding of God. In the doctrine of the Trinity, God is communal by nature. The one God is Father, Son, and Spirit. As God is fundamentally communal in God's own nature, so too is human life, made in the image of God, communal. This communitarian view has led the Roman Catholic tradition to examine the political, social, and economic spheres of life together as one: *imago dei*. Human beings are individuals, but they achieve their individuality only by and through their relationship with others. In this Christian tradition a Trinitarian lens helps one to appreciate the integral relationship of individual human identity with the communal nature of human life. One cannot isolate the categories from each other. The two, individual human identity and the human community, are mutually implicative. In the Christian mystery of the Trinity each of the persons of the Trinity is distinct but can only be understood in relationship to other persons of the Trinity.

---

[9] Second Vatican Ecumenical Council, Pastoral Constitution on the Church in the Modern World, *Gaudium et Spes*, #12.

[10] Altmann, Alexander. "'Homo Imago Dei' in Jewish and Christian Theology." The Journal of Religion, vol. 48, no. 3, 1968, pp. 235–259. JSTOR, www.jstor.org/stable/1202149. Accessed 3 Apr. 2020.

9.5.2 The Common Good

Embedded in the concept of the *imago dei* is the notion of the "common good." Most Americans understand common good to mean the good of the majority (the will of the majority),[11] but that interpretation is incorrect in this tradition. Instead, the term common good refers to those conditions that are necessary for humans to flourish. Pope John XXIII defined it as "the sum total of conditions of social living, whereby persons are enabled more fully and readily to achieve their own perfection."[12] Social justice strives to create a society that enables its members to have access to these basic conditions, to take part in the common good. In his encyclical *Pacem in Terris*, Pope John XXIII wrote, "In our time the common good is chiefly guaranteed when personal rights and duties are maintained."[13] The idea of social justice is a cross, one could argue, between the traditional ideas of general justice and distributive justice.

The questions of social justice are concerned, by and large, with how a society is organized with respect to individual persons and the common good. The language of common good tries to focus on those conditions that human beings need to flourish. For example, an historical example of the use of the term "social justice" is the civil rights movement in the United States[14] in that it sought to ensure that the same rights were extended to all Americans. The civil rights movement was initially focused on making sure that all Americans, especially African Americans, were able to exercise the fundamental rights of American citizens, such as voting. One of the most prescient issues faced by the Civil Rights movement was the issue of voting rights for African American citizens. In a broad sense this was a fundamental question about how a society was organized. Other major questions of the Civil Rights movement had to do with issues of segregation, in education and housing, and education itself. Again, each of these questions raised issues about how American society at the time was organized; as such, they were questions of social justice.

In examining organizations, and how they function in society, there is a natural link between modern governmental structures and their role in social justice, given that governments play crucial roles in the organization of society as a whole. The language of justice in the Catholic tradition is founded on the notion of dignity of the human person, which is the fundamental object of concern in the tradition of

---

[11] Wildes, Kevin Wm. (2008) "The Rebirth of a City: Birth and Achievement of the Ethics Review Board," *Seattle Journal for Social Justice*: Vol. 7: Iss. 1, Article 5. Available at: https://digitalcommons.law.seattleu.edu/sjsj/vol7/iss1/5

[12] Pope John XXIII *Mater et Magistra* – "Mother and Teacher" (1961), paragraph 65.

[13] In our time, the common good is chiefly guaranteed when personal rights and duties are maintained.

[14] *Civil Rights Movement in American Law, History, and Politics*, Austin Sarat, editor, (Cambridge, UK: Cambridge University Press, 2016).

Catholic social thought.[15] In this tradition, the language of human dignity is tied to the idea of community; in essence, the language of justice is inextricably bound to the language of community and the dignity of the person. As mentioned, this tradition of justice is distinct from atomistic accounts of many modern philosophers, which often begin with the person in isolation from others.

9.5.3 Public Ethics and Social Justice

The language of justice in the Catholic tradition from which we have been borrowing is founded on the notion of dignity of the human person—the fundamental object of concern in the tradition of Catholic social thought. In this tradition, the language of human dignity is tied to the idea of community; in essence, the language of justice is inextricably bound to the language of community and the dignity of the person. This tradition of justice is distinct from atomistic accounts of many modern philosophers.

9.5.4 The Common Good: Imago Dei

As was mentioned earlier the concept of human beings, made in the *imago dei* is integrally related to the way the notion of the "common good" is developed in this tradition. This tradition assumes that there is a common, human anthropology, and the idea of the common good refers to the conditions that are needed for human beings to flourish. These are the conditions which would allow the person to achieve their own perfection.

It is in light of these foundational assumptions about a common anthropology and the ability to identify common conditions for social living that the Catholic tradition moves to speak of "social justice" which is concerned with creating a society that enables its members to have access to these basic conditions, to take part in the common good. In this traditions the idea of social justice is a cross between general justice and distributive justice. Social justice examines how a society is organized with respect to the common good of its members where the language of common good focuses on those conditions that human beings need to flourish.

As was mentioned earlier a good historical example of the concept of social justice historically in the United States is the civil rights movement insofar as the Movement sought to ensure that the same rights were extended to all Americans, particularly African Americans. The civil rights movement was focused on making sure that all Americans, especially African Americans, were able to exercise fundamental rights, such as voting. In many ways, the development of governmental

---

[15] The Second Vatican Council, *Gaudium et Spes*, no. 76.

structures, laws, and regulations can be seen as an exercise in social justice in that these structures are charged with making sure governmental structures respond efficiently and effectively for all citizens.

9.5.5 Implications for Organizations and Justice in Postmodern Societies

It is clear, both in management theory and in terms of organizational ethics that organizations need to remain focused on their identities and missions as foundational starting points for how they are organized and how they operate. The focus on identity and mission is crucial for how an organization operates ethically in a pluralistic, secular world, and it is important for how an organization uses its resources of time, talent, and opportunity. In a finite world of limited resources an organization will need to be clear on why and how resources are used and what the procedures are for making decisions about the allocation and stewardship of resources. The nature of such accountability should be internal to the organization, with implementation by the employees of an organization and oversight by the appropriate level of the organization's management structure. However, accountability for stewardship can often be external as well, extending to payers, funders, regulators, students, patients, and families that are involved with the organization. So, while the allocation of resources may be primarily a "management" decision, it can have implications far beyond the day-to-day operations of the organization in terms of accountability and the ability to raise additional resources.

Living with limits, for any organization, ought to lead to a constant focus on the mission and identity of the organization, as well as to a focus on its planning and procedures. An organization may want to be X, but it needs to achieve steps A, B, and C in order to achieve X. The organization's planning ought to reflect its long-term goals and the steps that have been identified which are necessary to achieve those goals. In this way the planning for the organization becomes a way to map out its use of resources; the budget of an organization then becomes a planning document. The budget of an organization ought to reflect the organization's planning documents, while the planning documents should be a key to the organization's budget.

Both the aspirations and planning of organizations are always accompanied by the reality that organizational resources are, and will always be, limited. Those limits force an organization to make allocation decisions that need to be justified. Part of the justification for allocation needs to address the mission and identity of the organization. Another part of the justification is the strategic plan of the organization, which should help to shape answers as to why certain allocations are given priority. Furthermore, in a postmodern, secular society organizations need to be cautious about appeals to "justice", in view of the many different stipulations and understandings of the term "justice". What may be most helpful, in such a diverse context, is for the procedures and outcomes regarding allocation to be clearly and publicly expressed, at least within the organization. This understanding, or implication of this understanding, of justice is widespread in contemporary multicultural postmodern, secular societies where the processes for such decisions are clear and publicly expressed and where the processes can be monitored.

9.6 Conclusions

Chapter 8 developed and argued for the position that, for an organization to be ethical in a postmodern, secular society, the organization needs to be clear about its mission and identity and open, at least on some level, to being accountable with regard to the organization's mission and identity to those within the organization and the broader society. This chapter continued to develop that line of thought by arguing that organizations need to develop and use resources in a way that is public and accountable. In a postmodern, morally pluralistic society an organization should be clear about its identity and the outcomes it hopes to achieve but also about the procedures that determine how resources are allocated in light of its identity, mission, and hoped- for goals.

Throughout this book we have thematically addressed the importance of organizational identity, even to the point of the relationship of mission and identity to developing budgets and allocating resources, prioritizing programs, and living with limits. Now, the investigation needs to take another step and examine how organizations can maintain their identities while working with other organizations and individuals in a diverse secular society.

Summary of the Main Points

1. Organizational Mission and Limits for an Organization
2. Social Sin and the Language of Justice
3. Organizational Keys to Stewardship: Mission and Social Justice
4. Justice Within and Organization
5. Social Justice and the Language of Justice in a Postmodern Society
    (a) Social Justice and Society
    (b) The Common Good
    (c) Public Ethics and Social Justice
    (d) The Common Good: Imago Dei
    (e) Implications for Organizations and Justice in Postmodern Societies
6. Conclusions

Chapter 10
Compromise, Cooperation, and Toleration: Maintaining Organizational Identity in a Pluralistic Society in an Age of Innovation

In exploring organizational ethics in postmodern, secular societies, this book has already highlighted the foundational importance of the identity and mission of any organization. The identity and mission of an organization are foundational for the *moral identity* of an organization. For organizations in health care and education, the identity and mission of the organization are the starting points for evaluating how well an organization functions ethically in both its internal life and life in the broader society. Identity and mission, however they are specified, should serve as the foundational points for thinking about the ethics of an organization and how it operates in a secular, postmodern society with the potential for moral diversity. As with individual moral agents in a diverse, morally pluralistic world, we begin by looking organizations, and their moral commitments, as moral agents, which has been the focus of this book.

In the light of questions on the topic of organizational identity and mission, the second part of this book explored the range of internal structures that can be implemented and used by an organization to create and sustain a moral identity. These structures can be helpful for organizations to both articulate and maintain identity and chosen moral character. Both identity and mission, however they might be labeled, are necessary conditions for understanding how ethical questions can be addressed both internally and externally by an organization when it exists in a morally pluralistic, postmodern society. In such morally diverse societies, it is crucial that any agent understand the agent's own identity and moral values. This is a necessary condition for both individual agents and organizations if they are to engage with other agents and maintain moral integrity.

Now, the third section of this book is exploring the reality that organizations rarely function in isolation in a complex postmodern society. Organizations certainly deal with the society in which they live, and they deal with individual moral agents as well. But organizations also deal with other organizations that may have their own identities and moral commitments.

K. W. Wildes, S.J., *Organizational Ethics and Moral Integrity in Secular Societies*, Philosophical Studies in Contemporary Culture 29,
https://doi.org/10.1007/978-3-031-39097-5_10

So, as we move beyond the examination of the internal life of an organization, which was the focus of Part Two, we need to ask how an organization can maintain its own moral identity and values and work with other organizations in a secular, postmodern society.

Few, if any, organizations exist in a self-contained universe. So, we need to explore how organizations can act with moral integrity as they work with other organizations. Organizations most frequently have partnerships or working arrangements with other organizations.

Organizations also respond to the society in which they exist through the works of government regulatory agencies, individual moral agents, and they respond and work as well with other organizations. Therefore, we need to continue our investigation into how an organization might function, in a secular, postmodern society, with other organizations as well as with public, social structures and still maintain its identity and moral commitments. As we explore the different ways that organizations can build relationships with other organizations, it is worth stating the obvious: the basic identity of an organization should be the foundation for how the organization develops relationships with other organizations and with society in general.

Let us think, for a moment, of the example of one approach: an organization might decide to *only* deal with people who share the moral views of the organization and not with others with different moral views, as is the case for some religious organizations. Alternatively, another organization might be willing to engage with whomever wants to use its services, regardless of differences in moral views between the cooperating parties. However, the adoption of such attitudes by an organization runs the risk of a loss of identity, perhaps over time, by the organization. One might imagine a spectrum of engagement by organizations with other organizations that hold different identities, moral values, and ways of proceeding. Given either end of the spectrum of how organizations respond to other, different organizations and the geography in between these two ends, it is important to recognize the reality that, not only may organizations have different, particular identities, but they may also have different views and approaches as to how to engage the society around them. No matter how an organization approaches arrangements with other organizations, it is important for organizations to recognize that they exist in a social setting often with changing and developing environments, which may lead to the need for an organization to consider changes and developments. Changes in the surrounding environment mean that organizations need to respond to their surroundings— changing environments. In such environments, organizations themselves are rarely stagnant and will often change, adapt, and develop over time in response to a changing environment, if they are to continue to exist and serve.

In addition to examining how we might also think about organizational innovation and change, we need to consider questions of how organizations can respond to changing environments in which they find themselves by forming partnerships or working arrangements with other organizations and agencies. Often, in responding to changing environments, needs, and opportunities around them, organizations may decide to create partnerships with other organizations or form some other type of cooperative venture with other organizations that will allow them to respond to new needs and opportunities. If we are to develop a full, thoughtful analysis of organizations and ethics, we need to think about the questions of identity and integrity as starting points in creating such partnerships. How might we think about such partnerships in terms of organizational identity and integrity? We often focus exclusively on the individual agent's decision-making and ignore organizational decisions, or how organizations can cooperate with others. An agent needs to decide if she or he wants to join with other agents in a particular endeavor. In such decisions an organization needs to think thorough how its moral commitments and identity as an organization align with the moral commitments of other organizations with which it is working. However, we need to consider a few questions. How can we think through such organizational agency and partnerships in terms of an organization's moral identity and agency? How can such partnerships and working relationships be formed so that an organization can maintain its identity and, with it, its integrity? A first step an organization can take to resolve these questions is to grasp a sense of its own identity and moral values.

10.1 Organizational Identity and Integrity

As has been argued throughout this book, particularly in Chap. 5, the identity of a moral agent, whether the agent is a person or an organization, is foundational for ethical discourse and decisions in a postmodern, morally diverse, secular society. The identity of an agent is a crucial and basic measure for assessing the integrity of the agent. The questions of identity and integrity are the key starting points for this type of discussion and investigation; they were explored earlier in the Second Part of this book. As has been argued earlier in the book, integrity and its content-full meaning, for a person or an organization, will depend on the fundamental moral commitments that are made by a person or organization.[1] These foundational commitments shape the identity of the agent and embody the moral values of the agent. Any discussion of integrity, it has been argued, is integrally related to the identity of the agent, whether an individual person or organization.

While the integrity of a moral agent relies on fundamental moral commitments of the agent for meaningful content, at the same time, as it has been argued in this book, secular societies are places where one often not only finds diverse but also sometimes competing and conflicting moral visions. These circumstances open up the possibility that two moral agents, with very different sets of moral values, may both still be living lives of moral integrity. In such a society, the moral agent needs

[1] K. Wildes, "Institutional Integrity: Toleration, Approval, and Holy War or 'Always True to You in My Fashion'", *Journal of Medicine and Philosophy* 16 (April 1991), 211–220.

to consider if and how to cooperate with other moral agents who may have different moral commitments and agendas. This requirement is certainly true for individual agents. However, with individual agents one can resolve a problem caused by different moral visions through the process of free and informed consent and agreement. The same challenge that exists for individual agents can also exist for organizations. However, for a complete analysis, we need to think through how organizations can engage in cooperative arrangements with other organizations and individuals that may have different views and moral values. In situations where people with different moral visions must work together around a moral project, like health care, they need to think about how they understand the ideas of moral compromise and cooperation.

According to the account of integrity articulated in Chaps. 5 and 6 of this book, one can develop how one might think about the idea of compromise, based on the concept of integrity, by articulating the ways in which an organization can live in a morally pluralistic world that involves cooperation with other individuals or organizations with very different views. One can argue that there is a range of possible responses for organizations with particular moral identities, as they encounter and work with others, with different moral visions, in a secular, postmodern society. At one end of the spectrum of responses, an organization can withdraw from the secular arena. One can find several examples of this response in religious communities that set up, for example, education and health care organizations for their communities and which operate by a strict code of ethics espoused by their religious traditions. On the other hand, at the other end of the spectrum, there is the possibility that an organization may lose its identity.

Alternatively, one can conceptualize ways in which an organization can engage the world around it and, at the same time, try to maintain its fundamental identity.

In examining these questions in a broader landscape of secular, morally diverse societies, one can imagine and articulate a possible range of responses that organizations can make to the ethical challenges they face in the world. One might conceptualize the scale as moving from approval to condemnation, with a number of responses of toleration that lie between the two extremes. Organizations, in health care or education, can give approval through their actions, such as public statements or institutional honors. For example, when a university bestows an honorary degree, or a hospital gives an award, it is usually for work that a person has done or will do for the institution or which is in line with the mission of the organization. There is a sense, however, that such honors "endorse" not only the work that has been done but also the person who is being honored. That person is honored as a model for the institution. In another example, one might think of St. Valentine's as having a hospital chaplain available day and night to care for the spiritual and sacramental needs of any patient or staff member. The organization commits its resources to such a service and may highlight this in its public profile communicated through literature and advertising material. The work of the chaplain touches the core of the mission of St. Valentine's hospital. The chaplain's work is one that has earned the hospital's endorsement and approval.

At the other end of the scale of possible responses by organizations, one finds the response of condemnation and what might become a "holy war". At this end of the range, an organization not only withholds approval but also expresses strong disapproval by putting all of its resources to work to resist the challenge, refusing to cooperate in any way. For example, if a local law required St. Valentine's hospital to perform abortions, one could imagine the hospital utilizing its resources to fight such a requirement in every political and legal arena. On the other hand, a religious university, faced with a law that required the indoctrination of its students in atheism might commit its resources to a legal battle to overturn such a requirement. Failure to alter the situation might lead to an extreme response: civil disobedience or the forgoing of public funding of any type to prevent the institution from being forced to cooperate with evil. It is imaginable that an institution, like a citizen, might employ force to protect its values.

Toleration should be thought of as a response that falls between the responses of approval and condemnation. Toleration has a very different meaning from both of those terms, and it is often misunderstood and misinterpreted as approval. Often, we fail to understand the meaning of toleration; as stated, many confuse it with approval, which it is not. At its root, toleration means to "endure". Many of us "endure" situations of which we do not approve. Indeed, in many ways institutions, which participate in the public domain, must tolerate situations that are, at best, incongruous with their institutional identities. However, there are various gradations of "toleration". The first gradation, closest to approval, is to tolerate but neither approve nor disapprove. For example, a university may be committed to the free expression of ideas and thus tolerate speakers and groups who are intolerant. In such cases, university officials may judge that it is best simply to say nothing. One might think of a group of students within a Catholic university who form The St. Pius V Club to honor the canonized members of the Holy Inquisition. While the university might not endorse the club, a Catholic institution might decide to tolerate such a club and would undoubtedly find it best to say nothing. A hospital might tolerate spiritual healers as long as they did not interfere with the primary work of the hospital.

There is yet another level of toleration by which health care or educational organizations may tolerate a situation but still articulate organizational concern about it. Some members of the staff of St. Valentine's may invite a speaker to talk on in vitro fertilization or Physician Assisted Suicide. The hospital may tolerate the speaker and yet voice its concern over parts of the speaker's remarks or point out that there are other views on the topic which should be represented. A university may have concern over the content of leaflets being distributed on campus and voice its concern as well.

Another level of organizational response is that of toleration with disapproval. A religious university may tolerate a speaker defending atheism or apartheid and yet publicly disapprove of the content of the lecture. The lecture is tolerated, because the university holds other values as fundamental to its identity as a university, such as free speech or academic inquiry and argument that are important to the institution and at the heart of its self-identity. One can think, for example, of performances of the *Vagina Monologues* on the campuses of Catholic colleges and universities as an example. Alternatively, a Catholic hospital may tolerate, but not approve of, a speaker on AIDS who endorses the use of condoms and sexual practices that are not permitted by the Church.

Yet another level of response on the scale is toleration that emerges as active opposition. In this response, the problematic situation may be such that the institution would seek to change the state of affairs through legal action. The institution may decide to address the matter legally and live with the result. At this level, we are still a step away from "holy war", in view that the institution will tolerate the results of the legal battle. For example, a group at St. Valentine's might seek to force the institution to include information about condoms in its social service counseling for HIV patients and to dispense condoms to all such patients. The hospital might oppose such demands with appropriate legal action. Similarly, one might imagine a Christian university confronted with the formation of a Young Fornicators League. It would not surprise anyone if the university decided to oppose the League with legal means. However, in both cases one could imagine the institutions living with, although condemning, the results of the court ruling if such results were adverse. There are gradations even within this level. The situation could be such that an institution decided to use all possible legal appeals. However, one could imagine that in the course of litigation an institution will have to weigh its use of resources in such litigation and decide to limit legal appeals.

In summary, organizations can respond to situations in a number of ways. The scale for organizational response can range between approval and condemnation, with the idea of approval indeed having several gradations. The scale looks like this:

1. Approval
2. Toleration and silence
3. Toleration and the expression of concern
4. Toleration and explicit disapproval
5. Toleration and opposition
6. Condemnation
7. Holy War

This range of responses provides the basis for a language for organizations to speak both internally and externally to the broader, diverse, secular society. In a way, organizations are able to speak to both their internal and external audiences about who they are, as organizations, in the situation of the time through decisions and policies. They speak, surely, in how they announce and monitor their missions. They also speak in how they build internal cultures, which should reflect the identity, mission, and vision of the organization. Finally, they also speak by how they engage the society, and organizations, around them. The use of institutional resources can be understood, cautiously, as a way of speaking and voicing toleration, approval, or condemnation.

10.2 Organizational Speech: Policies and the Allocation of Resources

In thinking about organizations as moral agents, it is important to examine not only organizational actions but also to identify how organizations can speak as moral agents. It is clear that one can generally say, correctly, that organizations speak through their actions.

However, there are at least two other key forms of organizational speech that an organization can use. These two forms are organizational actions, but they are, quite often, internal actions and ways for an organization to speak. The two most prominent forms of organizational speech, as actions, are the adoption of policies and the allocation of resources.

Policies can be positive in promoting the values of an organization, or they can be prohibitive in forbidding certain activities that are counter to the identity of the organization. In either case organizations speak, through their policies, to what is the organization's identity and what are its values. An organization's policies potentially cover a wide range of activities, which might range from the hiring and orientation of personnel to codes of conduct and discipline.

The allocation of resources by an organization, or any moral agent, is yet another way that an organization can speak to its values and commitments in so far as the allocation of resources is an indicator of what any moral agent values. If one takes this approach, one should be able to read an organization's budget as a mission statement and thereby know, to some extent, what the organization values. For example, if an organization says in its mission statement that the organization is committed to X, whatever X may be, but in reviewing the organization's budget one discovers there are no resources allocated for X, one can say that the organization is at the very least deceiving itself.

When we think about the resources of an organization, we need to think beyond money alone. The use of organizational resources, such as money, space, personnel, time, and talent, is another important aspect of organizational life and a way in which organizations speak. The use of resources can be best read through the lens of this scale. The budget of an organization is more than accounting. It is a planning document that should reflect the identity, mission, and vision of the organization. Resources, especially monetary ones, come often from a mixture of public and private sources. Such a funding mixture will carry with it designations and regulations that an institution may have to tolerate. This may well be described as "toleration" but not approval. Allowing a group to use its resources is not necessarily itself an approval of what the group supports. Rather, resource allocation needs to be understood as a very subtle and nuanced form of institutional language—a language that has more voices than simply approval or condemnation.

10.3 Cooperation with Other Organizations

Organizations are rarely, if ever, self-contained, so we need to consider how organizations can cooperate and work with other organizations or how organizations can work with society as a whole. To address these types of questions, we will borrow from a tradition in Roman Catholic moral thought about cooperation. This model is not held up as the definitive model on how to address the challenges of organizations working with other organizations. However, it is used as a well-developed moral tradition that takes into consideration institutions and organizations working with others, particularly if the organizations do not share the exact same moral commitments.

This tradition has a well-developed understanding of cooperation and the problems that are inherent when organizations enter into cooperative ventures with other organizations with different moral commitments. This tradition of thought has a well-developed set of categories for how organizations can cooperate with others when one of the cooperators is involved in what may be viewed as an action or policy that is wrong or "evil".

This tradition makes what can be a helpful distinction between material and formal cooperation with evil.[2] To understand this distinction, and its use, one needs to conceptualize a moral system that understands some acts, such as murder, to be intrinsically evil. To cooperate with any evil act has meant that one concurs, in some way, with the evil act of another. Formal cooperation takes place when one shares the intention of the agent who is performing the sinful act—for example, when one is, knowingly, the getaway driver in a bank robbery. Material cooperation takes place when someone contributes to the sinful or evil act without sharing in the intention. Someone materially cooperates when engaging in an act that supports the other, such as a cab driver who drives a woman for an abortion. The action contributes to the whole, but it is done without sharing in the intention. Material cooperation can be either immediate or mediate. It is immediate if it is part of the act. It is mediated if it is somehow "at a distance". Often classical writers have spoken about mediate material cooperation as being either proximate or remote.

There are clear limits to this language and distinction of cooperation, but the concepts present one way to think about how organizations can act with other organizations. The tradition of the distinction will be more carefully explored in Chap. 11 when we explore the geography of organizational and corporate partnerships. It is a distinction that can also be developed in a way that is too legalistic or Jesuitical. The language can be understood as if there is some type of absolute measure that can tell one where she or he stands in relationship to an evil act. The distinction is also limited by the view that there are discrete acts in the world that can be identified.

At the same time, however, the distinction offers an important way to think about organizations, as well as individuals, that are trying to preserve their moral

---

[2] Kevin L. Flannery, *Cooperation with Evil: Thomistic Tools of Analysis*, (Washington, DC: Catholic University of America Press, 2019).

identities and integrity in a morally diverse world. It reminds us that for some people and organizations there are moral evils that ought not to be supported in any way. In recent years, the distinction has taken on an important role in Catholic health care as a way to think through the range of possible relationships that Catholic institutions can have with other institutions that engage in practices viewed as wrong or inconsistent with the mission and identity of the organization. The view has been taken that, cooperative arrangements were possible, insofar as they were material and "the object of material cooperation should be as distant as possible from the wrongdoer's act."[3]

To understand the language of this distinction, an important, underlying assumption posits that there are some acts which should be understood as morally evil. For example, there has been a long discussion, in Roman Catholic moral thought, about certain acts that are to be considered as "intrinsically evil moral acts".[4] However framed, this is an example of a tradition that identifies certain actions as moral evils in the world. If such evils exist, the question arises as to how one should approach such evils. In an ideal perfect world, one would simply avoid them and have nothing to do with them. However, this is not a perfect world. So Catholic moral theology developed a schema for discerning the actions by which people and organizations can cooperate with others in an imperfect world.

Chapter 11 offers a more developed account of these distinctions and their relationship to moral evil and wrongdoing. The distinction relies on a philosophical distinction drawn from the Aristotelian-Thomistic tradition of metaphysics in which a substance is composed of form and matter. The form is the essence or the core of a being. The material aspect of a substance is what particularizes a particular being, while the essence makes it be what it is. In the same way, one can also talk about acts as has having form and matter. The form is the essence of an act.

Essential to identifying the form of an act is not only the physical action itself but the intention as well. To cooperate formally is to participate in the act and share the intention of the agent.

Material cooperation is when one acts in a way that contributes to the evil/sinful act without approving of it or sharing in the intention of the agent. This occurs when A helps B by an act that is not sinful/evil and without approving of what B does. Material cooperation can be either immediate or mediate. Material cooperation is immediate when the object of the cooperator is the same as the object of the wrongdoer. Immediate material cooperation is wrong except in some instances of duress. Mediate material cooperation occurs when the cooperator's action is distinguishable from the wrongdoer's and can be justified for a proportionate reason. Mediate material cooperation can be further broken down into proximate or remote cooperation. It is proximate when the help is intimately concerned with the act of another and remote if the help given is not closely tied to the wrongful act.

---

[3] *Religious Directives Catholic Health Care Services*, United States Conference of Catholic Bishops, (Washington Ethical and, DC: United States Catholic Conference, 2018), Part Six.

[4] J. Bretzke, J. (2014). Debating "Intrinsic Evil". *Horizons*, 41(1), 116–129. doi:10.1017/hor.2014.30

In this tradition, as in most moral traditions, there is an important role for the freedom of the agent. When agents are coerced in their actions, and their freedom is compromised or diminished, so the moral assessment of the action changes. That said, one would need to examine how the freedom of organizations can be limited. Often such limits take place through other organizational actors or governmental regulation.

10.4 Integrity and Compromise

While the goal of this chapter is to expand and continue the discussion about organizational identity and integrity, which were explored earlier in Chaps. 5 and 6, it will be helpful if we continue to explore the notion of integrity based on the individual person as a starting point for our exploration of the range of organizational responses. It is important, at this point, to link together the notions of integrity and compromise.

In all of our exploration, it is important to remember that the identity of an organization is foundational to its relationships with other organizations, government, people, and society. In this way, we will have a clearer sense of the idea of integrity before tackling the more complicated notion of organizational integrity. When we think of integrity, we usually think of it in terms of an individual maintaining his or her moral commitments. Unfortunately, in popular culture we often think of integrity in a binary way. People often say that an agent, whether an organization or individual person, either has, or does not have, integrity. However, as has been argued earlier, the virtue of integrity is not an all or nothing proposition, in that it depends on the agent's other moral commitments. Therefore, we need to think about how to assess integrity, particularly for organizations, in a diverse, morally pluralistic society, because both organizations and contemporary secular societies are complex and diverse in terms of moral views.

As situations of conflict emerge in a person's life, the hierarchy of moral values and commitments is crucial to determining which resolutions are acceptable without abandoning the fundamental moral projects, which constitute one's conception of the moral life. Such ordering leads to a prioritization. If there is an internal conflict of values that demands a compromise, one will have to know which commitments are most central to know what can, and cannot, be given up in effecting a compromise. The second point is that this model of integrity can lead to the development of a model of compromise.

For many people integrity is often understood, essentially, as consistency. This view of integrity as consistency is straightforward. A person has a set of moral commitments, no matter how they may be articulated (principles, rules, virtues), and the person seeks to stick to those commitments. The opposite of this notion of integrity is any idea of compromise. However, this construal of integrity involves a number of views and assumptions that need to be challenged.

One should ask why consistency by itself is an incomplete model for integrity. In response to that question, one can argue that the consistency model of integrity is too simple.

For example, it does not give a way to think through conflicting moral commitments. One can see the problem of conflict within the lives of individual moral agents. One does not even have to open up the complicated issues of moral pluralism and diversity. Most people have confronted the problem of conflicting moral demands, such as the decision to keep or break a promise to one person in order to respond to the request of another person. Much of our moral thinking is shaped by conflicting demands and trying to judge what is the right thing to do. On the other hand, one can understand the simplicity of the integrity-as-consistency model by reflecting on the difficulties of applying a rule. First, people often assume that rules can simply be applied to particular cases. People often have no sense that it is often difficult to figure out what is the right rule to apply to a particular situation. Wittgenstein pointed out that rules do not tell us when and how they should be applied. One often finds examples of this problem in sporting events when there is a controversy over a call made by a referee or judge. Such calls are often controversial; no matter how much we use instant replay, the situation requires human judgment on (1) whether or not there has been an infraction and (2) if so, which rule has been violated. In bioethics, for example, one might think of examples from end-of-life care. An individual may have a commitment to the preservation of life. However, consistency, understood as always doing the same thing, would lead to a mindless vitalism and a misuse of resources.

Moral controversies are often contentious, because the event or decision can be described in different ways and because different rules can be applied. One has only to look at numerous cases of decisions at the end of life to see how differently the same case can be described.

Therefore, while consistency is an element of integrity, consistency alone does not give a full picture of integrity. Moral controversies often involve competing moral commitments and a decision to choose among them or to rank them. If we assume that integrity is a second order virtue, with the task of ordering our moral lives, consistency alone will not give a full account of integrity.

Integrity can and should be understood, however, in a much broader and richer way than as a model of consistency; that is, people have values, both moral and non-moral, which they wish to maintain and projects they wish to pursue. These projects and commitments shape their lives. This sense of integrity is not simply a matter of narrow consistency in one's life. Rather, it usually reflects a ranking of goals and values, which leads to a balancing of different projects and to the directing of commitments over time. Integrity requires dealing with conflicting demands. Integrity requires judgment.

This dynamic or moral judgment and discernment takes us back to the first point about integrity: integrity is integral to its relationship to a person's or an organization's first order moral commitments. Integrity needs content, and that content comes from the commitments of the moral agent. The exercise of integrity will involve a judgment and discernment of the balancing and ordering of the first order moral commitments and a decision about how they should be applied in different circumstances. Why should there be compromise at all? We live in an imperfect world. There are numerous ways to account for its imperfections, but one key element is the recognition that the world is finite and a place where we are limited and the options imperfect.

The recognition of compromise is the recognition that the practical world, the world of ethical decisions, is one that is limited and finite. It is not an ideal world in which every moral value can be fully realized. Rather, it is a world of limits, where one has limited options.

Therefore, individuals and organizations often must compromise. However, to enter into the give and take of compromise, one needs a sense of the moral values to which one is committed and a ranking of these values. Without a sense of the central value commitments, a person or an institution will not stand for anything. Without some ranking of the values, a person or organization will not know which values can be compromised and which cannot.

Utilizing this understanding of integrity means that an organization would have to articulate an understanding of its "mission", values, and projects[5] in order to effectively preserve its moral integrity. Such a public statement would inform interested parties how the institution sees itself and why it is in "business". Such a statement ought to shape the business practices it adopts. Such an articulation can do even more, however. It can help the institution understand its own commitments, their foundations, and their relationship one to another. With this view of integrity, an institution can move beyond identifying itself simply by what it will not do to a positive view of what it is trying to achieve; such institutional self-understanding allows for the possibility of compromise. Not all of the commitments of an organization, in its mission, are univocally valued. Some are less fundamental than others. This understanding of integrity is a crucial first step to help the organization avoid the Scylla and Charybdis of the loss of self-identity on the one hand, or the withdrawal of the organization from the public context to the safety of isolation on the other. In a secular society, with different moral values and visions, there are also different views of what is morally appropriate medicine and health care. If an institution is to make its way in this world, it will be important for it to have a vision of its moral commitments and their ranking.

The importance of such reflection is made evident in legal cases such as that of Beverly Requena.[6] Mrs. Requena, suffering from amyotrophic lateral sclerosis (ALS), asked not to undergo artificial feeding or administration of fluids. St. Clare's, the hospital in which she was a patient, developed a policy stating that the institution would not participate in the withholding or withdrawal of artificial feeding or fluids. The policy, however, was established after Mrs.

[5] See Chap. 5 of this book.

[6] Superior Court of New Jersey, Appellate Division, *Re Requena*, 442–486, decided October 6, 1986.

Requena's admission to the hospital. St. Clare's had sought to honor her request by transferring her to a nearby hospital. Mrs. Requena asked that she not be compelled to leave St. Clare's after having been there for fifteen months and establishing relationships of trust with the staff.

In deciding the case, the courts supported Mrs. Requena's request to remain at St. Clare's and refuse the artificial feeding and fluids. One of the reasons for the court's decision was the hospital's failure to develop and announce a policy in a timely fashion. The Appellate Court wrote:

> An equitable consideration here is that Beverly Requena had no notice of St. Clare's policy against withholding artificial feeding or fluids until July of 1986. The balance to be struck here is between the hospital's right to enforce its regulation and fundamental rights of the patient. Under the circumstances, we find no waiver or estoppel against Beverly Requena who *had no notice of the regulation prior to her admission or for 15 months thereafter* (Requena, emphasis added).[7]

The court seems to support the hospital's right to have such regulations, but at the same time, it also held the institution responsible for its failure to communicate its moral commitments in a timely fashion. In writing about the effects of moral pluralism on the practice of medicine, Alasdair MacIntyre has offered some remarks that are appropriate to the Requena case and the issues of institutional identity and integrity.[8]

Where a community of moral and metaphysical beliefs is lacking, trust between strangers becomes much more questionable than when we can safely assume such a community. Nobody can rely on anyone else's judgments on his or her behalf until he or she knows what the other person believes. It follows that nobody can accept the moral authority of another simply in virtue of his professional position.

While MacIntyre's remarks are focused on the importance of patient autonomy and patient-directed activity, the remarks implicitly address the need for persons and organizations, such as HCOs and educational organizations, to spell out what they believe. The practice of health care in the terrain of moral strangers means that the consent and agreement of participants is crucial to the justification of any choice or practice. Institutional statements of moral commitments are a means for honest participation in the pluralistic world of medicine. Such statements, and the process of formulating them, can also enable the institution to take a positive, proactive stance in the world, rather than assuming a reactive, defensive stance to unfolding events.

---

[7] Superior Court of New Jersey, Appellate Division, *Re Requena*, 442–486, decided October 6, 1986.

[8] MacIntyre, A.: 1977, 'Patients as agents', in S.F. Spicker and H.T. Engelhardt, Jr. (eds.), *Philosophical Medical Ethics: Its Nature and Significance*, Philosophy and Medicine Vol. 3, D. Reidel Publishing Company, Dordrecht, Holland, pp. 189–212.

10.5 Innovation and Mission

Organizations live in a social context, and most societies are open to change and development. This means that organizations, particularly in health care and education, will need to adapt to a changing environment. In both contemporary health care and higher education, one will often find discussions about innovation; this topic is not surprising, given both the rapid, ongoing developments in substance and material as well as new, evolving models of delivery in each area and concerns about rising costs in both education and health care. The topic of innovation has been widely discussed and studied in both health care and related delivery systems of care.

However, at this point, I would suggest that a lot of this talk is fueled by concerns about cost for education and health care and, with it, the unstated assumption that innovation might make it more affordable.

I would also suggest that the idea of innovation is very much a part of certain cultures, including American culture. Some modern and postmodern cultures are biased toward the "new" and the "innovative". Often, when something is being marketed the chief virtue of the product is heralded as "new". However, it is worthwhile to evaluate the new and innovative, for an organization, in terms of the mission and identity of the organization. It is in the light of mission and identity that one can determine if and how the innovation can serve the organization. The mission and identity of an organization, in education and health care, must serve as the Archimedean point for direction and decision-making for the organization.

In recent years, education, particularly higher education, has provided numerous examples of innovation and technology. The development of the Internet, along with cheap and effective computing technologies, has certainly influenced how higher education operates. The uses of these technologies depend on the mission of an educational organization and the type of education it is attempting to offer. However, according to one observation, while there may be ways to accomplish tasks more efficiently, that does not mean the substantive work of those tasks is necessarily improved by the way in which they were accomplished. We must remember that any innovation, technological or otherwise, needs to be evaluated in terms of the mission and identity of an organization and what it wants to accomplish.

In the contemporary health care and education areas, the development of new and different technologies is ongoing, including both new technologies and replacement technologies that change the way we deliver services. The continual development of technologies often leads to calls for innovation. In health care, there is a variety of structures, such as professional standards, state licensing, and the threat of litigation, which affects and governs the introduction of innovative techniques and practices. Education is a more wide-open area, and here the goals, objectives, and mission of an organization should play an important role in guiding innovation.

When considering innovation in education or health care, key questions must be asked.

First, what is the purpose of the innovation and how does it serve the mission of the organization? If a proposed innovation does not serve the mission of the organization, it may not be worth doing.[9] The consideration of mission is crucial to the evaluation of any innovation, in order to assess what it can accomplish and to evaluate whether the innovation will detract from or disturb the mission and identity of the organization.

These evaluative questions are crucial in the development, implementation, and evaluation of any innovation in an organization in health care or education. One might characterize the evaluation of innovations, in light of the mission of an organization, as a question about the "mission alignment" of the innovation.

10.6 Conclusions

In this chapter, we have explored the terrain of how organizations, with particular moral identities and missions, can live in a postmodern, morally diverse secular society and work with others, whether individuals, organizations, or society as a whole. We have also explored questions of how such organizations can change and evolve and still maintain identity and mission. These questions are very important for organizations, as they operate in a secular, morally diverse, postmodern society and work with other organizations in education and health care that may not share the same identities and values.

If one starts with the foundational stone of an organization—its mission and identity—one can examine how an organization in education or health care can work, and cooperate, with other organizations that have different identities and missions, all the while retaining its own moral integrity. Many of these questions can be helpful for an organization, as it sorts through issues of compliance with government regulations. The geography of responses developed here is drawn from the moral traditions of the Roman Catholic community, which has a long history of Church-affiliated health care and educational organizations involved directly in the world.

What has been developed in this chapter is one possible scheme or scaffolding of ideas that can be used to evaluate relationships between organizations and provide a way to think about how an organization can be involved in and with not only a diverse, secular society but other organizations in the same society and still maintain its particular identity.

[9] Kate Evner and Noah Pickus, The Right Kind of Innovation", *Inside Higher Ed*, July 25 2018.

Summary of the Main Points

1. Organizational Identity and Integrity
2. Organizational Speech: Policies and the Allocation of Resources
3. Cooperation
4. Integrity and Compromise
5. Innovation and Mission

Chapter 11
Living with Limits: Organizations, Justice, and Injustice in Postmodern Societies

In this exploration of organizations and how they can be understood as moral actors in a secular, postmodern society, it has been argued, particularly in Part Two, that to evaluate any organization as a moral actor, we should begin with the organization's articulation of its own identity and its moral commitments. The articulation of the organization's moral values is important for the organization, but it is also important for assessing its interactions with the wider, morally diverse, secular society. The awareness of an organization's moral commitments, by the organization and by other members of the society in which it operates, is important for civil cooperation in a secular society. Secular societies in the postmodern age open, in principle, to moral diversity. In these societies it will be important for all moral agents to be aware of their own moral commitments and to be able to articulate those commitments to other moral actors in order to cooperate with them. Such moral awareness, of an organization and its environment, is important, if the organization is to remain anchored in its identity. Moral awareness of its identity is also important for how an organization can interact with other organizations and the society in which it operates. A postmodern, secular society, as argued earlier and explored in Chaps. 3 and 4, will be open, in principle, to moral pluralism and diversity because of the secular nature of the society. So, it follows that a sense of moral identity by an organization will be essential for how the organization can successfully interact, morally, in such a morally diverse society and still maintain its own identity and mission. Of course, this assumes that an organization has an identity and mission that it wants to maintain.

This chapter will develop another reason as to why it is important to understand an organization's self-identity and mission. That reason is the reality of limits. Every human being and every organization live in a limited world. There are limits to time, opportunity, talent, and resources. In our contemporary world we do not, normally, think or discuss the subject of "limits". When we do think about limits, we usually think about how we can overcome them! Because of the way we normally think and operate, trying to think about limits is like trying to conceive the

K. W. Wildes, S.J., *Organizational Ethics and Moral Integrity in Secular Societies*, Philosophical Studies in Contemporary Culture 29,
https://doi.org/10.1007/978-3-031-39097-5_11

philosophical category of "nothingness".[1] However, like the existential state of nothingness for human beings, the condition of limits represents an important existential, and practical, reality for organizations. Indeed, I would argue, that limits are a reality for the finite world generally and that, in a finite, created world, the reality of limits is always present. There are limits in time, talent, material, and opportunity, for example.

Yet, limits are not something that human beings or organizations often think about explicitly. But, as existentialist thinkers like Sartre and Heidegger have pointed out the human condition is defined, in some respects, by its limits in time and, ultimately, in death. In light of the arguments of this book it will be argued here that an organization's self-identity and moral commitments ought to be foundational in how it deals with limits. As with human beings, an organization cannot be everything to everyone. The organization will need to determine how it lives in a world of limited time and resources. Any organization will need to live with the dialectical tension that exists between its identity and the vision of what it hopes to accomplish and the limits of what it can do at any particular moment.

An organization's self-identity will not only be important, morally, for how it addresses the realities of limits, but the organization's identity is also important for how the organization participates in the society in which it exits, as explored, in part, in Chap. 10. This chapter will also argue that an organization needs to understand that it exists in a finite world, where the organization's resources, the resources of its collaborators, and the resources of the surrounding world are limited. Both organizations, and the world around them, are finite. In the face of limits, which are manifest in terms of time, talent, and resources, organizations will need to determine how best to structure themselves and their relationships with others, whether organizational partners, users of services, individual agents, or government agencies, so that they can give an accounting for their use of resources. Faced with limits how does an organization use its resources? How are an organization's relationships with other organizations structured to support the identity and the credibility of the organization in a diverse, secular society? The two questions intersect around an organization's identity. The question with regard to an organization's use of resources and the question with regard to an organization's relationship with other organizations both recognize the finite nature of the world and the importance of an organization's identity in searching for answers. The use of resources by an organization or any moral agent, is a pragmatic measure of what the agent values.

One of the constant challenges for any organization or, for that matter, the society in which it functions, is the ever-present limits to the resources available to an organization or to society in general for that matter. Organizations, like all moral actors, need to think about the reality of the limits and use of resources. So, an often-unspoken ethical question, for any moral agent, whether an individual,

[1] Jean-Paul Sartre, *Being and Nothingness,* trans. Hazel Barnes , (New York: Washington Square Press, 1943).

organization, or society, is how the finite resources available to a moral agent should be used.

Because organizations in health care and education almost always use common or shared resources that derive from the societies in which they are situated, we need to examine how resources can be ethically distributed both within an organization and by a society. The language that is most often used for these types of questions about the distribution of resources is the language of "justice". As we further explore how organizations can participate, ethically, in morally pluralistic, secular societies, we need to examine how the language of "justice" might be used to understand and assess the participation of organizations in secular, morally diverse societies. One problem, however, is that the language of "justice" can be defined, applied, and stipulated in several different ways. And, because of the different ways it can be defined and applied, the term can carry so many different meanings as to become, practically speaking, meaningless in multicultural, secular societies. So, to advance the analysis and argument, we should think about what that language might mean and how it might be, appropriately or inappropriately, used.

The use of the language of justice can be of particular importance for organizations in health care and education. The services of organizations in health care and education cannot be easily imaged in the way we normally think about companies, organizations, and products or services. To begin, both health care and education are areas heavily supported, at least in part, by common, public resources in a secular society. And, because resources are not unlimited, in any society, we need to find a way to think about the reality of limits, what that reality means for organizations, and how that reality can be confronted by the organization. One important reason for reflecting on the language of justice is that when moral agents, individuals or organizations, confront the reality of limits, they often use the moral language of justice to address questions regarding the process and distribution of resources.

11.1 Finitude: Living with Limits

Individuals in the First World rarely reflect on limits as part of their lives. But limits are part of human life in almost all aspects, and the reality of limits is part of almost every decision. Human beings cannot do everything. They cannot be everywhere. They are limited in space and time. They are also limited in their talents. In fact, philosophers like Heidegger and other existentialists would argue that the limitations of human life, particularly in death, are key to the search for meaning in human life.[2]

[2] Harvey, Sharon R. "Environmental Problem-Solving and Heidegger's Phenomenology: Addressing Our Technical Relation to Nature." *Environmental Philosophy* 6, no. 2 (2009): 59–72. http://www.jstor.org/stable/26168017. See also, Martin Heidegger, *Being and Time*, trans. John Macquarrie and Edward Robinsk, Blackwell Publishers, Oxford, UK, 1962.

Nevertheless, those living in contemporary, secular societies rarely or explicitly think about limits. Rather they usually think about finding ways to transcend limitations. The absence of a discussion about, or consciousness of, limitations is particularly apparent in American culture, which, historically, has seen its potential as boundless.[3] This is a nation that has been shaped historically by the westward expansion and the new frontier of outer space. Some will argue that the lack of a sense of limits, culturally, has contributed to the environmental issues which the nation is now experiencing. In the area of health care, generally, America as a nation and its culture do not confront death or, perhaps better, see death as a limit to be overcome.

The limits and limitation of human life, in all their dimensions, are a challenging reality for many people, particularly Americans, to understand. But the reality is that human beings are finite creatures. Though contemporary cultures often appeal to the idea of human beings as limitless, that is an illusion. Human beings are creatures that often push the boundaries and go beyond limits that exist. The great westward expansion in the United States is one historical example. At the time, there seemed to be unlimited possibilities for the expansion of the nation. Or, one might think of the USA-Soviet race to the moon and outer space as another example of a social desire to push beyond defined limits to new, unlimited possibilities. In each of these we see historical examples of the human struggle with human finitude, and we find historical examples that helped to fuel American self-understanding of unlimited possibilities.

Ultimately, however, the human condition is limited by space, time, knowledge, opportunities, and, in the end, death.[4] The existentialist philosophers of the twentieth century provocatively and thoughtfully pointed out that the human condition is ultimately limited by death. No matter what people might assume in their day-to-day lives, or what their culture might communicate, human beings do not have unlimited lives. Human beings are finite creatures who will die. But the end of life is not the only limit with which human beings live. In their day-to- day lives humans are limited in their talents, abilities, and resources. From a Christian perspective, and from the perspective of many religions, human beings are finite, limited creatures. They are finite and limited by nature. However, the reality of human finitude is often overlooked, or forgotten and hidden, in contemporary secular cultures.

Even though it is often overlooked, or, perhaps, deliberately ignored, the reality of human finitude is a very important background assumption not only for understanding individual human life but also for understanding social structures, like organizations in health care and education. The different types of organizations in both education and health care are created, in some deep sense, to help human beings overcome their finitude and limitations. Yet, human life will always be limited, and, one can argue, the reality of human finitude is always important for ethical reflection. However, it is often overlooked. We are finite creatures, and we cannot do everything for everyone, so we need to make choices about how to use our resources.

---

[3] David Kamp, "Rethinking the American Dream", *Vanity Fair*, April 2009.

[4] Solomon, Robert C. "Existentialism, Emotions, and the Cultural Limits of Rationality." *Philosophy East and West* 42, no. 4 (1992): 597–621.

It can be argued that one can identify a natural link between reflections on human finitude and religious institutions and organizations, which address questions of meaning in response to the reality of finite, limited existence. In some ways one can also argue that the development of the different systems of health care and education are cultural and systemic responses to aspects of human finitude. One can argue that medicine, education, and religion are driven by a response to the same fundamental human experience: the experience of finitude. The practice of medicine confronts, again and again, the finite nature of human existence in suffering, sickness, death, and the limits of resources. This confrontation with finitude is also an impetus for the religious experience of many human beings who seek to understand the meaning of human life in the face of suffering and death, which is at the heart of so many religious experiences. And the quest for knowledge is a quest to overcome human limitations. The dilemmas of medical ethics present a unique meeting place for religion and medicine. In a different way, education, no matter how it is structured, responds to a fundamental human need to overcome the limits of human knowledge.

Organizations in health care and education must also come face to face with the experience of limits, in materials and resources, just like other organizations. But, organizations in health care and education also confront the limits of human life in the cultural and social hopes for ongoing progress, development, and the improvement of human life. Health care, in society, is often more than simply repairing what has gone wrong for a person who gets sick; it is also a way of improving the quality of a person's life. Education is often seen as more than simply helping someone develop the knowledge, wisdom, and skills needed to function and thrive in a society; education is also a way to open new doors and improve one's life. Both education and health care have become linked to ideas of human progress and development, so it may seem antithetical to consider the reality of limits and limitations when thinking about organizations, in either since both hold a promise of progress.

Given the moral and social importance of organizations in health care and education, along with the economic impact of these organizations on the life of a community, it is natural that important social and ethical questions will arise concerning the allocation and use of public resources to support these organizations in society. It should be clear that how choices regarding the allocation and use of resources are structured will depend on the nation and its history and culture. So, there is no single model for every society. Indeed, if one surveys industrialized nations one will find a range of models for how the goods of health care and education are delivered in a nation.

At this writing, for example, the United States spent \$3.8 trillion on health care, or just under eighteen percent (18%) of the GDP in 2019.[5] In terms of education, the

[5]Centers for Medicare and Medicaid Services, 2019, https://www.cms.gov/Research-Statistics-Data-and-Systems/Statistics-Trends-and-Reports/NationalHealthExpendData/NationalHealthAccountsHistorical and American Health Care: Health Care Spending and the Federal Budget, May 16, 8018, Committee for a Responsible Federal Budget, 1900 M Street, NW, Suite 859, Washington, DC 10036 www.crfb.org

United States spent approximately 6.2% of GDP on education.[6] So, in a combined snapshot, American society used approximately twenty-five percent of its collective resources on the two areas of health care and education. Now, to be clear, the total numbers cited here are aggregate numbers, and they include both public and private resources combined in a country.

In exploring the allocation and the use of resources for health care and education, there are important questions when trying to understand ethical issues for the use of resources in health care and educational organizations. This chapter argues that the ethical questions about the allocation and use of resources need to be addressed on at least three levels by moral agents, including organizations and nations. The first level is that of individual moral agents. This is the level of the individual student or patient or their families and how they decide to use their resources. Answers by the individual moral agent about how resources should be used depend primarily on the values and choices of the individual patient, student, or family.

A full discussion about decision-making and the use of resources is beyond the scope of this book and investigation, given that resources often involve both public investment as well as private investment. However, it is important to note that neither health care nor education can be understood, adequately, by simply using a model of individual consumer choice. One reason a normal market model is not applicable is that the "product" in either health care or education is not privately developed in the way that many consumer products or services are developed.

Rather, both areas of health care and education are developed and sustained in some way by public investment that is often significant. And one can argue that public investment in education and health care allows the public to claim a voice in how resources are distributed and used.

Another level of decision-making with regard to the use of resources involves the budgeting process of an organization, a process that is commonplace among organizations and part of their everyday existence. This type of decision-making with regard to the allocation of resources is particularly evident in how an organization creates and implements its budget. In a finite world an organization has a certain, limited amount of funding and other resources it can deploy, and the organization must make decisions on how resources should be used. This question asks how an organization uses its resources. Decisions on the use of resources should be based on the organization's identity, mission, and values. In this way the planning process is not simply a budgeting exercise; instead, it should be an exercise regarding the values of an organization. The third level of the question about resources concerns their use by the whole society. This chapter focuses on questions about how an organization allocates and uses it resources—the second pertinent question. However, in exploring this type of question, one opens the door to exploring how the larger society sets priorities for funding areas like health care and education.

[6] https://ourworldindata.org/grapher/us-education-expenditure-as-share-of-gdp-public-and-private-institutions

How organizations address their particular use of limited resources may take different forms, depending upon the organization in question. Most organizations typically allocate their resources through a budgetary process, which should be known within the organization. In many ways a budget ought to be understood as a "planning document",[7] as it articulates how an organization plans to use it resources. There are a number of important factors, which can vary, in how an organization addresses the limits of its resources. One important factor is the expectations of the source of resources. For example, a grant from a foundation or a gift from a benefactor will carry with it expectations on how the resources provided by the grant will be used. The other factor, which should be very important, is the mission and identity of the organization; the use of resources should align with the mission and identity of an organization. One way organizations address these limits is through efforts to find more resources through, for example, fund raising, or increasing revenue by increasing patient or student populations or developing new programs. An organization acknowledges the limits of its resources in its act of creating an annual budget, which is a planning document concerned with how resources will be used.

The questions surrounding the allocation of resources really confront us with similar problems in two different venues. Essentially, the allocation of resources for education and health care confronts the challenge of how to deal with our finitude and the limits of our resources. We do not have unlimited resources, as individuals or as a society, so the question becomes how do we allocate and use the resources we have? The key ethical question is about how to allocate, and use, the resources that a society, or organization, has. Then, in the light of how a society responds to the question of how it uses its resources, organizations, in health care and education, need to articulate how, and why, they will use the resources that they have. At both levels, the broader social level and the level of the organization, the question of allocation and use of resources is often addressed by using the language of justice. However, as has been argued, the use of the term justice needs to be understood within the context of the language in which it is being used.[8]

11.2 Justice and the Language of Procedures

Before we turn, explicitly, to the questions concerning justice and the allocation of resources in a society, it is important to address how the idea of justice can be applied to life *within* an organization first. This is because there are at least two different arenas for the questions of justice and distribution. There are the questions of justice for the wider society, and there are the questions of justice internal to the organization. While the internal issues and questions of resource allocation are

---

[7] I owe this idea of a budget as a planning document to Rev. William Byron, S.J.

[8] Alasdair MacIntyre, *Whose Justice? Which Rationality?* (Notre Dame,: University of Notre Dame Press, 1988).

important for organizations and need to be addressed, there should be a link in an organization between how they are addressed and the culture and operations of the organization. For example, if one conceives of an organization's budget as a planning document, then there ought to be some link between the budget and the planning of an organization and its mission. One ought to be able to read the budget and strategic plan of an organization as complementary documents that tell a story about the organization. If, for example, a health care organization speaks of a mission of service to the poor and underserved but has nothing in its budget for uncompensated care, one can conclude that the organization is deceiving itself in its mission or planning statements. In the same way, if an educational organization speaks of being committed to students with financial need but has no structures or processes for assisting them with financial advising, or if it has nothing in its budget allocated to enable such students to attend the school, the school is deceiving itself and the public.

The allocation of resources by organizations in education and health care provides a clear picture of what the organization values. If we think about the use of resources in education and health care as an important ethical question that needs to be explored, we can then begin the exploration by classifying these questions into two general categories. First there is the question of how an organization allocates and uses the resources it has. The first type of ethical question for educational or health care organizations is concerned with how resources are allocated *within* the organization. To answer this question, one will have to know who has the authority, within the organization, to make decisions about allocation.

The question concerning the allocation of resources by an organization is not only a question about the mission and identity of an organization, but it also raises the question regarding the process by which the organization makes decisions about the allocation of resources. Anchored in mission and identity, the organization should have procedures for the allocation of resources that are reflective of the mission, identity, and culture of the organization. The allocation of resources raises questions about the proper procedures for making decisions pertaining to that allocation, within an organization, and making sure they are followed. The questions of procedures also offer a glimpse into the culture of an organization and how it proceeds. How these questions are answered by an organization will often vary from organization to organization. Organizations are not ideal platonic forms separated from time and space. They are created with a mission and purpose and with a way of proceeding. From the viewpoint of postmodern, secular ethics, it is important that an organization articulate and follow its own procedures for the allocation of resources and follow through with implementation.

Within any organization there should be clear procedures regarding these decisions and the decision-making process, and these processes should be known within the organization. In many cases internal questions about the allocation of resources will depend in large measure on the appropriate processes and the culture, within an organization, for making and carrying out these decisions. The questions about justice and the allocation of resources, within an organization, are questions about both the organization's procedures and the organization's mission, vision, and planning. If one understands a budget as a planning document, it follows that an organization's budget ought to reflect an allocation of resources which mirrors the plans and vision of the organization. At the same time, the method of developing a budget for an organization ought to align with the values, commitments, and culture of an organization. The internal structures of an organization should align with the mission, identity, and culture of the organization, while the procedures for allocating resources should also be grounded in the organization's mission, identity, and culture. We should also note that within the process of allocating resources there ought to be procedures which would allow parts of the organization to appeal budgetary and resource allocation decisions.

However, it is important to remember that organizations in health care and education, no matter how they are structured, are to varying degrees *social* organizations, and their resources, rarely, are simply private resources for disposal by a private organization. Some of an organization's resources may often come from some sort of government or private investment. And often resources, which are supported by government or private donors, have some type of restriction or dedicated use which directs how the organization can deploy them. Often the resources for health care and educational organizations are mixed in that they derive certainly from private sources but also from public investments like tax incentives. No matter the sources of their resources, organizations will face limits on the use of resources that will depend, in part, on the source of the resources and the restrictions that have been put into place by that source of funding.

While health care and education are, in many ways, individual goods, they are also social goods. These organizations offer goods for the individual patient and student, but they also offer benefits for the whole community in that the knowledge basis for health care and education is social and based in the community. It follows that the decisions about allocating resources in society are not only questions addressed within an organization but also social questions that need to be addressed by a society in general.

However, *any and every* choice about the allocation of resources, whether the choice is a decision made within an organization or by a society, should also confront the underlying reality that resources are limited; therefore, choices should reflect what one hopes to achieve by using resources in a particular way. In a world of limited resources every determination about where to assign resources is also a negation in that it is an implicit decision about where resources will not be allocated. In a finite, limited world there are no unlimited resources. And, when we confront issues about resources in health care and education, we should recognize that one of the questions that should be addressed by organizations is the question of how to appropriately allocate limited resources. It is only when people are faced with limits on their resources, whether time, talent, or money, that they can make thoughtful decisions about how to allocate the limited resources they have.

In day-to-day life, many decisions about the allocation of resources are made by individual moral agents, yet most people who make these decisions do not think about such decisions beyond their own personal choices. People have limited time, and they need to allocate it. A person makes decisions about doing A and B but not activity C, because the person does not have enough time to do C, or one makes the choice to do C on another day. Each day people make decisions about where and how to allocate resources of time, talent, or money that are limited. Simply put, in diverse, secular societies the market model, which relies on individual choice, is the basis we most often use for allocating resources.

However, the goods of health care and education raise, at least, one additional layer of reality, which complicates decision-making, because health care and education are not, usually, simply the allocation of individual resources. Resources in health care and education are, in some way, *pooled* resources. Both areas encompass the use of private resources in that patients do pay for some elements of their care, while in education, students and their families pay tuition and offer resources in support of schools. However, in education, as in health care, tuition is rarely the full cost of the student's education. So, from the start the "market-exchange" model is an inadequate model to understand by what manner these services are paid. At the very least, the market model is incomplete, given that both health care and education benefit from support by the societies in which they exist.

Also, while there are a variety of forms that financing can take, these organizations in health care and education are often the beneficiaries of public resources in terms of direct dollars paid for patient care or educational services financed through tax incentives. In this sense these organizations, most often, are problematic; they do not fit neatly into a free market model, because they are supported or developed, to some extent, with public resources. This also raises, as an ethical question, the issue of who has the authority to allocate the resources and how such decisions should be made.

Many decisions about the allocation of resources, in secular, morally pluralistic societies, are made by using a modified market model of consumer choice and relying on individual, consumer decisions. The market model allows individuals to make their own choices about how their resources should be deployed. The market-consumer model works well particularly in a diverse society by allowing moral agents to make their own choices about the allocation of resources. However decision-making for organizations, particularly in education and health care, becomes more complex, because the resources that are used are a combination of resources from both public and private sources.

However, when resources are held in common, as is the case for many resources in health care and education, the questions surrounding resource allocation become more complicated in terms of public policy and ethics. When we turn to organizations of any type, but especially those in education and health care, the ethical justification of the individual consumer market is often not adequate to account for the nuances of a situation.

This chapter has argued that there are at least two distinct, though related, lenses through which to view questions asked and discussed with regard to the allocation of resources. The first lens, which has been discussed, looks to the question of how resources are allocated *within* an organization. This question asks how an organization uses its own resources and the resources that have been allocated to it. An organization's mission and identity should be central components in answering this question. The second lens looks to the question of the allocation of resources in terms of the whole society, while questions of resource use and allocation are often discussed by using the ethical language of *justice*. However, the language of justice is complex and can be specified in a number of different ways, according to the different forms of justice.

However, our primary focus here is on procedural justice in the allocation of resources in society and procedural justice in how an organization utilizes the resources that it has.

When examining organizations in health care and education we need to examine the relationship of the organizations to the wider society in which they exist and operate. One question, for either type of organization, will concern the organization's source of resources. Are they public resources, or private, or a mixture of the two? Any source of resources will, undoubtedly, have some restrictions and expectations attached to the use of the resources. Both of these two types of organizations rarely, if ever, exist on their own in contemporary health care and educational practice. First, they are governed by the rules of the secular societies in which they exist and operate. Second, in many of these societies these organizations are supported by common resources of the society.

However, organizations in health care and education present a somewhat different challenge, as they are not particular, individual agents deciding how to use their own resources. The first challenge involves the recognition that how they are structured and organized varies from nation to nation. One has only to look at the OECD (Organization for Economic Co- operation and Development)[9] comparative data to see how health care sectors are variously organized from one nation to the next. So, one of the first questions, when examining this area, is to see how a particular nation organizes its education and health care sectors.

One way to begin thinking through this part of our exploration is to make a distinction between public and private health care and education. And, while this distinction can be useful, to a degree, the explanatory power of the distinct differences is limited, particularly in countries like the United States, where the lines between public and private are not always as clearly drawn as one might assume. For example, in health care, while both public and private health care organizations exist, individuals are able to make use of either type of organization, and often both, because of the way health insurance protocols are structured. And health care provider organizations are open to patients. In a similar way, in education, there are public and private educational opportunities and systems available to individuals, but again, people often have the opportunity to use either type of system because of programs like vouchers or scholarship programs.

While there are variations among different societies as to how health care and education are structured and financed, both health care and education often have a mixture of public and private resources in many secular societies. Therefore, at least two important areas need to be investigated in examining the questions of organizations and resource allocation. The first type of question has to do with the

[9] http://www.oecd.org/

organization itself and how it uses the resources that it has at its disposal. In many ways, at first glance, this is an important internal question which should be capable of being answered in light of the organization's mission, identity, and planning. So, there can be a question about how resources are allocated within an organization. The evaluation of how resources are allocated within an organization should depend in many ways upon the organization's mission, vision, and strategic plan and the way it is organized, internally.

A second type of question about the allocation of resources goes beyond any particular organization and asks how a society allocates resources to areas like health care and education and their organizations. This second type of question is concerned with the method of *how* a society determines the level of resources that should be devoted to any particular area of social life, like public safety or health care and education.

It is important to note that, in a postmodern, secular society, there is not a "correct" answer to these types of questions. Rather, the second type of question, which often varies from society to society, also changes in the history of a particular society. How a society responds to these types of questions will depend, at any given moment, on how a society views the importance of, and the need for, health care and education compared to other social needs, as well as the broader questions with regard to the pool of resources a society has at any given time. And, how a society responds will be influenced by how the society itself is organized and who has a "voice" in the processes of allocation.

To address issues of allocation, postmodern, secular societies frequently use a market model for the exchange of goods, which works well, ethically, for most goods. However, the goods of education and health care are rarely or strictly private goods, as they are supported by both private and public investment. And, furthermore, these goods are often overseen by society through an array of regulatory structures. The public investment both directly in health care and education and in the underlying infrastructure of both areas means that we need to find additional moral language to examine how they are organized.

11.3 Social Justice

It is with caution that I introduce the term "social justice" to this discussion and analysis. My caution comes from several different concerns. The first concern is that this book has been developed to examine ethical issues in multicultural, secular societies. The reason for the caution is that, like most terms in ethical language, "social justice" has a wide variety of stipulations and understandings. As such, it can easily be misunderstood in morally diverse societies.

Furthermore, when the term is used, it is often used as the assertion of a self-evident principle or as a conclusion, rather than as a premise in an argument. And, when the term is taken out of the context of a particular moral language or understanding and used in a diverse moral culture, the term can contribute more Babel and slogans than analysis and argument.

However, we should first remember that, like any ethical term, "social justice" should be understood within the language game in which it is used. Terms like "killing" and "murder" are distinct in their meanings even if they are used for a similar or same physical reality. The language game within which a term is used sets out the boundaries for its use and application.

So, the term "social justice" needs to be understood within the context of the language game in which it is being used.

In this book I use the term social justice as it was developed traditionally in Catholic moral thought. As pointed out earlier in the book, traditional Roman Catholic ethical thought was framed in the language of natural law as a philosophical language that could be known by natural reason. In that tradition the term social justice is used in light of assumptions about the dignity of the human person. The human person has been the fundamental object of concern in the tradition of Catholic social thought. In this tradition the language of the human person and human dignity is fundamentally tied to the idea of community and a normative human anthropology.

In light of assumptions about human anthropology, the language of justice is inextricably bound to the language of community and the dignity of the person. In this tradition, the idea of justice is fundamentally different from atomistic social accounts of justice or totalitarian accounts, both of which are prevalent in many modern philosophies and understandings of society and the moral claims that can be made. The Catholic tradition of social justice calls for us to balance these two extremes and provides a way to think of an alternative middle road. On the one hand the tradition has a focus on the community, but it also has a focus on the individual person and understands both as interconnected.

Why is the Catholic tradition of social justice so tied to the relationship among the human person, human dignity, and community? The fundamental assumption is that the human person is made in the image of God (*imago dei*). This language is based in the Hebrew and Christian scriptures and was developed by theologians and philosophers in the early Church and through the Middle Ages. One theme that runs through the development of the language is that of the human person as the *imago dei*, which is a Trinitarian understanding of God.[10] As God is fundamentally communal in God's own nature, so too human life, made in the image of God, is communal.

The concept of the *imago dei* links the ideas of the humanities and social justice. This communitarian view of reality, which ties together God and humanity, as well as human beings with one another, leads this tradition to examine the political, social, and economic structures of human life. They are interrelated and, in this tradition, need to be examined together.

---

[10] http://www.vatican.va/archive/hist_councils/ii_vatican_council/documents/vat-ii_cons_19651207_gaudium-et-spes_en.html

A key set of assumptions, often unarticulated in this tradition, presents the ideas that the human person is a reflection of the *imago dei* and that human dignity is a concept which is tied to the idea of the "common good." How so? The language of common good can be a challenge for many contemporary individuals to understand. Most Americans, for example, would understand common good to mean the summative good of the majority of people or the will of the majority. However, this interpretation could also be used to justify forms of authoritarianism, and that interpretation would be an incorrect interpretation of the language of common good in Roman Catholic thought. The notion of common good in Roman Catholic thought refers to those conditions that are necessary for human flourishing. Pope John XXIII defined the common good as "the sum total of conditions of social living, whereby persons are enabled more fully and readily to achieve their own perfection."[11] Now, it is clear that one of the background assumptions of this tradition posits that certain assumptions are made about human anthropology, insofar as one can articulate a common understanding of the conditions needed for human life which transcended particular cultures.

Social justice represents the ethical concern that a society should be organized in such a way that enables its members to have access to these basic conditions. In his encyclical *Pacem et Terris*, John XXIII said that "in our time the common good is chiefly guaranteed when personal rights and duties are maintained."[12] The use of the term social justice is tied, in the Catholic intellectual tradition, to assumptions about human anthropology. From this anthropology one can argue for a basic set of human "needs" or basic goods that are needed by people such as life itself, housing, food, and medical care, along with other basic protections such as freedom from harm or assault. The idea of social justice is a cross, one could argue, between general justice and distributive justice, insofar as one can argue that the object of social justice is concerned with how a society is organized with respect to the common good of all members of the society. So, it is concerned with general organizational justice and the justice of access to the common good.

What does that mean? In the Roman Catholic tradition, the language of common good is focused on those conditions needed by human beings to flourish as human beings. So, in this tradition the language of social justice is concerned with the access of people to the basic conditions for human life. And this tradition assumes a basic, normative anthropology which is foundational for the basic conditions of human life.

One may disagree with the anthropological assumptions of this tradition. However, one can make the argument that the goods of both health care and education are supported, at some basic level of investment, by the investment of public resources. And, from this, one can argue that members of the community should have access to the basic goods created by public investments.

---

[11] *Mater et Magister*, # 65.

[12] John XXIII, 11 April, 1963, *Pacem in Terris*, #60.

The Civil Rights movement in the United States provides an excellent historical example of this sense of social justice in that one of the goals of the movement was to ensure that the same rights were extended to all Americans. One key insight from this tradition is that one can use an ethical lens to *examine how a society is organized*. The Civil Rights movement opened up society for many citizens by taking steps against segregation and discrimination in how society was and is organized. And, not surprisingly, it can be argued that both health care and education fall under the ambit of social organization. In using the lenses of social justice, one asks important questions about how a society, generally, is organized. This question about how society is organized is an important question for social organizations, such as those in health care and education, to ask about themselves. The category of social justice should mean that the organization needs to examine both how it is organized in its internal operations, as well as how it is organized in relation to the wider, secular society.

11.4 Organizations, Social Prejudice, and Organizational Sin

If one can develop the concept of social justice in relation to how an organization or society is organized, so too, it seems, one should address the use of the category of social or organizational evil or wrongdoing. In a postmodern, secular society, which is in principle open to moral pluralism, one might think the element of social evil or wrongdoing is limited, given the potential moral diversity of such societies and the potential diversity of moral views. However, even though there are many different accounts of moral wrongdoing and moral goodness, given the procedural nature of postmodern, secular societies, one should be able to think through the boundaries for social or organizational wrongdoing. There is no doubt that the outlines for organizational and social wrongdoing will be far weaker than many might hope. So, it is helpful to remember that we are examining organizations in a postmodern, secular society which, in principle, is open to moral pluralism. This means, as argued in Chap. 3, that the only common ethical language for a secular society essentially is procedural, which is clearly defined in a society, and relies on the free consent of moral agents.

In a secular, postmodern society, the language of justice can be utilized in several ways, often leading to confusion. However, in examining organizations it is helpful to use the language of justice to examine the way an organization operates internally and the way a society operates in general in relationship to the organizations in health care and education. The issues of internal procedures and justice were examined in the second part of this chapter. The key points on this topic are that an organization have clear procedures for its members, as well as clear procedures for arbitration and appeal.

For a secular society in general, which in principle is open to moral diversity, it would seem that the discrimination against a particular group by any *public*, social structure would be a social sin. Historically one might think of examples that excluded people from participation in a secular society because of race or gender. There are many historical examples in the procedures of voting, employment, or housing for example that were devised to exclude people based on race. In the United States, for example, the *Jim Crow* laws and restrictions, enacted in the late nineteenth and early twentieth centuries, legalized forms of discrimination in a secular society. Those legal restrictions limited opportunities in education, housing, jobs, and voting rights for African American citizens. All of these laws and practices were passed and implemented under the guise of creating the legal structures for a "separate but equal" society.

The main point, for this investigation of organizations, is simply that we need to examine the way a society in general is organized from the ethical perspectives of secular, postmodernism. Organizations can and should have their own identities and ways of proceeding. But, in the moral diversity of a postmodern, secular society, organizations need to be clear about their identities and their procedures for operating and what it means for their use of resources.

The questions of justice, for an organization, involve both how an organization participates in the broader, secular society and how it lives within itself. Both the internal and external lives of organizations will depend on the mission and identity of an organization, as well as the society in which it exists.

What are the implications of the idea of social justice practiced by organizations participating in secular, post-modern societies? There are at least two ways we can use the lens of justice to examine organizations. The one lens looks at the organization itself, its procedures, and how it is structured. However, the starting point for this type of examination should go back to the organization's mission and identity. In a diverse, secular society it is important for an organization to be clear about its own identity and moral commitments. That self-understanding should give rise to internal procedures for how it deals with questions of justice. For example, if an educational organization says that it is committed to the success of underserved students in its statements of mission and identity, it would seem that the organization ought to have internal procedures which are designed to help meet that goal and commitment. Analogously if a health care organization articulates a commitment to the poor and underserved in its mission and identity statements, it too should have in place measures and procedures to meet these commitments.

These are simply examples by which a diverse, secular society can look at the public commitments of an organization to its use of resources. It also gives a lens by which a society can assess, in some way, whether an organization is living justly by its own commitments.

11.5 Organizations and Social Sin

The focus of this book has been on organizations; however, organizations do not exist by themselves. Organizations are part of the broader society in which they exist. And, in this work, we have been examining organizations as part of postmodern, secular societies. Up until this point in the book we have focused on the examination of the internal structures of organizations. However, it is important to recognize the broader social context for organizations, because that context will so be influential in shaping how particular organizations respond to the society in which they exist. Organizations are shaped by the society in which they are formed and in which they live, and societies shape what organizations are and how they respond ethically.

Understanding this reality is particularly important for how we understand and assess organizations in health care and education, given their strong ties to the societies in which they exist. A for-profit business organization can, in principle, pick up and move anywhere, and this reality is often used as a bargaining ploy for business organizations in developing local tax incentives. However, organizations in health care and education are most often more closely tied to their local communities through the needs they may serve and the way they are structured.

Sometimes, for example, organizations in health care and education are tied to their locale through structures of regulation.

We have seen in Chaps. 7 and 8 how ongoing examination and assessment of an organization is often carried out, in the United States at least, through various processes of certification and accreditation. However, we also need to acknowledge that organizations, because they are human constructions, can assume various human shortcomings like social sin and prejudices common in a society. In the context of a postmodern, secular society, robust criteria to articulate social sin and prejudice will not exist. However, we can identify some criteria that can be helpful in examining organizations.

11.6 Conclusions

This chapter has explored the reality of limits as a fundamental element of the ethical questions confronting organizations in health care and education. Human beings and human organizations exist in a finite world, and so decisions need to be made in view of the limits of this world. In most cases there will not be enough resources to do everything for everyone. Individual agents make decisions all the time on how to allocate and use their resources of time, talent, or money.

The issues of allocation and justice will always have at least two dimensions. One involves the decisions made within an organization as to how it should allocate resources. These questions can be answered by the identity of the organization, its mission, and the procedures it has established to develop answers to such questions. The other dimension of allocation is the social dimension, which turns on the question of how a society decides to allocate resources. Societies need to make decisions on how to allocate and use resources, especially in terms of social goods, like education and health care, as well as other social goods like safety and protection, and how they are balanced against one another. The ethical challenge for any secular society is to establish procedures that are public and well known. The assessment of the use of goods should, in some way, be publicly known to investors, whether consumers, donors, or government investors, so that they can understand how the organization has confronted the reality of its limits.

Understanding the ethical challenges of confronting limits is important for any moral agent or organization. And, these issues are tied to the links of the organization to the society around it. We know, from examples like the Jim Crow laws, that societies are not stagnant. They change, grow, and develop. It is therefore important in this investigation to reflect on how social organizations, like those in education and health care, can deal with the changing needs of the society around them.

Summary of the Main Points

1. Finitude: Living with Limits
2. Justice and the Language of Procedures
3. Social Justice
4. Organizations, Social Prejudice, and Organizational Sin
5. Organizations and Social Sin

Part IV
Changing Societies and Changing Organizations

Chapter 12
Organizations and the Changing Needs of Society

Since the Introduction to this investigation, and throughout, it has been argued that there are often three levels to many ethical decisions. The first level has to do with what individual moral agents decide to do. The third level is concerned with what a society decides to do about a particular moral issue and this often entails acting through, law, policy or regulation. The second level of moral decisions has been the focus of this book and that is the level that focuses on what organizations do as moral actors. Organizations exist between individual agents and society as a whole. And organizations are particularly important in the areas of health care and education.

This book has focused on some of the key questions surrounding how to understand organizations as moral actors, particularly organizations in health care and education, in post- modern, secular societies. While the book has focused on organizations, hopefully this investigation will also provide a way to think more carefully about the postmodern condition and how we think and talk about ethics in postmodern, secular societies, as well as provide a way to better understand these societies. Because organizations in health care and education are social organizations with moral commitments, they provide yet another lens through which to view, and think about, addressing ethical questions in postmodern, secular societies. Organizations in education and health care, at minimum, have moral dimensions or elements in their missions, depending on the identity of the organization. No matter the mission and identity of an organization, or the moral values to which an organization is committed, organizations in education and health care are moral actors in diverse, secular societies, which can be, in principle, morally pluralistic. So, as moral actors, these organizations challenge us in how we think

This Chapter grew out of a question asked by Professor Laurence B. McCullough, PhD., Adjunct Professor of Ethics in Obstetrics and Gynecology, Weill Medical College of Cornell University and Distinguished Emeritus Professor, Baylor College of Medicine, at a lecture and presentation given on this book at a symposium titled "Organizing Ethics: Rethinking Ethics in Health Care and Education", St. Edward's University, Austin, TX, November 4, 2019.

K. W. Wildes, S.J., *Organizational Ethics and Moral Integrity in Secular Societies*, Philosophical Studies in Contemporary Culture 29,
https://doi.org/10.1007/978-3-031-39097-5_12

about questions of how to respect the moral identities and values of organizations in a morally diverse secular society. Furthermore, the existence of these organizations, as moral actors, should push us to think further about the questions of moral pluralism in postmodern, secular societies. In addressing organizations in health care and education we can expand the discussion and analysis of postmodern, secular societies beyond an analysis of individual moral agents and the role and limits of governmental authority.

A significant part of the investigation in this book, particularly in the chapters in the second part of the book, have focused on the internal life of organizations in health care and education, with particular attention given to the questions of how these organizations can be structured in light of their missions and identities and how these structures can help the organizations live with integrity in a secular, morally pluralistic society. The book has also explored how organizations can function and live with integrity in secular, postmodern, morally pluralistic societies. The book's exploration has examined how organizations can deal with other moral agents in a society that is morally diverse, and it has examined how organizations can have relationships with other organizations with different moral commitments and yet still live with integrity.

The focus, throughout this book, has been on how we can think about the organization as a moral actor. However, organizations do not exist in isolation. Organizations, particularly those in health care and education, exist in social contexts, and they respond to some of the needs of human beings in a particular society and social context. That is why an examination of either education or health care in one country or region often shows that organizations in education and health care differ, in structure and practice, from similar organizations in other countries or regions. While there are similarities, the likenesses are more like family resemblances.[1] So, as part of the investigation of this book, we need to consider questions about what happens to a social organization, in education and health care, if the society in which the organization operates changes significantly. Changes can and do occur in societies that can alter the context for these organizations in a way that makes the organizations no longer needed for the purposes for which they were founded. A society may change in such a manner that eliminate the reasons for which an organization was originally founded. Or a society may change in a way that creates new needs which should be addressed. The organizational question is what happens to social organizations when society, and the social context for need, changes?

For example, many Catholic schools in the United States were started in the nineteenth century as a response to discrimination against Catholics, at the time, in public education. Over time that discrimination came to an end, and Catholic schools were challenged to rethink their missions and ongoing operations. Once again, it is helpful to state the obvious. Organizations exist in a social environment and to address particular needs in those environments. However, it is important to

[1] Ludwig Wittgenstein, *Philosophical Investigations*, (London: Blackwell, 1953).

recognize that organizations live in changing environments, and these social environments may change in ways that affect the reasons for the mission and identity of an organization.

Throughout this book it has been assumed that there is a dialogical relationship between social organizations, like those in education and health care, and the societies in which they live and work. While the focus of this book has been on the organization, we also need to consider what happens to the organization if and when the society changes. These organizations exist in relationship to the society around them, but societies are rarely stagnant and rather change, develop, or decline. It follows that in an investigation of social organizations, like those in education and health care, we need to ask how to think about organizations if the social environment around them changes in such a way that significantly challenges the mission of an organization to the point where, on honest evaluation, the mission of the organization is no longer needed. We know that societies can and do change, and they sometimes change dramatically. So, as we examine the landscape of organizational ethics, we need to consider how organizations are related to their surrounding societies and how they can address dramatic social change and respond to these changing circumstances with integrity.

Because organizations live within a society, and define themselves, in part, in relationship to particular needs in a society, organizations should be responsive to changes and developments in the society in which they exist. Such responsiveness by organizations to social needs and social changes is particularly important for social organizations in health care and education, which are linked to their social settings. However, as it was emphasized in the second part of this book, organizations need to have both a clear sense of their own identities, histories, and purposes when faced with changing societies, and they need to have structures which monitor their missions and identities and which allocate resources according to identity and purpose. Beyond the internal structures that monitor the identity of an organization there should also be other structures which monitor a dialectical relationship between organizations in health care and education and the societies in which they are situated.

12.1 The Dialectic Between Organizations and Societies: What Do Societies Expect from Organizations in Health Care and Education?

With the various methods to evaluate the work of organizations developed and outlined in the second section of this book, the third section of the book examined some of the ways in which organizations can move outside of themselves and collaborate, with other organizations, in a diverse secular society. Of course, the identity and mission of an organization should establish both the foundation for and the limits of an organization's collaborations with other organizations and groups.

This book has examined the different aspects of the relationships between organizations that can exist, as well as their relationships to the societies in which they exist. One way to examine this relationship is through the experience of working with other organizations. In any collaborative effort either with other organizations or with society, a key challenge, for each organization that is involved, is how each organization can remain faithful to its own fundamental identity and mission when it works with other organizations in health care and education that may have different identities and missions. Such collaboration with other organizations always carries the risk that any organization involved can lose sight of its fundamental mission and identity and even lose its identity over time. So, one challenge for such collaborative endeavors is how an organization can still maintain its own organizational identity and integrity in such collaborative endeavors.

Now, before concluding the investigation into organizations as moral actors, it is important to raise at least one further set of questions for organizations that often goes *unasked* by organizations themselves, associations to which they belong, or by society in general.

Throughout this book, it has been assumed that organizations in health care and education need to be understood within the context of their relationship to the secular, postmodern society in which they are situated. One can say that there is a dialectical relationship between an organization and the society in which the organization is located. We have examined the questions of change and development from *within* the perspective of an organization. However, before concluding this investigation we need to ask another question, which is about the possibility of change in the broader society in which organizations find themselves. This book has assumed a dialogical relationship between organizations, in health care and education, and the societies in which they are located. The analysis of this book has focused on the belief that the foundation and starting point for organizational ethics begin with the mission and identity of an organization. What is often unspoken is the assumption that the missions and identities of organizations are developed and articulated in relationship to the society in which they exist. So, in order to complete this examination of the ethics of organizations we need to ask what happens to an organization if a society evolves and changes in such a way that the mission of the organization is no longer needed.

I should point out that while this type of significant change in a society is unlikely, it is an important to ask, as it is a "limits" question. This book has spent a considerable amount of time and effort examining changes within an organization. What happens if the social environment in which an organization exists changes in such a way that the society no longer needs the organization?

In one sense the societies in which organizations find themselves are dialogical partners with organizations in health care and education. Societies are central to the environment, and the mission, of any social organization, like those in health care and education. And it is also important to acknowledge that societies can change, and organizations can find themselves in a changed or changing environment. And, because organizations in health care and education are social organizations, one needs to examine the question of what happens to any organization if the social circumstances change in such a way that the mission of the organization is no longer necessary in the context of a particular society. How should social organizations, like those in education or health care, respond to changes in a society, considering that social changes can affect the primary purpose and mission of an organization? What happens if changes in a society are such that the original need, for which an organization was founded, no longer exists?

Historically one can see examples of this type of change when one considers the changes which took place in health care, affecting health care organizations, with the passage of legislation that created the *Medicare* and *Medicaid* programs in the United States, which became law in 1965.[2] The creation of the new programs dramatically changed the social environments that many organizations had been designed to serve. Other examples, in the United States, of social changes that affected organizations in health care and education were the passage of the *Affordable Care Act*[3] and the *No Child Left Behind* [4] legislation. These pieces of legislation, which were signed into law in 2010 and 2001, respectively, significantly changed the operational and social contexts for organizations in both education and health care in American society. The changes ushered in by the laws have often touched on the very missions and identities of many health care and educational organizations. As we have explored the ethical nature of social organizations in health care and education, it seems that we need to also ask what happens to organizations, and their missions, when such dramatic social changes occur in a society.

Organizations are historical creations that are created at particular times and situated in particular social environments. They exist in societies, and they are created to serve and address identifiable needs in those societies. Organizations in education and health care exist in a dialogical relationship with the needs of the secular societies around them. While we have been examining how organizations can manage change, we need to ask and consider a broader, and more challenging, question about the social environment in which an organization exists. What happens to an organization if the society in which it exists changes in such a way that there is no longer a need for the particular mission of the organization?

Governmental interventions, on behalf of the broader secular society, are historical reminders that social organizations in education and health care cannot be fully analyzed on an isolated basis, as if they existed in isolation from the rest of society. Most of the time organizations, rightly so, focus on day-to-day existence and improving their services in light of their missions, identities, and long-term strategic planning initiatives. However, when an organization engages in long-term planning, these planning exercises and assessments should include a current environmental assessment of the society in which the organization exists. Such an assessment is

---

[2]The legislation can be found in Stat. 286, Pages 286 – 423, Law Number Public Law 89–97, Date Approved July 30, 1965.

[3]Public Law 111–148 111th Congress, an Act Entitled *The Patient Protection and Affordable Care Act.*

[4]Pub.L. 107–110, 115 Stat. 1425, enacted January 8, 2002. *The Elementary and Secondary Education Act* (aka, The No Child Left Behind Act of 2004).

important for any organization but particularly important for social organizations, like those in education and health care. An important question for a long-term planning initiative is the question of whether the organization is still, or will be, needed in society.

There are at least two possible reasons why organizations do not typically consider dramatic social change. One reason is that most organizations are often focused on changes in their particular environments and do not look beyond local changes to see that sometime changes can signal long-term social changes which may have an impact beyond the organization. Another reason that organizations often do not consider dramatic social change is simply because societies rarely undergo the types of dramatic social changes that would significantly alter, or even end, the purpose and mission of an organization. However, societies do change. This is why it is very important for any organization to perform some type of scan of its surrounding environment, and the society in which the organization lives and works, and ask about the social needs for the work of the organization in the society. In this book we have focused, by-in-large, on the internal life of the organization. However, we should not think of organizations as if they exist in isolation from the societies in which they live and, hopefully, serve. The chapters in the third section of this book have explored different possible ways that an organization can be related to the society in which it lives.

Yet another reason that organizations often fail to understand the potential impact of a changing society is that organizations often do not ask questions about, or reflect upon, the ongoing need for their mission. They simply assume the mission is important and relevant. One reason for this lack of reflection is that the leadership of organizations, in particular boards of trustees or directors, serve for limited periods of time and often tend to focus on the immediate and near-term issues facing an organization. An organization's executive leadership often tends to stay focused on near-term issues as well.

Another reason that organizations, in health care and education, can fail to grasp the impact of a changing society around them is that, oftentimes, those in leadership positions are blinded, in part, by the good work the organization has done and is doing. If assumptions like that shape one's mindset, it will be challenging to imagine the work of the organization coming to an end or the social context changing sufficiently to obviate the need for the work of the organization. And yet our current age is filled with examples of how social changes, outside of organizations, affect the missions of organizations. New technologies and financial developments have changed, and continue to change, the ways in which people are educated or receive medical and health care. For a number of good reasons—financial, medical, and ethical—the structures by which health care is delivered have changed, and now, everything that can possibly be done to avoid hospitalizing patients has become a goal.

It requires a certain discipline, imagination, and culture within an organization for the organization to engage in honest and ongoing environmental scans and assessments of what it offers. And it requires further honesty and freedom to ask if the organization is still needed. Has the social environment changed, or is it changing in such a way that the needs which shaped the organization are no longer present or no longer present in the same way? Certainly, the ongoing evolutions in technology in both education and health care should cause an organization to ask fundamental questions about its mission and model for doing business.

Throughout this book, we have been examining some of the questions of how organizations can maintain and monitor their identities, and fulfill their missions, in the midst of changes in society. Organizations need to respond to these broader social changes, given that they do not exist apart from society but *within* society to serve the particular needs of a society. It is important to remember that both health care and educational organizations are not modeled on some abstract, timeless platonic form or ideal which exists outside of space, time, and history.

Rather both types of organizations are social organizations,[5] and societies and circumstances often change. Organizations in education and health care not only exist in the midst of a society, but they also exist to serve the needs of society. There is, to a certain extent, a dialogical relationship between social organizations in education and health care and the larger secular society in which they find themselves. In addition, we know that contemporary, postmodern societies are not static. They are open to change. Therefore, an organization needs to think about, and explore, questions about what happens to organizations when societies, in which they are situated historically, change and how external social changes can affect the missions and purposes for which organizations were created also change. That line of questioning and exploration raises the possibility that, given social changes, the needs for which an organization was created may no longer exist. Organizations, frequently, are not comfortable asking these types of environmental questions.

An organization's mission and identity, as has been argued throughout this book, ought to be fundamental to an organization's way of proceeding and a guide to the organization's ethical behavior, as well as to its relationship with the society around it. The mission and identity should identify the population the organization aspires to serve and how it serves the needs of that population in the context of the broader society which surrounds it. So, it may be uncomfortable for an organization, or the people in the organization, to ask if an organization still serves the needs of a society or if those needs still exist. Is the mission of the organization still needed in the society? These are questions that still need to be asked. They are questions that can help to guide the process for an organization concerning its evolving mission and identity in a changing world. Moreover, asking these types of questions can help an organization better serve a society and live out its mission. In addition, asking these questions, when asked thoroughly and honestly, may lead to the conclusion that, given changed social circumstances, an organization's mission may be at an end.

This type of reflection, questioning, and exploration suggests that an organization should engage in an ongoing reflection about its mission, purpose, and the needs of the society in which it finds itself. These are necessary questions for which

[5] See, K. Wildes, "The Crisis of Medicine: Philosophy and the Social Construction of Medicine", *Kennedy Institute of Ethics Journal* 11 (2001): 75–91. Also in, "Bioethics as Social Philosophy", *Social Philosophy & Policy* 19 (2002):113–125. Reprinted in *Bioethics*, eds. E. F. Paul, F.D. Miller, Jr., J. Paul, (Cambridge: Cambridge University Press, 2002), 113–125.

there is no singular answer, or set of answers. Rather, in an organization's response to its environment, it is important for the organization to develop a method and set of questions for thinking about the changing circumstances in which the organization finds itself. Organizations need to engage, with some regularity, in what many people refer to as an "environmental scan." We also need to identify different methods for developing answers to these types of questions, even if those answers lead to the conclusion that the mission of the organization is no longer needed. In this way, an organization may be able to make judgments about its future.

12.2 Social Sins and Social Organizations

Most of the time when we use moral language we do so to address the particular actions of individuals. However, in the last century those who study and reflect on questions of ethics have come to talk moral about "social sin" and social wrong doing. When we use the social lens to frame an ethical problem the way we view a problem changes. When we use a social lens to view something that is wrong in a society it changes our understanding of an ethical problem and it changes the diagnosis for solutions to the problem. The phrase "social sin" can be used to refer to a structure which oppresses a human being and "social justice" can be understood as steps which are taken to address a social sin.

To understand the category of social sin or social justice one might look at the historical example of the work that was done in the United States to address issues of Civil Rights. Many everyday issues faced by the African American community were systemically related to ways the particular community had been addressed by society. Housing, education, voting rights, are all examples where a society could impede progress for generations of a whole group of people. In the Civil Rights legislation the United States took steps which changed the ways organizations could operate in a society.

There were a variety of issues, related to the race of citizens, which were embedded in law and public policy. The behavior of African Americans was regulated, in many States, through laws. The right to vote was restricted, along with the right to participate in the open housing market, for examples. Issues such as voting rights, fair housing, employment and education all fell under the umbrella of the Civil Right Act[6] and these legislative interventions were concerned with how a society was organized. In addressing particular issues in social organization these efforts also addressed how organizations, within a society, could function.

For the work of this investigation, which looks at organizations as moral agents in a society, it is important to identify the relationship between questions in how a society is organized and issues in how an organization is put together and functions in a society. As it was argued in the First Part of this book organizations exist in a

[6] Pub. L. 88–352.

social space between individual agents and society as a whole. As such, organizations may well reflect the social sins and failings of a society but, at the same time, they will be important when and if a society decided to take steps to address particular moral wrongs that are systemically practiced in a society. As this investigation of organizations draws to a close it is important to realize that many ethical questions faced by organizations can only be fully addressed if the issues are addressed by the society as a whole.

12.3 The Evolution of Organizations: The Innovation Imperative

Again, returning to what has been argued earlier, particular organizations are defined both by their missions *and* by the societies within which they exist. The mission of the organization is developed in response to needs within a society. There is a dialectical relationship between the mission of the organization and its social setting and social needs. This is the case for *any* organization, not only those in health care or education. It is also the case for for-profit organizations, as well as for nonprofit organizations. Organizations in any area are often created to serve particular needs that are perceived within a given society at a given time in history.

These needs, along with the purpose of the organization, are usually identified in the mission and vision statements of an organization. Therefore, and again returning to the obvious, organizations have a relationship to the societies in which they are situated, and they serve particular needs within a society and particular social settings.

However, societies, like organizations, are not static. Societies can, and often do, change and develop, and, in some cases, they may even go out of existence. Therefore, in carrying out a thorough analysis of the ethics of an organization in health care or education, we need to explore not only how the organization can adapt but even ask the question of whether or not it *should* adapt, if the needs of a particular society in which it serves, and for which it was created, radically change or even if those needs cease to exist. For example, in education in the United States today, there are new and emerging forms of "credentialing"[7] for individuals in particular occupational fields and specialties. The importance of credentialing, no matter how it is done, depends on the professional associations and the wider society to determine what "counts" as an appropriate credential. One advantage of credentialing is that it provides an independent assessment, for the broader, secular society, of

[7] National Center for Complimentary and Integrative Health, NIH: Credentialing, Licensing, Education, https://www.nccih.nih.gov/health/credentialing-licensing-and-education#:~:text=%20Credentialing%2C%20Licensing%2C%20and%20Education%20%201%20The,Complementary%20Health%20Practitioner.%20Understand%20your%20state...%20Mor e%20

the organization's claims of what it says it can do. In a sense, credentialing fulfills a "truth in advertising" standard, which is important in diverse, secular societies.

Credentialing and certification of organizations by society also raise questions about how existing organizations should adapt to new and changing social realities and standards. That is, organizations are created at particular points in time with particular missions, which anchor their identities (e.g. a Catholic hospital or university). However, the mission and identity of an organization should be interrelated. The mission of an organization is tied to the identity of the organization, but the specification of the mission is also tied to the needs of the particular society in which an organization lives. Most often organizations, like those in health care and education, are involved in evaluative processes to assess how they are doing in light of their specific missions. Nevertheless, we often fail to ask a more foundational question: whether a particular mission is still needed by a particular society. Societies change and evolve, and social needs, which may have been identified at one time, may no longer exist later.

One might think, for example of the many hospitals that were created originally as "charity hospitals" to serve the uninsured in the United States. As mentioned earlier in this book, changes in the broader society, such as implementation of *The Affordable Care Act* and the expansion of Medicaid, can mean that such organizations, as they have existed, may no longer be necessary. Or, another question asks how they should adapt to remain relevant under different circumstances. We might also consider, in education, what happens when there is an expansion of opportunities through the development of local community colleges or other publicly funded avenues of education, opening doors and offering new opportunities for students.

In thinking about organizational identity and mission, one always needs to consider the dialectical relationship that exists between organizations and society, particularly in health care and education, which serves social needs in some way. Because societies are not static, how organizations can adapt to the changing circumstances of the societies they serve, and the changing needs of populations within those societies, becomes a question of relevancy and importance.

Organizations in health care and education are particularly vulnerable to external social changes from at least two directions, and they need to respond to the changes in society around them. One change is from the broader direction of society and involves what a society would expect from social organizations in health care and education. Shifting social challenges can happen in many ways, but organizations need to be attentive to changes in social needs and expectations, as well as to the evolution of the regulation of health care and educational organizations as a form of social expression. One example of this challenge facing American education today, for example, is the socially perceived relationship of education to employment. While people will often say that education is important for employment, they often have different models of "education" in mind. So, again, it is important for an educational organization to be clear about the model of education if offers and to which it is committed.

If organizations in health care and education are shaped, in part, by the societies in which they live, it is important for an individual organization to look beyond itself and ask questions about the society and its needs. This type of environmental awareness by an organization helps to shape the way it specifies its mission in a contemporary vision statement. Based on the reality that societies do change, an organization may find that the original purpose and mission of the organization has now been met in other ways and is no longer needed.

As part of an environmental awareness, it will also be important for any organization in education or health care to engage in an ongoing process of assessing the "needs" for the mission and services of the organization within a particular society. Broader social changes may have significantly changed or eliminated the need for which the organization was founded. Or other demographic changes may have taken place and significantly altered the needs that shaped the mission and identity of the organization.

In the history of a particular organization, one may find that the needs for which the organization was created to serve no longer exist because of changes in the broader society. For example, the evolution of a community college system or other forms of public education may answer a social need that had been identified and served by a number of independent colleges or universities through their missions. So, a social organization needs to ask itself what happens when the surrounding environment changes in such a way that the need, which sparked the mission of an organization, is no longer present in a society. Changing social and environmental circumstances should cause an organization to reflect on basic questions about its mission and identity and how it should adapt to changing circumstances. Or, an organization may raise the question of whether it does indeed need to adapt. However, the circumstances may be such that the trustees of an organization may conclude that the society has changed in such ways that the mission of the organization is no longer needed.

12.4 Changing Societies and Changing Needs: Alternative Credentials and the Conclusion of a Mission

This book has stressed the importance of the missions and identities of organizations, particularly for organizations in education and health care in contemporary, postmodern secular societies. In the book, we have assumed a dialectical relationship between an organization in health care and education and the society in which exists. Mission lies at the heart of organizational identity, while identity is crucial for organizations in morally and culturally diverse secular societies. In addition, as has been investigated, it is crucial for organizations in health care and education to continually evaluate, and be evaluated, in terms of how well the organization is living out its identity and mission. The book has also argued that it is important for an organization to evaluate its mission, and how it is expressed, in light of contemporary, changing needs and circumstances.

However, this type of reflection, for an organization, may also lead to challenging questions and disturbing conclusions. One fundamental question is whether the mission of an organization should be concluded. The "mission" of an organization should be at the heart of the life of an organization. And, as it has been argued in this book, an organization needs to revisit its mission periodically and, perhaps, restate it. An organization may find, for example, that the population(s) for which the organization was created to serve either no longer exists or no longer needs to be served in the same way. One can imagine, for example, a higher education organization that was established to serve first generation students in a society. But, because of social changes in the surrounding society, that population may now be well served. So, an organization will need to examine the context of its work, in light of its mission, and it may need to rethink its mission and purpose, in light of its contemporary circumstances. It may be that the initial purpose of the organization is no longer needed, because the need is being met in some other way. For example, public investment in community colleges nationwide may affect the traditional need for some organizations in higher education. On the other hand, the evolution of online education may also affect the need for some organizations in higher education or, at the very least, the way they deliver their services. The development of clinics and urgent care centers may dramatically affect traditional need for other types of health care organizations.

These questions and reflections are not offered as an "answer" but as a set of questions for any organization, particularly those in higher education and health care, in secular, postmodern societies. As has been argued, in a postmodern, secular society these organizations need to be clear about their own identities and missions. In addition, as part of their organizational cultures, organizations need to reflect, in an ongoing way, about how well they are living out mission and identity. Such reflection means that organizations will need to be aware of how the societies in which they are situated are changing and developing. Such an awareness will be founded on analysis of a thorough, up-to-date environmental scan of the society in which the organization is located. That implies, as well, that organizations will need to think through how their particular organizations are responding to changes in the societies around them. Such reflection will serve as the basis for evaluation and change.

However, there is one possibility, in principle, that is embedded in these questions and should not be omitted from this exploration. It is possible, in light of changes in the social context in which an organization exists, that the mission of the organization is understood as completed or that the mission is no longer needed in a society because of changes in that society. For example, a health care organization, which was created to take care of patients with certain needs, or patients who fit into certain categories, may no longer be needed in a society because of changes in the society that allowed these needs to be met in other ways. For example, changes to a nation's health care policy, like the development of Medicare and Medicaid and implementation of the Affordable Care Act's provisions, can significantly change the needs in a society for certain types of organizations. Alternatively, significant changes in a society's education law or funding for educational or health care organizations could affect the need for these organizations in a society.

All of these observations lead to two separate, but important, sets of questions that need to be asked by an organization, as it evaluates its work as a whole. The one set of questions has to do with the internal life of an organization and how well it is living out its identity and mission. The other set of questions asks whether the mission is needed, any longer, by the society the organization has served.

These types of questions, particularly the second type on social need, are difficult for any organization to ask, because the answers may be difficult for an organization to assimilate.

Organizations, particularly in education and health care, are often conceived with a noble purpose. In addition, organizations are focused oftentimes on how they can fulfill their missions or how to do better. However, it may be missed that, given changes in society, the mission may no longer be necessary. A society may have changed its policies or laws to address the needs for which an organization was started, and the need may no longer be present. Alternatively, the organization did such an excellent job meeting the needs for which it was created that it inspired changes in the society which, in turn, led to other developments that occurred to meet those needs. These types of changes or developments may be unlikely, but they cannot be ruled out. In addition, if an organization, in health care or education, is honest with itself, it will assess not only its work but also the social context in which it is working.

12.5 Conclusions

There are several important reasons, in the structures of organizations, as to why it is difficult for an organization to execute a serious assessment of its purpose and mission. One reason these very fundamental questions are often neglected by an organization can be attributed to the involvement of the organization's employees in the details of their day-to-day jobs and positions. Very few individuals, except the chief executive, are required to ask about, or take responsibility for, the entire organization. So, very few people have the need to ask about the organization as a whole. One might respond that it is the job of the trustees of the organization to think about the whole entity—its present, past, and future. Organizations in health care and education are held in trust for the public good, and the trustees are the stewards of these organizations. However, by their nature boards are limited. Members serve for limited terms, which is good for the organization. Essentially, we recognize that at organizations, individuals, at all levels, find themselves immersed in the questions of immediate needs and operations, failing to ask questions regarding long-term concerns: the purpose of the organization and the needs of society.

Summary of the Main Points

1. What Do Societies Expect from Health Care and Education?
2. Social Sins and Organizations
   (a) Institutional racism
   (b) Social determinants and barriers to health & education
3. The Evolution of Organizations: The Innovation Imperative
4. Changing Societies and Changing Needs: Alternative Credentials
5. The Conclusion of an Organization's Mission

Chapter 13
Trust in Organizations and Trust in Society

This book has focused on how secular, morally diverse societies can think about organizations in health care and education as moral agents. Organizations act, through their policies and procedures to affect directly individual patients and students, as well as their families, and society. Social organizations in education and health care respond not only to the needs of particular students and patients but also to the needs of the society in which they live and through their actions organizations affect the society around them. The focus of the investigation of this book has been to examine how we can think about organizations in health care and education as moral actors in the context of postmodern, secular societies. These societies are secular, and so, in principle, these societies are open to moral pluralism and to the challenges of thinking about organizations. To understand more fully the challenges of moral pluralism in secular societies we should not limit our thinking only to government, governmental agencies, or individual agents.

We need to expand our analysis to think about organizations as moral actors. Doing this will help us to understand with greater depth the ethical complexities of postmodern, secular societies.

Therefore, in addition to examining organizations in education and health care, the investigation also provides a heuristic device to think about and understand moral discourse in postmodern, secular societies.

The process of examining organizations in health care and education raises important questions about how, ethically, postmodern, secular societies can function. We often examine secular, postmodern societies in terms of diverse ethical questions and how secular societies can, regulate morally such questions. However, the challenges of moral pluralism go beyond the questions involving individual agents, governments, and moral diversity in secular societies.

Organizations are moral actors. However, organizations in education and health care create a different category of ethical issues for several reasons. First, the work of health care and educational organizations is interwoven with ethical assumptions. So, the services these organizations deliver and how these organizations deliver

K. W. Wildes, S.J., *Organizational Ethics and Moral Integrity in Secular Societies*, Philosophical Studies in Contemporary Culture 29,
https://doi.org/10.1007/978-3-031-39097-5_13

their services are freighted with ethical values. Second, in addition to their own moral commitments, these organizations deal with people who are, in some way, in vulnerable states. Because of illness, ignorance, or the way these services are paid for, people using the services of these social organizations are not, in a strict sense, informed consumers. In addition, organizations in health care and education often use public or shared resources, as well as private resources. This means that the model of a private, consumer exchange is not easily applied. Furthermore, because of the duality of public investment and the need to protect vulnerable citizens, organizations in health care and education are regulated within different societies. The questions about the use of common resources, as well as questions about offering goods that are understood as public, lay the ethical groundwork for public oversight and regulation of these organizations.

This book has focused on organizations in health care and education for several reasons. Most important among them, there is always a moral dimension, even if minimal, in the nature of the work done by organizations in education and health care. Further, these organizations are often dealing with people who are in need or disadvantaged in some way. The model of the informed consumer, giving free and informed consent, is often ethically inadequate to capture many of the exchanges for people seeking assistance from health care and educational organizations. In addition to the fact that people who seek services from these organizations may not be fully informed consumers, people often seek the services of these organizations because *they themselves, or someone they love,* are in need. The exchanges between people and organizations in health care and education are, often, not like ordinary commercial exchanges in the market for goods or services that people can freely decide to purchase.

The moral character of these organizations, whatever they may be, makes them an important heuristic to understand better ethical discourse in postmodern, secular societies. Such societies, given their secular nature, are, in principle, open to moral diversity. That diversity presents not only challenges and limits for the moral authority of government and law in regulating behavior and allocating resources, but the reality of moral diversity presents challenges for how we can understand and morally regulate organizations in health care and education. Therefore, first, it is important to understand that organizations in education and health care, which can be moral agents. This book examined, in Part Two, how an organization can be structured, internally, so as to maintain its identity and moral commitments, no matter what they might be, and still function in a secular, morally pluralistic society. Beyond the internal life of an organization, the book has examined how organizations, with moral identities, can work with other organizations in a morally diverse society, in general, and maintain identity and moral commitments.

The book has also examined ways in which a diverse, secular society can verify the identity of an organization, as a moral actor, on behalf of other members of society, whether individual moral agents, other organizations, or government agencies. Understanding the identity of *any* organization can be challenging. However, the challenges of organizational identity can become more difficult when one needs to consider an organization's moral commitments and how it can, and cannot, work with other organizations or society in general. In a secular society, the primary measure for any organization in relationship to the rest of society is some form of the standard of "truth in advertising." In assessing the ethical identity of an organization, we need to ask if the organization is what it says it is. Can the moral identity of an organization be verified? We also need to consider and evaluate whether an organization delivers the services it promises, in education and health care, to people. This type of evaluation is important for building trust in the organization and for building reputation. Oftentimes trust in an organization depends upon one's personal experience of the organization or the trust that others may have placed in the organization, which is communicated through the reputation of the organization.

There are several ways that people, in diverse, secular societies, can make decisions to trust organizations in health care and education. One way, which can be easily overlooked, is simply through the experience of "word of mouth". This is often a key way that people find their way to certain educational organizations. They learn about an organization from others, and they learn about the experiences of others with an educational or health care organization.

Aside from personal experience, reputation, and "word of mouth" verification, there are other ways to measure and judge whether an organization is what it says it is. There are various ways in which organizations in health care and education can be certified by agencies outside of the organization. In education, the processes of accreditation, on the state, federal, and specialized levels, are a way to know that an educational organization can be trusted and that it is what it says it is. In health care, there are numerous accrediting, licensure, and certifying processes that have been brought into play for organizations; these processes verify the abilities of organizations and give them license to assist patients. Analogously, there are numerous licensing processes for the professionals who work for these organizations.

The processes for certification, accreditation, and licensure are essentially ways to assure people of truth in advertising in the specialized areas of health care and education. Processes like these are important for verifying an organization's mission and identity, and they can be important for building public confidence that the organization is faithful to its mission and identity and capable of fulfilling its mission. Indeed, the appendices to this book provide specific examples of how organizations can be measured and certified essentially for identity and mission. These processes can also serve as an important step in building trust in the mission of an organization.

13.1 The Changing Needs of Society and the Evolution of an Organization's Mission

As has been noted throughout this book, our moral language in the Anglo-American world has been developed and is most often utilized to address the particular acts of individual persons or the particular acts and policies of businesses or governments. This book has attempted to explore and examine, in a systematic way, some of the moral terrain that exists between individual agents and society as a whole where organizations are the moral agents. The traditional area of business ethics explores the terrain of organizations in business. However, this book has focused on organizations that are traditionally understood as "not-for-profit" organizations in health care and education. The book has sought to understand how these organizations can be evaluated, as moral actors, in postmodern, secular societies. After examining the postmodern condition and the challenges it presents for discourse and arguments in ethics, the analysis of this book has focused on the identities and missions of organizations in health care and education. These two areas have been of particular interest, because they each have a moral dimension in the work they do. While organizations in health care and education can differ significantly, they work within assumptions, though perhaps differing, about what is the human good. Throughout this book, it has been argued that the mission and identity of an organization should be foundational for understanding and assessing the ethical behavior of the organization in a postmodern, secular society.

The second section of the book examined the idea of organizational identity and the questions of how the identity of an organization can be related to and woven into the fabric and life of the organization through various structures. The second section also reviewed different ways that the missions and identities of organizations can be validated, particularly for moral agents who are outside of the organizations. Different forms of external evaluation of organizations, such as accreditation, certification, and regulation, allow organizations to functional ethically in a morally diverse society under a "truth in advertising" standard, which is of vital importance for moral exchanges in secular, postmodern societies. Organizations, particularly in education and health care, are not isolated monads. Organizations do not exist by themselves in isolation. Social organizations, such as those in education and health care, exist in the midst of society. They exist to serve the needs in the societies in which they exist, and it is not insignificant that these societies often regulate the activities of organizations, particularly in education and health care. However, we know that societies are not static. They change. So, we need to think about the questions of what happens to, and for, organizations when societies change, and the needs, for which the organizations were created, change or no longer exist.

Following what has been argued throughout this book, one can assume that there is no single answer to all of these questions. But these questions do raise a number of important considerations that should be contemplated by any organization to help guide its planning. When we consider organizations and the changing nature of the societies in which they serve, it is helpful to think about a method for asking these questions and to think through how to bring awareness, created from the answers to these questions, into the planning processes of an organization.

13.2 Evolution and Innovation of Social Organizations in Changing Societies

As said previously in this book, sometimes it is good to state what is "obvious" and ask questions about the obvious. It is important to remember that a great deal of human life, particularly in the life of societies, is involved with change and development. So, it is not surprising that the fields of health care and education are changing and developing in a variety of ways—especially with respect to new knowledge and new technologies. In both education and health care, there continues to be a growth in the knowledge base. Moreover, with the evolution of knowledge, there continues to be an evolution in the uses of technologies to support education and health care, as explored earlier in Chap. 3.

Moreover, the evolutionary nature of health care and educational organizations is an underlying theme in many discussions about health care and education. The theme of change plays out in at least two different arenas in education and health care. One is the area of technology and delivery of information and services. With the ongoing development of new technologies and new knowledge, change will often be a constant factor for health care and educational organizations. That theme should not be surprising, given that both types of organizations exist in and are essential parts of the secular societies in which they live and function. Furthermore, the fields of health care and education keep evolving not only with new knowledge and technologies but with the evolution of knowledge and technologies. With the evolution of new knowledge and technologies there will be changing standards for the vision of what it is to be educated, and there will be evolving standards for how we envision health. The evolutionary nature of these fields means that an organization in health care or education will need to adjust, adapt, and develop according to changes as they occur.

It is important to think about how we understand the evolving roles of technology in both education and health care. It can be argued that technology is neither good nor bad in itself but needs to be evaluated in the broader context of how technologies are used. Both health care and education are areas experiencing ongoing technological development in the contemporary world. With that in mind, we need to be thoughtful in how technological developments and innovations are approached. Given the earlier arguments in this book the touchstone of any evaluation should be the mission and identity of an organization; it seems clear that the mission of an organization should guide the organization's approach to innovation and technological developments.

There is often a cultural bias, particularly in the United States, that assumes the "new" is in fact better. However, by itself, that is not always an appropriate value assumption. The new is just that: new and not, necessarily, good or bad in itself. Rather, one can argue that most technological innovations are neither good nor bad in themselves. Rather, like any innovation, technological innovations need be evaluated within the context of their use, as well as the ancillary effects on other areas of life. For an organization, this would mean evaluating any technological innovation from the perspective of the mission and identity of the organization.

Mission and identity ought to be the Archimedean point by which we evaluate any innovation in health care and education. Mission and identity define what an organization is, what it does, why it does it, and, to some extent, how it does it. So, it makes sense that an organization should evaluate its use of new and developing technologies through the lens of the organization's mission and identity.

This ongoing evaluation of technology and change poses at least two fundamental questions for any organization. First, an organization needs to reflect on the question of how to evaluate and implement, or, perhaps, forgo, new knowledge and technology. An organization needs to be aware of a bias, certainly present in the contemporary, postmodern age, where it is assumed that the "new" is better. Often, in marketing a new version of an existing product the emphasis will center on the "newness" of the version with little attention to how it is better than the older, existing product. However, it is not necessarily the case that the "new" is better, and innovations need to be evaluated in light of an organization's mission and identity. Second, an organization, and society, should ask the question, as the wider society changes and evolves, of whether there is still a need for a particular organization, its mission, and what it offers. Social organizations like those in education and health care exist in dialectical relationship with the societies in which they exist. One can see, for example, in the recent history of health care in the United States, the changed and changing role of hospitals in the delivery of medical care. The roles of these organizations have and are changing because of the evolution of technology and how it has changed health care. In analogous ways the evolution of technology is affecting learning and the shape and missions of universities.

As has been argued throughout this book, organizations are living organisms, and they should, on an ongoing basis, evaluate themselves and their performances in light of their missions and identities in relationship to the societies they are serving and how well they are fulfilling their missions. Such evaluative processes can take different forms depending on the culture and history of an organization. However, the processes of accreditation and certification can be helpful for an organization in developing a self-critical, evaluative culture and the structures to support it; those processes can also be helpful to organizations in terms of their being viewed through the lens of society. Organizations should be evaluated by the society they serve in terms of how well they are performing their missions, living out identity, and serving society.

It is possible that these evaluative processes, both internal and external, reach the conclusion that the basic mission of an organization has been fulfilled or that the society it serves has changed so that the mission of the organization is no longer needed in a society because of changes in that society. For example, given certain changes in social policy, the need for an organization may no longer be present in a society. In the United States, for example, many private educational organizations emerged to meet the shortcomings of public education.

However, one might argue that social and educational changes in public education, over time, had eliminated the original needs for private education. Alternatively, changes in a particular field may mean that a particular type of organization is no longer required. For example, schools created to educate low income, economically poor students may no longer be needed if there is a certain development in public education. On the other hand, the health needs of a population may be better served by the development of neighborhood clinics that better serve certain populations than a hospital. In such a situation, an organization might go through a process of self- examination that leads to a new articulation of mission and vision that is faithful to the history of the organization and responsive to the needs of contemporary society. Alternatively, the trustees and leadership of an organization reach the conclusion that it is time to write the concluding chapter of the life of the organization.

In our social imagination, we rarely think of for-profit organizations ceasing to exist or going out of business. Yet, it does happen. In the United States a number of prominent, well- known for-profit corporations have either ceased to exist or been acquired by other companies and no longer exist. Companies like Compaq Computers, Eastern Airlines, Enron, Standard Oil, and General Foods have all ceased to exist or been acquired and transformed by other companies. These historical examples remind us that organizations are not eternal forms detached from history. They can come to an end. So, it makes sense that we should explore similar questions pertaining to the end of non-profit organizations in health care and education.

It is important to remember that both health care and education are developmental and not static. Both areas continue to grow and change. Such growth and change are driven by the reality that we continue to learn more and acquire more knowledge. Again, stating the obvious is important. For most of human history, we understood knowledge as something that was static and fixed. It was only in the late Modern Age that the Western world began to think of knowledge as something which can be grown and increased. Moreover, coupled with this view of increasing our knowledge and understanding, there was the evolution of technology to help further the expansion and use of knowledge. This fundamental social change in how we understand and use the expanding base of knowledge changes the way organizations in health care and education can evolve or, in fact, continue to exist.

13.3 Organizational Identity and the Changing Needs of a Society

There are many different factors that can lead, and sometimes force, an organization to change. The factors include problems and challenges within the organization, which affect its external reputation. The clergy sexual abuse scandal in the American Catholic Church is an example of a number of internal issues, within the organization, that led to changes in the way the organization operates. Alternatively, there can be social factors, such as a declining population of students considering higher education, or changes in federal or state law or insurance plans in health care that give many patients access to health care organizations. No matter the causes of the challenges, organizations have to respond to the changing environment in which they find themselves. The changes in surrounding circumstances will often mean that organizations cannot simply continue doing the same thing and operating in the same way. Furthermore, a failure to respond could pave the way for the end of the organization. Again, it is important to remember that organizations in health care and education are social organizations responding to a particular society and culture.

However, the fundamental question for any organization, but particularly those in education and health care, is how to respond to social changes that affect the organization's mission and purpose. It can be argued, based on the earlier work in this book in Part that the starting point for guiding change in an organization is the mission and identity of the organization. Through the various processes of evaluation, accreditation, and certification, those outside an organization are able to evaluate whether the organization is being faithful to its mission and living out its mission. The challenge, when facing a changed and changing environment, is for the organization to ask what steps the organization can take to address the circumstances of a changing environment. Then, the organization needs to evaluate proposed steps and plans in light of the mission and identity of the organization.

Let us consider some extreme examples. Suppose, for a moment, we are the trustees of a liberal arts college. However, there were significant changes in the society around us, and we are now facing severe enrollment shortfalls. One suggested way that we might attract and enroll more students would be to change the focus of our course offerings and become more like a traditional vocational school. The trustees might review such a proposal, evaluate the proposal, and decide not to follow the proposal, because to do so would forsake the mission of the school and, in fact, essentially lead to the creation of a new organization. Alternatively, one could think of a health care organization, which found that different insurance carriers were not reimbursing it for the ways it had traditionally practiced medicine. The organization could choose to adapt to the new demands of the insurance organizations or decide to look for ways to modify what had been done traditionally.

Other changing circumstances may also affect social organizations, like those in education and health care. An educational organization, for example, may have been founded to serve a particular population that was not being served at the time of the foundation. However, ensuing changes in society as well as legal developments led to the needs of that particular population being well served today. Alternatively, the organizations that finance health care, such as insurance companies or government agencies, might decide to no longer cover certain types of treatment or care. Environmental changes like these have a direct impact on an organization's mission and vision.

In all of this, one can argue that social organizations, like those in education and health care, need to find ways to adjust and adapt themselves, and their offerings, to the social demands they face. In making any such adjustment, the organization should keep its mission and identity at the forefront of its decisions about what it is and what it does. If an organization does this, the organization will set the range of responses that are possible for it. On the one hand, the organization may well decide to adapt to the changing circumstances in which it finds itself.

Alternatively, it may be that the organization is able to comply with the demands it faces but in a modified way. Finally, there may be times when an organization cannot respond to the demands and still be faithful to its identity and history, and its trustees face the decision of whether to end the organization.

These types of questions identify issues for organizations. However, they do still more.

They identify questions that can be raised about the larger social environment of a society in which health care and educational organizations exist. Social organizations, like those in health care and education, adapt to the societies in which they live. Moreover, these questions about organizations may lead to further explorations of how postmodern, secular societies should organize themselves for the delivery of social goods, like education and health care. But that is another, and further, exploration.

13.4 Mission and Identity: The Keys to Organizational Integrity

Throughout this book, it has been argued that the foundational starting point morally for any organization should be its mission and identity. What is the organization, and what is its purpose? In addition, given that it may well be that the historical circumstances which defined the purpose of an organization no longer exist. For example, an orphanage and school may have been set up to serve a certain population of children who were, at one time, neglected by society. However, it may be that the society has set up social programs to address the needs of that population of children. Or, educational programs may have been set up to serve the needs of particular populations, but, with the evolution of public education or changes in the population, those needs can now be met in other ways or are no longer present.

These broad, general examples are drawn from generalizations made about the histories and missions of many organizations in health care and education. They also reflect the reality that societies are not static. They change and develop. So, it is always possible that a society can change in such a way that the social needs identified in the founding of an organization have changed or, in some cases, ceased to exist. Many of U.S. President Lyndon Johnson's Great Society programs, for example, were created to meet the basic needs of citizens in health care and education, while such social changes can affect the social need for many organizations. The creation of systems of community colleges in many American states, for example, was another systemic change that altered higher education and affected, at least indirectly, the missions of many colleges and universities. The creation of federal programs like Medicaid created the possibility of making health care available to many people. The continuing evolution of health care precipitated by the Affordable Care Act has introduced the possibility of health care for nearly all Americans.

These historical examples remind us once again that organizations exist within the environment of the particular society in which they live. That means organizations will need to examine continually the social environments in which they live and serve. The changing dynamisms and structures of society will affect social organizations in education and health care. As societies change and develop, it will also mean that organizations, such as those in health care and education, will need to adapt how they can or should change and develop and still remain faithful to their identities and live with integrity. And, it will be important for organizations to ask the most fundamental question of all: is the organization still needed?

13.5 Conclusions

This chapter has continued to highlight and examine the relationship, which exists between organizations in education and health care and the societies around them. The first part of this book explored the idea of the identities of organizations and argued that they arise in response to needs within a society. This chapter has explored the idea that societies are, in most cases, not static but are developing and evolving. The changing society around an organization can affect organizations in health care and education simply because they are created, in part, to serve needs within a society. As the society changes and evolves, this development should affect the life of social organizations in health care and education. It may be that changes in a society require different kinds of responses and services from an organization. It may even be the case that changes in a society may mean that the society no longer needs the services of an organization and that the initial mission of the organization is completed.

Summary of the Main Points

1. The Changing Needs of Society held to shape the evolution of an organization and its Mission
2. Evolution and Innovation are part of social organizations in changing societies
3. Organizational Identity is key to meeting the Changing Needs of a Society
4. An Organization's mission and identity are the keys to maintaining organizational integrity

Chapter 14
Conclusion: True North: Organizational Mission and the Changing Needs of Society

- Intro and conclusion about objective morality S/S
- Importance of proceduralism, based in respect for persons
- Procedures as universal moral language
- Review chapters for summaries

This book has been an exploration of secular ethics in a Post-Modern, culturally diverse society. The book builds on the work of H.T. Engelhardt, Jr. and other thinkers who have explored ethical controversies in a secular society. However, the book has taken a different route in its investigation. Instead of examining particular acts and moral decisions, or the moral limits of governments in secular societies to control the choices of individual agents, this book has focused on a different set of moral actors: organizations.

Most organizations in a secular society are for-profit organizations governed by the laws and regulations for business organizations and commerce. The book has investigated organizations in education and health care that are traditionally classified as non-profit organizations and are seen to offer some benefit to the community. This investigation has argued that organizations in education and health care should to be assessed as moral actors in a secular society in terms of their self-identity, value commitments, and their relationship to society

Part I of this investigation has examined the language of how we can talk about organizations, which have a moral purpose, as moral actors in a post-modern, morally pluralistic, secular society. This book has argued, in Part I that social organizations in education and health care can be moral actors in secular, morally diverse societies. This investigation has focused on organizations in education and health

"True North" is a navigational expression in Cardinal Directions. To find "true north" is to find or proceed on the correct course or in the right direction. The expression is a reference to finding the position of the North Pole (e.g., by compass or by locating a pole star) to navigate properly. I use this phrase, here, because one of the goals of this book is to help organizations, in the fields of health care and education, find and keep their directions and true north.

K. W. Wildes, S.J., *Organizational Ethics and Moral Integrity in Secular Societies*, Philosophical Studies in Contemporary Culture 29,
https://doi.org/10.1007/978-3-031-39097-5_14

care, with particular moral commitments, can be influenced by their moral commitments. The moral commitments of social organizations should influence both the work of the organization and how it operates in the morally diverse, secular society. Unlike many business organizations, which have some minimal levels of moral commitments, organization in education and health should be shaped by deeper levels of moral commitments in how they care for the persons who seek their help and assistance. The object of the work of organizations in education and health care is the human person themselves.

The first part of this investigation identified the key concepts, tools, and language needed to investigate organizations, with moral identities, in post-modern, secular societies. This investigation has explored how such organizations, which have moral identities, can operate with moral integrity and be accountable for their identity and moral commitments (Chaps. 3 and 4) while operating with others in a morally diverse, secular society. Chapters 4 and 5 went on to further explore how we can develop a moral language that can be applied to organizations with moral identities in the context of a post-modern, secular society.

Part II of this investigation (Chaps. 6 and 7) explored how organizations, with a moral identity, can be structured internally to maintain their moral identity while they operate in a secular, postmodern society. This book has argued that it is important to remember that organizations in health care and education, because they are committed to some model of human flourishing, are inextricably linked to a set of moral values or viewpoint. However, different organizations in education and health care may have different moral commitments, different models of human flourishing, and different ways of proceeding. Organizations need to understand their own moral commitments if they are to operate with moral integrity internally and in a secular society.

It is important to understand that this investigation has focused on how organizations, which have their own moral identities, can operate in morally diverse, secular societies shaped by the post-modern condition. This investigation has not mapped out any one particular model for these organizations but instead it has examined the necessary conditions for how any organization, with moral commitments, can operate in a morally diverse, secular society.

Organizations with moral identities may face a number of challenges in secular societies because these societies can be settings for moral diversity and moral pluralism. One challenge these organizations with moral identities will need to face is how to maintain their identity and moral integrity, while still interacting with other agents in the morally diverse secular society around it. Organizations with a moral identity will face at least two types of challenges in maintaining their integrity. One challenge will be how to balance the identity and integrity of the organization while it works with other agents, which have different moral commitments.

Another challenge will be how to maintain the integrity of the organization's mission while addressing the changing needs of the society in which the organization lives.

This investigation has assumed that secular societies will be open, in principle, to diverse moral points of view and diverse ways of thinking about morality. It is be important for organizations, which have moral identities, to be clear about their moral commitments both to themselves and to other members of a morally, diverse secular society (Chaps. 6 and 7). Working with other organizations in education and health care, which have different moral commitments, will be a challenge for the integrity of any organization.

This investigation has argued that it should be important that the moral commitments of social organizations be integrated into the life and work of the organization. This investigation has also argued that the moral commitments of an organization be known publically in a morally diverse, secular society. In addressing the challenges of moral pluralism there will always be a real risk that an organization can compromise, or lose, its identity in its efforts to respond to, and speak to, the needs of the surrounding society.

The relationship between social organizations and the society in which they exist poses a number of risks for both social organizations as well as for the society in which they live. One obvious challenge, explored in the Second Part of this book, is how we can think and talk about organizations having moral identities and how we can think about them as moral actors in morally diverse societies. Too often we limit our language of moral agency to individuals or to government agencies. Considering organizations expands that category of who can be considered a moral agent in a secular society.

A further challenge for this investigation, explored in Part III of this book, is that we need to think about how morally diverse, secular societies can operate with organizations which have different moral identities as part of the society. When we include organizations in our ethical analysis of secular societies, we open a different set of questions, beyond those about individual agents and the moral authority of governments to regulate individuals. Now, we need to think about how to articulate the morally justified possibilities and limits for how secular governments can regulate organizations. This book has argued that we need to broaden our conceptual scheme to think about the extent to which secular societies might regulate organizations with particular moral identities. It is important to recognize that organizations with particular moral identities can enrich the moral diversity of such secular societies.

This book has followed Engelhardt's analysis and insights about ethics in secular societies and their openness to moral and cultural pluralism. However, this investigation has expanded the framework of his investigations. Engelhardt focused on the choices made by particular moral agents and the moral authority of government to regulate moral choices in secular societies. Within this framework, he argued for the importance of free choice and consent by moral agents as the foundations for moral discourse in secular societies and for the moral limits to government authority. This book, however, has argued that we should expand the cast of moral actors in secular societies beyond individual agents and beyond government authorities, which regulate the choices of individual agents. This book has argued that *every* organization can be considered a moral actor in secular societies insofar as organizations make and keep promises concerning the goods and services an organization offers and delivers.

Organizations can be committed to a set of moral values, no matter how thick or how thin they might be, which underlie the moral character of an organization.[1] Every organization can be judged as a moral actor to the degree that the organization makes and keeps its promises. Even organizations that are primarily commercial enterprises can be judged by this standard.

Beyond honesty in advertising, along with clear, public procedures for consumers, most organizations in secular societies will not have a developed moral identity that is more than the ethical canons of commerce. Most organizations are commercial enterprises and have no particular moral purpose beyond the minimal moral requirements of truth telling in advertising, selling, delivering commercial services or goods, and keeping promises. These organizations can be assessed as moral actors through the framework of whether or not they advertise honestly and the degree to which they deliver the goods or services they promise.

However, this book has argued that social organizations in education and health care should be considered as content-full moral actors that can have moral identities in secular societies. If organizations in education and health care have an identity and moral commitments then they should be integral to its operations. Part I of this book examined how organizations should develop and maintain a moral identity in a secular, morally pluralistic society. It was argued that organizations, with moral identities, should be clear about the moral commitments of the organization and those commitments should be integrated into the culture and operations of the organization. Furthermore, it is important in secular, morally diverse societies, that organizations should be explicit and public about their moral identity and commitments if they are operating with others in secular, morally diverse societies. Such explicit commitments is both important for the internal integrity of the organization and for how the organization operates in a morally pluralistic, secular society.

The nature of the services delivered by social organizations in health care and education, along with the manner by which these services are delivered, will depend upon the particular identity, mission, and moral commitments of each social organization (Chap. 4).

However, in many secular societies social organizations in education and health care, because of their social nature, will be subject to some forms of oversight by the society in which they exist. In a secular, morally pluralistic society, it is important that every social organization be clear about its own identity, mission, and moral commitments so that the organization can maintain its own integrity and deal honestly with others in a morally diverse society. Such clarity is important both for the organization itself, so that it can know what it is, what it does, how it operates, and why it does what it does. Such clarity is important both for the organization but also

[1] K. Wildes, "Institutional Integrity: Toleration, Approval, and Holy War or 'Always True to You in My Fashion'", *Journal of Medicine and Philosophy* 16 (April 1991), 211–220; K. Wildes, "Institutional Identity, Integrity, and Conscience", *Kennedy Institute of Ethics Journal* 7, (1997), 413–419; K. Wildes, "Institutional Integrity in Health Care: Tony Soprano and Family Values", *Institutional Integrity in Health Care*, ed., A.S. Iltis, (Dordrecht: Kluwer Academic Publishers, 2003), 7–28.

for the ability of the organization to participate ethically in the secular society in which it lives and works. It is important that organizations, if they act as moral agents, be clear with those who use their services, other organizations with whom it might work, and the broader secular society.

The focus of this investigation has been an exploration of organizations in education and health care as they are content-full moral actors in a postmodern, secular society (Part I).

These two areas, education and healthcare, are implicitly committed to some moral vision about the flourishing of human beings which influences the practices in education and healthcare. As argued in this book, organizations in education and health care are shaped by the content-full moral views that are held by the organization. Organizations, which hold moral views, should identify the moral commitments of the organization in the ongoing planning and operations of the organization. In addition, organizations with particular moral commitments need to identify explicitly those commitments for the morally diverse, secular society around them in which they operate. In this way, they can deal honestly with individuals, other organizations, and society as a whole.

Given the vulnerability of patients, students, and their families and parents, who are the objects of health care and education, these organizations cannot operate only by a consumer model of the market. Society should take steps to protect those who use need the services of organizations in education and health care. In addition to protecting the confidential nature of what happens to students and patients additional steps are taken to protect their privacy and the information of patients and students, which distinguishes these organizations from the ordinary commercial procedures. Often the steps for protection of patients and students are taken through processes of licensure and oversight by the appropriate authorities in education and health care assuring that minimal standard are met in education and health care.

This book has argued that because education and health care make some moral assumptions about what it is to be a human being then organizations in these areas should be considered as important in understanding the complexities of ethical questions and moral discourse in post-modern, secular societies. The potential moral diversity found in contemporary secular societies shapes the background and context for many social and ethical debates in these societies. This book has argued that ethical debates can involve organizations as moral actors, along with individual actors and the place of government authority in these debates. This book has argued that we need to consider organizations as potential moral actors, at least in the areas of education and health care, since these areas are often laced with, and framed by, moral assumptions and purpose.

The moral diversity in a secular society may be evidenced, in part, in the moral diversity of a society's social organizations. This investigation has argued that social organizations need to be clear, to themselves and to the society in which they operate, about the moral commitments and values to which the organization is committed. Social organizations in secular societies need to operate with a degree of moral integrity and they need to be clear, with those in the society around them, about their moral values and commitments. In addition, the argument of this book has been that it is important for there to be ways to verify the identity of social organizations and monitor the identity of these organizations over time. In this way, a society can know that the organization is what it claims to be and social organizations can build trust within a society even if others reject the moral commitments of the organization. This social trust is grounded in the identity and integrity of the organization such that others in a secular society can trust that the organization is what it claims to be.[2]

"*True north*" is a navigational term that refers to using the stars to find one's location in relationship to the North Pole. By using the stars, one will know where "true" north is and be able to navigate accurately, because one knows what true direction is. Important underlying questions explored in this book is how social organizations in education and health care in secular, morally pluralistic societies can know, articulate, and live their true north and navigate their way through the diverse and changing cultural and moral elements of the postmodern, secular societies in which they live.

This book, to some extent, was developed to challenge organizations, in health care and education, to identify and find ways to both articulate and maintain their own true north. The book has argued that, for organizations in postmodern, secular societies, there can be a variety of moral views, which influence the direction of an organization, and it is important to remember that in secular societies not all social organizations in health care or education will be the same. Each one can have a different "true north" and different moral views depending on their origin, identity, and mission. One of the challenges, for any organization, is to be clear about its own mission and identity and then to find ways to inculcate the organization's mission and identity into the fabric of the organization. If the mission and identity do not become part of the fabric of the organization then a social organization can become more like department stores selling a variety of merchandise and where the customer can find whatever he or she wants and where the 'customer is always right'. When this happens a social organization, which once had a particular identity and mission that shaped the organization and the services it offered, would cease to exist.

It is important to remember that social organizations, to some degree, exist in a dialogical relationship with the society in which the organization is situated. Such dialogical relationships, between social organizations and the society it serves, enables the social organizations and the society to both critique and complement each other. It is important that a social organization respond to needs within a society and they can be critical moral voices in a society because of their moral identity as organizations. It will be important for the society to be able to verify that social organization are what they claim to be through some public processes of certification (e.g., accreditation). The processes of certification or accreditation for social organizations verifies that the organization is what it says it is and helps to build trust, for the diverse, secular society, that the organization is what it claims to be.

[2] K. Wildes, S.J., "Institutional Integrity: Toleration, Approval, and Holy War or 'Always True to You in My Fashion'", *Journal of Medicine and Philosophy* 16 (April 1991), 211–220.

However, it is important to recognize that, for social organizations with particular identities and missions, there are real risks in the dialectical relationship with any particular society.

One needs to consider that there is a relationship between social organizations in education and health care and the societies in which they live and operate and it is possible that changes, in a society, will affect the society's needs for social organizations like those in health care and education. In addition, societies will have changing expectations about health care and education and the manner by which they are delivered. Therefore, one challenge for these social organizations will be to find ways of proceeding which will allow them to adapt to change, develop, and serve the changing needs of societies in which they find themselves while still maintaining the integrity of the organization. For any social organization, one needs to be conscious of the relationship between the mission and identity of the organization and the needs of a particular society.

There are risks for social organizations when they respond to changes in the societies in which they exist. One risk is that social organizations can become too rigid in their focus on their mission and identity and miss the changing needs of the society they were designed to serve. In such an approach one hears language like "This is who we are and this is what we have always done and this is the way we have always done it." The practical challenge of this response is to freeze the mission and identity of a social organization to a particular moment in time, which may no longer be appropriate for the society the organization, serves. This view does not allow the mission and identity of an organization to change, grow, or develop as the society it serves changes and develops and this view runs the risk of rendering the social organization irrelevant to the society it is supposed to serve.

Another risk, which is at the opposite end of the spectrum from this first response, is the risk where the rudder for the organization to navigate change is to follow the most current and recent social trends of the day. If the rudder for navigating change is to follow the latest changes or trends in a field or society, then the organization will be steered by the most recent trend and fashion in education and health care and not by its mission and identity.

Every social organization faces the real risk of losing its identity and mission if the organization becomes either too entrenched in the secular societies they serve or if the organizations become too isolated from the societies in which they function and serve. The true north of an organization should be found in its identity and mission. In its mission and its identity, the organization not only remembers its identity and purpose and it also finds the foundations for its value commitments as well as its way of proceeding in its relationship with the morally diverse, secular society in which it lives. It is important for an organization to be clear, to itself at least, about its mission and identity, as they should guide the organization's culture, the way it hires and orients new members, the way it treats and evaluates existing members, the way it evaluates itself, and the way it deals with the world outside the organization. Only when an organization knows its mission and identity can the organization operate with moral integrity in a diverse, secular, postmodern society. It is only when an organization has a sense of its own identity, mission, and history, that it can make decisions about its development in response to changes in society. This dialogical awareness, by a social organization, will be an essential element to how the organization can change and develop in response to changes in the society it serves.

Because of moral diversity in secular societies, organizations in such societies each organization needs to have their own "true north." This term is used as the title of this chapter because, as I have noted, "True North" is a navigational expression in Cardinal Directions and to find "true north" is to find or proceed on the correct course. The expression is a reference to finding the position of the North Pole (e.g., by compass or by locating a pole star) to navigate properly. A social organization will need to know its own true north and how its true north defines the relationship of the organization to the secular society in which it lives. That is each social organization will need to know its identity and mission, which will tell its correct direction and way of proceeding. As a consequences schools, universities, and health care facilities can exist side by side and be remarkably different because they each have their own mission and identity. The distinctiveness of identity and mission for each social organization makes it difficult to establish meaningful comparative measures, such as those done in annual studies by *U.S. News and World Report*, by which to evaluate social organizations. Social organizations each have their own distinct missions and identities, which can make it difficult for meaningful comparisons.

In morally and culturally diverse secular societies, it is important for a social organization to know its identity and its mission for two reasons. First, this allows the organization to both know and follow its own true north and navigate the challenges of operating in a secular, morally pluralistic society while remaining true to itself. Second, if the organizations knows its mission and identity it allows the organization to operate honestly with others in a diverse, secular society. Such organizational honesty is a crucial underpinning for the practice of informed consents in morally, culturally diverse secular societies. It is important that an organization make its mission and identity clear to individuals who might seek to use its services and to other organizations with which it might collaborate or do business, as well as to the regulatory agencies of the secular society in which it lives and works. For an organization to operate in morally and culturally diverse societies, and maintain its own moral clarity and integrity, the organization will need to be clear to both itself and the society about its identity and moral commitments.

For organizations in education and health care there will often be the temptation to follow the current trends in the field of the organization and become "all things to all people." Consequently, it can be easy for social organizations to lose sight of their particular mission and identity and become a supermarket of services, which relies on consumer choice. This book was developed, in part, as a way to help organizations think about their own identities and missions, no matter what they are, and how to realize their identities and missions as integral parts of the life and work of the organization. Mission and identity need to be more than a coversheet for a board report or a glossy public relations production. As this book has argued mission and identity need to be integral to the organization—its vision, planning, and allocation of resources. Mission and identity should be built into the structure and culture of the organization and should be the true north of the organization.

Hopefully, this book has accomplished at least two goals that can help secular, postmodern societies think about organizations as moral actors. First, the book has brought together a set of problems and challenges in ethics that is not often addressed in contemporary, secular societies and postmodern thought. These are the challenges of ethical issues, which arise for organizations, which understand themselves as moral actors in a secular, morally diverse world. In secular societies, we argue about the moral authority of society and its role in setting limits for individual freedoms and choices in postmodern, secular societies. While we do investigate organizations in the area of business ethics, however we rarely examine the ethical issues that are involved when organizations, which are traditionally regarded in some societies as non-profit or charitable entities, are the principal moral actors in the delivery of services.

Nevertheless, recent experiences have taught us that these organizations need to be examined in society, in part because they can act badly.

This book, hopefully, can also help to expand the conversation about ethics in secular societies beyond only investigating how we can talk about ethics and individual agents and their actions, or investigating the justifications for, and the limits of, government authority and regulation. This book has investigated a different species of ethical actor in secular societies, and these are the questions, which recognize that organizations can be moral actors and decision makers in the fields of education and health care. So, rather than limiting the scope of our ethical investigation to questions about individual agents or government authority regarding the regulation of agents, we should include organizations as moral actors when we examine ethical issues in secular societies. These organizations fill an important social space, as moral actors, which exists between individual agents, and society as a whole. In that social space organizations are important not only for delivering certain goods and services, but they are important as moral actors that make ethical choices about their goods and services through organizational policies and their use of resources. These types of decisions about policies and procedures shapes the moral discourse that affects people in their day-to-day lives, as well as other organizations with which they might partner or interact.

The second reason to focus on organizations in education and health care is that, in dealing with patients and students, these organizations are assisting people who have particular needs for the services, in health care and education. Patients and students do not fit easily into our normal model of consumer exchange. Transactions involving health care and educational organizations do not follow the normal model of exchange for goods or services, because the people who engage the services of these organizations often do so to help themselves flourish as human beings and not something external to being human. As argued in the first part of this book, in this way organizations in health care and education play a fiduciary role for their patients or students unlike commercial business organizations. They are not simply selling services, but their services are about the overall good of the patient, student, and families.

Furthermore, society takes steps to ensure that people can trust these organizations for the services they offer.

We know, however, in recent years, that several non-profit organizations have acted egregiously, toward their patients, students, benefactors, and supporters and eroded public trust. In some way, these violations of public trust have contributed to the work of this book and investigation. This book has focused on the questions of ethics for non-profit organizations in education and health care, because normally we assume that these organizations have particular ethical commitments, no matter how varied, in secular, postmodern societies. In many ways, these types of organizations rely on an assumption of social trust, as they address the needs of people who are often viewed as vulnerable in society.

The book has focused on organizations in education and health care specifically because the work of these organizations is inextricably bound up with some level of moral commitments. The moral commitments of organizations in health care and educations should frame why an organization does what it does and, often, how the work of the organization is carried out. This investigation, hopefully, can also help us look beyond organizations and expand how we think, talk, explore, and analyze ethical questions in postmodern secular societies. In examining organizations as moral actors the tools of our ethical analysis is expanded beyond examining what other individuals or government agencies. Organizations make decisions and act by implementing policy and, in doing so, direct and affect the actions of other moral agents. At the same time, in examining organizations as moral agents we also recognize that there are broader questions about how a society is organized in terms of health care and education. These about how a society is organized go beyond the focus of this particular investigation.

Indeed, social organizations in health care and education can also be important moral voices in secular societies in addressing and criticizing social practices, for example, that have been historically racist, sexist, or discriminatory, or social practices, which provide inadequate education or inadequate services for health care. Social organizations, like those in education and health care, with particular identities and moral commitments, can be a moral voice in a morally diverse, secular society *if* an organization so chooses. Often, the role of being a moral critic in a society can be tied to the organization's mission and identity.

The second section of this book explored how an organization can both have and maintain its identity and so live with integrity in a morally diverse, secular society. Social organizations, such as those in education and health care, exist in the midst of society, and they exist to serve the needs in the societies in which they exist. In turn, these societies often regulate the activities of organizations, particularly in education and health care. However, we know that societies are not static, and they often change and evolve, as do the needs of a society. Therefore, we need to think about how to ask the questions about what happens to organizations when societies around them change, and the needs, for which the organizations were created, change or, perhaps, no longer exist.

Following the themes that have been argued throughout this book, one can conclude that there is no one set of answers, in a morally pluralistic, secular society, to the questions about organizations and their relationship with other organizations or with their relationship to society as a whole. In fact, this book has argued that there can be a range of responses to this relationship that are defined by the identity and mission of the organization. However, questions about the relationship of social organizations to society do raise a number of important considerations that should be asked by any organization in order to help guide the organization's own self-assessment, planning for the future, and decisions about cooperative ventures with other organizations. When we consider organizations in the context of the changing nature of societies it is important to think about an appropriate method, tied to the mission, identity, and culture of the organization, to ask these questions and to think through integration of the answers with the planning processes of an organization.

In examining organizations in health care and education, this book has intentionally avoided the topics of public health and public education. The reader, however, should not draw the wrong inferences from what is missing! Make no mistake; these are important topics and considerations for any society. However, there are two reasons for *not* exploring these topics in this book. First, as has been argued from the beginning, this book has been focused on exploring the intermediate structures of the organizations in health care and education as moral actors.

These organizations are intermediate structures, which are largely overlooked in discussions of health care, education, ethics, and public policy. In addition, a focus on public health or public education is a different topic, beyond the focus of this book. Investigations of public health and public education are inevitably tied to questions about how a society is organized. Those questions about how a society is organized are important, but they call for a different investigation. Second, the topics of *public* health and education, as part of a secular society, rest, primarily, on policy decisions made by each society. Furthermore, public health care and public education involve additional issues and policy questions that require their own ethical analysis and should be developed in another work about ethics and public policy.

14.1 Mission and Identity: The True North for Organizational Integrity

It has been argued throughout this book that the foundational starting point, morally, for any organization in a secular society should be the organization's mission and identity. Am organizations need to be clear about what it is, its purpose and what its moral commitments are, and its way of proceeding. The organization needs to demonstrate that its moral commitments guide how the organization conducts itself with individuals, other organizations, and society in general. Organizations like those in health care and education do not live out identity and mission in isolation. We know that societies differ from each other and we know that societies can change and develop. In addition, we can ascertain that change and development in a society will mean that social organizations, like those in health care and education, will also need to judge how to adapt to a changing society.

Given the evolving nature of secular societies, every social organization needs to be aware that the original social and historical circumstances, which helped to shape the mission, purpose, and identity of an organization, may change over time as societies change. In fact, the need for social organizations may even cease to exist over time. This book has been focused on changes that can take place within an organization. However, societies, and the needs of a society, may change thus affecting social organizations. For example, an orphanage or a school may have been set up to serve a certain population of children who were, at one time, neglected by society. However, it may be that the society, over time, has developed social programs to address the needs of that population of children, so that they are now well served. Therefore, it is possible that a society will change in such a way that the needs, which led to the establishment of the orphanage and the school, may no longer exist. Alternatively, educational organizations may have certain programs that were set up to serve the needs of particular populations of people, however, with the evolution of public education or changes in the population, those needs can now be met in other ways; or, because of other changes, the programs may no longer be needed in the contemporary society. These types of changes, while dramatic, are always possible in principle. However, they need to be developed and assessed by the organization in relationship to the needs of a society. This is one of the reasons why social organizations, like those in education and health care, should engage in a continual environmental study as part of the organization's planning process.

There are many examples of for-profit organizations that failed to understand innovation and adapt to changing times and which went out of business. One thinks, for example, of Pan American World Airways or Borders bookstores. These examples also remind us of the reality that societies are not static. They change and develop. Therefore, it is always possible that a society will change in such a way that the social needs, which were identified in the founding of a social organization, have changed or, in some cases, ceased to exist. Many of U.S. President Lyndon Johnson's *Great Society* programs, for example, were created to meet the basic needs of many citizens in health care and education. The creation of systems of community colleges in many American states, for example, was another systemic, social change and which altered higher education and affected, at least indirectly, the missions of many colleges and universities. The passage and implementation of *No Child Left Behind*, under former President G.W. Bush, changed the social context for early education in the United States.[3] The creation of federal programs like Medicaid opened the possibility of making health care available to many people.[4]

[3] https://www.govinfo.gov/link/plaw/107/public/110?link-type=html

[4] Joseph A. Califano, "Seeing is Believing – The Enduring Legacy of Lyndon Johnson" Kaiser Family Foundation, May 19, 2008, Washington, DC. http://www.lbjlibrary.org/lyndon-baines-johnson/perspectives-and-essays/seeing-is- believing-the-enduring-legacy-of-lyndon-johnson; Wilson, Robert H., Glickman, Norman J. and Lynn, Laurence E., *LBJ's Neglected Legacy: How Lyndon Johnson Reshaped Domestic Policy and Government*, New York, USA: University of Texas Press, 2021. https://doi.org/10.7560/300541

The further evolution of the health care industry by the *Affordable Care Act*[5] opened up and developed the possibility of health care for nearly all Americans.

These historical examples are offered simply as reminders that social organizations in education and health care are not isolated from the societies in which they exist. Rather, they are situated in the context of a broader social environment of a particular society and the needs and expectations of the society. The social context of organizations reminds us that there is a dialectical relationship between social organizations, like those in health care and education, and the society in general. This realization means that organizations need to examine continually the changing dynamics and structures in the particular society around them might affect organizations. Furthermore, as societies change and develop organizations, such as those in health care and education, will need to adapt to how the organization can or should change and develop and still remain faithful to its identity and live with integrity. In addition, it will be important for organizations to ask the most fundamental question of all: does the purpose for which the organization was created still exist? Does the social need for the organization still exist?

These very fundamental questions call for an organization to be aware of the social environment in which it lives and to be mindful of its history, identity, and mission. In addition, they call for the organization to face questions about society, and itself, with honesty.

14.2 Mission and Identity: The Rudder for Innovation and the Evolution of Organizations in Changing Societies

Sometimes it is good to state what is often assumed as "obvious" and question it. It is also important to remember that a great deal of human life, particularly the social life of societies, is involved with change and development. Therefore, it is not surprising that the fields of health care and education are both fields that change and develop in a variety of ways because of new knowledge, new technologies, and new ways of proceeding. In both education and health care there continues to be a growth in the knowledge bases of both areas. Moreover, with the evolution of knowledge there can be an evolution in the technologies to support education and health care, as explored in Chap. 3.

Moreover, the developmental and changing nature of the health care and educational fields is an underlying *challenge* for any discussion of organizations in those fields. The challenge of change plays out in at least two different arenas in education and health. One arena is the area of technology and the delivery of information and services. With the ongoing development of new technologies and new knowledge, change will often be a constant factor in health care and educational organizations.

[5] https://www.healthcare.gov/where-can-i-read-the-affordable-care-act

That theme of change should not be surprising, given that both types of organizations exist in and are essential parts of the secular societies in which they live and function. Furthermore, both the fields of health care and education keep evolving with new knowledge and technologies. The evolutionary nature of these fields means that the organization in health care or education will need to adjust, adapt, and develop according to the changes as they occur.

In identifying and addressing questions of ethics and organizations it is also important to think about how to consider the evolving roles of technology within an organization and the ethical questions that are raised by these evolving roles. There are often two, different and extreme reactions to technology. One is what I often call an "American" extreme where people assume that they need to have the newest version of a particular technology. What matters, in this view, is simply that the person has "the latest" without an evaluation of the value of "the latest". The other extreme can be referred to as the "luddite"[6] approach to technology and innovation: the refusal to pay attention to changes in technology or in the field itself. I would argue that it is a better approach is to think of technology as neither good nor bad in itself but that any technology needs to be evaluated in the broader context of an organization's identity, purpose, moral commitments, and the vision of how the technology is to be used. Technology ought not to be an end in itself but a means to ends that we have determined, and it should be evaluated according to whether it helps to achieve those ends.

Both health care and education are important social goods of ongoing developments in the contemporary world. Both areas develop from the continued expansion of knowledge and technology in each area. With that in mind, organizations need to be thoughtful about how developments and innovations are approached. Given the earlier arguments in this book, the touchstone of any evaluation should be the mission and identity of the organization. There is often a cultural bias, particularly in societies like the United States, which assumes that whatever is "new" is in fact better. However, by itself, that is not always an appropriate value assumption. The new is just that: it is new and not, necessarily, better, good, or bad in itself. Rather, one can argue that most technological innovations are neither good nor bad in themselves. Instead, like any innovation, technological innovations need be evaluated within the context of their use as well as the ancillary effects on other areas of life.

The discussion and evaluation of technology and change pose at least two fundamental questions for any organization. First, every organization needs to reflect on the questions of how to evaluate, implement, or forego, new knowledge and technology. Both the processes of evaluation and implementation should be guided by the mission and identity of the organization. Every organization needs to be aware of a bias, certainly present in the contemporary, postmodern age, where it is often assumed by people that the "new" is necessarily better than what preceded it. Often, in marketing a new version of an already existing product will emphasize the "newness" of the most recent version, with little attention to how the product is actually

[6] https://en.wikipedia.org/wiki/Neo-Luddism#cite_note-2

better than the older, existing product. However, it is not necessarily the case that the "new" is better, and innovations need to be evaluated in light of an organization's mission and identity. The organization needs to evaluate how a new innovation or technology, whatever it may be, actually advances the mission and identity of the organization. Again, the mission of the organization should be the key measure by which decisions are made.

Second, as the wider society changes and evolves, along with the fields of education and health care, an organization should ask the ultimate foundational questions from time to time. These are questions like whether or not there is *still a need for a particular organization,* its mission, its way of proceeding, and for what it offers a society. These are very difficult questions for any organization to ask, and often these questions, because they touch the foundation of the mission and identity of an organization, are not asked by organizations. In many ways, most organizations, particularly non-profit organizations, are not set up by way of their structures, cultures, or their corporate imaginations to ask questions of whether or not the mission of the organization is relevant or important to the society the organization serves.

Because of market forces, for-profit organizations are forced to examine themselves and their missions because of their relationship to market forces. Declining use of a product or service may indicate that the product or service is no longer needed. However, organizations in the non-profit world of education or health care may not always have such "market" indicators, given that in postmodern, secular societies, health care or education are rarely set up according to typical market models. Furthermore, the governance of these organizations, set up with trustees serving for limited terms, may not be able to best measure important, slow shifts or changes that can challenge the organization. Nor may those in governance have the collective imagination to think that a society could reach a point where there was no need for a particular organization.

No matter the situation or structure, it is important for any organization to find ways to ask the fundamental questions, as part of long-term planning, about the ongoing social need for the organization and whether the organization should continue to exist. If an organization exists in a dialectical relationship with the society around it, it is quite possible that the society will have evolved in such a way that the organization is no longer necessary. This type of question is very hard for an organization to ask about itself. Social organizations, like those in education and health care, exist in dialectical relationship with the societies in which they exist, and they are often consumed in the day-to-day operational questions involving their work and their missions. However, one can see, for example, in the recent history of health care in the United States, the changed and changing role of hospitals in the delivery of medical care, as well as the dramatic changes that have come to the way medical care is delivered. The roles of these organizations have changed, and are changing, because of the evolution of knowledge, as well as technology in medicine and how it is changing the delivery of health care services. In analogous ways, the evolution of technology is affecting learning and the shape and missions of universities.

Now, it has been argued throughout this book, organizations are living entities that are situated in a society. Moreover, as living entities, organizations should, on a regular basis, evaluate themselves, based on their identities and missions, in relationship to society and its needs, and ask how well an organization is serving society, meeting its needs for continuing service, and fulfilling the mission of the organization. Such evaluative processes can take different forms, depending on the culture and history of an organization and the nature of the society it serves. No matter what form it takes this evaluative process should be done at regular, periodic intervals. The processes of accreditation and certification by outside groups can be helpful in developing a self-critical, evaluative culture for the organization and the structures to support it. In addition, these processes of accreditation and certification can be helpful for the secular society to give the society confidence in terms of how well they are performing their missions and living out their identities in relationship to the needs of society.

However, one needs to keep in mind that it is always possible that these evaluative processes may lead to the conclusion that the basic mission of an organization has been fulfilled or that the society, served by the organization, has changed in such a way that the mission of the organization is no longer needed because of changes that have happened in a society.

Alternatively, it may be that changes in a field might mean that a particular type of organization is on longer required. For example, schools created to educate low income, economically poor students may no longer be needed if there is a significant development in public education in a city or region. On the other hand, the health needs of a population may be better served by the development of the delivery model of neighborhood clinics that could better serve certain populations rather than a particular hospital model. In such situations, an organization could go through a process of self-examination that leads to a new articulation of mission and vision, which is faithful to the history of the organization and responsive to the needs of contemporary society. Conversely, the trustees and leadership of an organization could reach the conclusion that it is time to write the concluding chapter of the life of the organization. The most obvious point, often missed, is that social organizations like those in education and health care may need to change and adjust due to changes in the broader society.

These questions are particularly challenging for any organization to address. In our social imagination, we rarely think of for-profit organizations ceasing to exist and going out of business. Yet, it does happen. In the United States a number of prominent, well-known for-profit corporations have either ceased to exist or been acquired by other companies and no longer exist, or they have morphed into other entities. Companies like Compaq Computers, Eastern Airlines, Enron, Standard Oil, and General Foods have all ceased to exist or been acquired and transformed by other companies. These historical examples remind us that organizations do not exist like platonic eternal forms that are detached from history. They can change, and they can come to an end. So, it makes sense that we should explore similar questions about non-profit organizations in health care and education coming to an end. What happens to an organization in education or health care if its mission comes to an end? Perhaps what is most important is that social organizations, like those in health care and education, should always consider these questions as a way to remind them of the fundamental, basic work of the organization. What happens if the mission has been accomplished or if the mission is no longer needed in a society?

It is important to remember that both health care and education are fields that are developmental and not static. Knowledge in these areas is developmental at almost every level. The underlying reality is that knowledge, which is the work of both health care and education, develops, changes, and grows. Furthermore, knowledge does not always develop in a straight line or incrementally. Sometimes we discover that what we "knew" was incorrect, and new knowledge helps us to correct errors of past assumptions and enables us to move forward. Both the areas of health care and education continue to grow, change, correct themselves, and expand, because the knowledge bases, which support them, continue to grow, change, and develop. Such growth and change are driven by the reality that we continue to learn more, acquire more knowledge, and correct mistakes of what we thought we "knew" in the past. Understanding this, about the nature of knowledge in education and health care, is important for the understanding the nature and the work of organizations in both education and health care.

14.3 True North: Organizational Identity and Mission and the Changing Needs of a Society

This book it has been argued that there are different factors that can lead or, sometimes, force an organization to change. The factors can include problems and challenges within the organization that affect its external reputation or its ability to fulfill its mission. The clergy sexual abuse scandal in the American Catholic Church is an example of an issue that has been both internal and external not only to the Church in general but also to organizations in education and health care which are affiliated with the Church. These scandals have affected the abilities of organizations to fulfill their missions and they have also affected how these organizations can operate. Internal scandals or ineffectiveness can undermine the trust that a society, and people, put in an organization.

Alternatively, there can be social factors, outside the organization, such as a declining population of students who are considering higher education, or changes in federal or state laws and regulations, or in insurance plans in health care, that give many more patients access to health care organizations. No matter what they are, these types of external changes create challenges for these social organizations, which will need to respond to the changing social environment in which they find themselves. The changes in the surrounding environment will often mean those organizations cannot simply continue doing the same thing or operating in the same way as in the past. A failure to respond to changes in the social environment could damage or even end the mission of the organization. Again, it is important to remember that organizations in health care and education are organizations that need to respond to the needs of the particular society and culture in which they are situated.

The fundamental question, particularly for social organizations in education and health care, is how an organization should respond to social changes that affect the organization's mission and purpose. It can be argued, based on the work in the second part of this book that the starting point for evaluating change for an organization is found in the mission and identity of the organization. In the various processes of evaluation, accreditation, and certification, those outside the organization can evaluate whether the organization is being faithful to its own mission and whether it is living out the mission and identity of the organization. Simply put, they can respond to the most basic questions of whether the organization is what it claims to be and whether it is doing what it promises to do.

However, in asking these questions it is important to recognize that organizations in health care and education are *social* organizations and acknowledge that the second starting point for social organizations, after mission, is the society in which the organization is situated. The challenge, when confronting a changing social environment, is for an organization to ask what steps it should take to maintain its identity and mission and to meet the changing social environment. The organization needs to evaluate the changing social environment in light of its mission and identity. .

In thinking about the nature of organizations as moral actors, it is also important to recognize that organizations in health care and education exist, to some degree, in a dialectical relationship with the societies in which they live. These organizations are created to respond to needs within a particular social context. At the same time, depending on their missions and identities, these organizations can also be witnesses to the moral commitments held by the organizations and, at the same time, critics of the societies in which the organizations exist. Health care and educational organizations in the Jim Crow south, for example, existed in a good moral position to criticize the practices of society. Health care organizations in the United States today can raise challenges to accepted practices of abortion or assisted suicide by becoming living witnesses to the care of newborns, the practices of adoption, and care for dying patients.

Let us consider some extreme examples of the dialogical relationship between organizations and society. Suppose, for a moment, we are the trustees of a liberal arts college. However, there have been significant changes in the society in which the college exists, and the college is now facing significant enrollment and thus financial shortfalls. One way that we might attract and enroll more students would be to change the focus of our educational programs and become more like a more traditional vocational school. The trustees might review the proposal, evaluate it, and decide not to follow the recommendation, because to do so would forsake the mission of the school and, in fact, essentially lead to the creation of a new organization.

Alternatively, one could think of a health care organization that was no longer being reimbursed by different insurance carriers for the ways it had traditionally practiced medicine. The organization could adapt to the new demands of the insurance organizations or look for ways to modify what had been done traditionally. The most basic question will be what the organization can do, in light of its mission and identity, which would allow it to remain financially solvent.

Changes in the social environment will often affect social organizations like those in education and health care. An educational organization, for example, may have been founded to serve a particular population of students that was not being served at the time of the foundation. However, with changes in society or legal changes the needs of that particular population may be well-served today. Alternatively, the organizations that finance health care, such as insurance companies or government agencies, may decide no longer to cover certain types of treatment or care. Environmental and social changes like these will have a direct impact on the organization's mission and vision. At this point, in this exploration, it is important to note the potential for social changes and the effects that they may have on social organizations in health care or education.

In light of their relationship to society, one can argue that social organizations in education and health care need to find ways to assess and adapt themselves to the changing social needs of the society around them; only in this way can they be responsive to the needs and demands of a society. However, in adapting to the changing needs of a society social organizations should keep their mission and identity at the forefront in its decision-making, as they should be the true north for the organization's decision making and how the organization accomplishes its mission. The mission of an organization is a fundamental way in which an organization articulates and lives out it identity. If an organization does this, the organization should be able to establish a range of responses to the social situation it serves, while still remaining faithful to its identity and mission and serving the society in which it exists.

While it has not been extensively developed in this book, it should be clear that social organizations, like those in education and health care, exist in a dialogical relationship with the society around them. In addition, we need to keep in mind that both organizations and societies are dynamic and changing. Therefore, in thinking about organizations we need to keep in mind the real possibility that there may be situations where an organization cannot respond to the demands and needs of its surrounding society and still remain faithful to its identity and history. For example, a society may change and come to value a very different model of education (i.e. technical) than the model an educational organization would view as appropriate because of its mission and identity. In those circumstances, the organization's trustees may well make a decision to either end the organization, as its mission no longer matches the needs of a society. Alternatively, the organization's trustees may decide to significantly change the mission, and identity, of the organization so that it emerges as a new and different organization. In either case, the organization, as it has understood itself historically, will no longer exist.

These types of questions identify fundamental issues for organizations, and they identify questions about the relationship of an organization's mission and identity to the society in which it lives and works. These types of questions cannot be resolved only by examining some point in the past. Rather, these are questions that require an examination of the ongoing dialogical relationship between social organizations and the cultures and societies in which the organizations exist and serve. They are questions that any social organization should consider, but they are questions, which go beyond any particular social organizations. There are questions about the society in which a social organization serves and the needs of the society. For social organizations in education and health care, it is important to remember not only that the fields of health care and education will change and develop but it is also important to remember that the societies which organizations serve can change and develop. This awareness should require that the social organizations, like those in education and health care, will need to consider carefully how they can addresses the current and changing needs of a society and not serve a society which existed in the past and which no longer exists.

This book has been an examination of *social* organizations in education and health care. These organizations serve particular needs of people in societies and they also serve the societies as a whole in which they are situated. Though unarticulated in this investigation, it should be clear that these social organizations exist in relationship to the society in which they are located and they are established to serve particular needs of the societies they serve. The most basic lens we can use to evaluate these organizations in education and health care is the lens, which examines how well they fulfill their announced mission and serve patients and students.

However, these organizations also exist in a relationship with the broader society in which they exist.

The relationship between social organizations to the society in which they exist is a dialogical one in that both society and social organizations in education and health care can raise questions about the other and respond to the needs of each other. This is one reason why social organizations like those in education and health care will often vary from society to society because the needs of societies in which they exist will vary. So social organizations like those in education and health care may be very different from society to society.

We should also recognize that social organizations within a particular society may change and develop over time as the society changes and develops. Social organizations in education and health care, in the United States, for example changed when the broader secular society adopted *No Child Left Behind* in education and the *Affordable Care Act* in health care. As a society changes and develops over time so too social organizations in education and health care will change and develop in response to social changes.

The dialogue between societies and social organizations can, and should, be an important way to raise questions about a society, how the organization exists, its needs, how the society is structured, the way the social needs of a society are met, and how a society is organized.[7] Questions about how a society is organized, can be

---

[7] Kevin Wm. Wildes, S.J., "Creating Critical Care Resources: Implications for Distributive Justice", *Allocating Scarce Medical Resources: Roman Catholic Perspectives,* eds. H.T. Engelhardt, Jr., Mark J. Cherry, (Washington, DC: Georgetown University Press, 2002), 200–211. See also, Kevin Wildes, S.J., "The Rebirth of a City: Birth and Achievement of the Ethics Review Board", *Seattle Journal for Social Justice* 7 (2009): 127–138.

raised by social organizations in health care and education because they provide important insights into the life of a society. The questions about how a society is organized are important questions that can be raised under the rubric of social justice, which is a lens by which one can ask ethical questions about how a society is organized. By examining social organizations, like those in education and health care, one can identify an important set of lenses, which can lead to questions about how postmodern, secular societies might be organized for the delivery of the social goods. However, the questions of social justice and the organization of a postmodern, secular society, represent a different set of questions beyond the explorations of this book.

As it was argued at the beginning of this book, ethical questions about organizations fall in an often-unexplored middle range of ethical questions in secular societies. People often look at particular cases and questions in education and health care. While questions about organizations often frame what is done in particular cases or questions they are distinct moral actors from the individuals involved or society as a whole. The other lens we often use, when examining ethical questions in health care or education in contemporary, secular societies is the perspective of social policy when we ask about how a society should approach a particular ethical question. This book has addressed a different set of questions and investigated how organizations can function as moral agents. Organizations occupy a middle ground and social space between individual cases and particular actors on the one hand, and the questions of social policy and how a society is organized on the other hand. Social organizations, like those in education and health care, occupy this middle ground. Social organizations live within a society and its regulations and laws on the one hand and they respond to the freedom of individuals to make choices and act on the other hand. Social organizations, at least those in education and health care, need to respond to the oversight of society as a whole as well as when they respond to the choices of individual agents.

The questions about ethics and social organizations are important questions because of their impact on the organization, the decisions of individual agents, and the society in which the organization operates. Hopefully, the investigation of this book will help to expand our ability to examine organizations in education and health care as moral actors in secular societies.

However, it should be obvious from this investigation that one cannot understand social organizations by themselves. To develop a more complete understanding of social organizations as moral actors one needs to achieve a greater clarity about how the society, in which the organization exists, is organized and how a particular society understands its ethical obligations to its members for health care and education. Those questions will give a broader and more comprehensive framework for evaluating social organizations in health care and education.

However, the questions about how a society is organized, and its obligations to its citizens, are questions for another, and different, investigation.

Correction to: Organizational Ethics and Moral Integrity in Secular Societies

Correction to: K. W. Wildes, S.J., *Organizational Ethics and Moral Integrity in Secular Societies*, Philosophical Studies in Contemporary Culture 29, https://doi.org/10.1007/978-3-031-39097-5

The book was inadvertently published with omission of the founding editor and series editor names and incorrect associate editor name and editorial board members. The correct editor names have now been updated as: Founding Editor: H. Tristram Engelhardt Jr., Editor: Mark J. Cherry, Associate Editor: James Stacey Taylor, Editorial Board: David H. Bradshaw, Peter Jaworski, Terry Pinkard, C. Griffin Trotter, and Kevin Wm. Wildes.

The updated original version for this book can be found at https://doi.org/10.1007/978-3-031-39097-5

K. W. Wildes, S.J., *Organizational Ethics and Moral Integrity in Secular Societies*, Philosophical Studies in Contemporary Culture 29,
https://doi.org/10.1007/978-3-031-39097-5_15

Introduction to Resources for This Book

This book examines how organizations in health care and education, which have particular moral identities, can be understood as moral agents and how they can operate with integrity in a secular, morally and culturally diverse, society and still maintain their own moral identity and integrity. The Resources listed in this appendix are examples of organizational associations, in education and health care, which have articulated criteria for organizations to be members of the particular association. These criteria provide a way to evaluate the identity of an organization who is a member of the particular associations.

The resources listed in this appendix are examples that accompany the investigation of this book. They are particularly relevant to the Second Section of this book that examines organizational integrity and identity. The documents in these sources are offered as *examples* to some of the questions raised in this book and as resources that can help readers understand more clearly the conceptual issues raised in this book.

The documents cited in this appendix are also examples of how an association of organizations might provide a way to validate the identity of organizations who are members of the association. The documents also provide examples of a way to assess how well an organization is living out the identity it professes.

(A) Association of Jesuit Colleges and Universities, *Some Characteristics of Jesuit Colleges and Universities: A Self-Evaluation Instrument*, (The Jesuit Conference, Washington, DC: 2010)

This is a consensus statement explains the defining character and apostolic rationale of the Jesuit colleges and universities, articulates their manner of collaboration and governance, and addresses a set of key relationships vital to engaging positively in the common Jesuit apostolic mission.

K. W. Wildes, S.J., *Organizational Ethics and Moral Integrity in Secular Societies*, Philosophical Studies in Contemporary Culture 29,
https://doi.org/10.1007/978-3-031-39097-5

https://static1.squarespace.com/static/55d1dd88e4b0dee65a6594f0/t/612fafa56362bb224b00f773/1630515115139/A+Guide+for+Mission+Reflection_09-21.pdf

(B) Association of Jesuit Colleges and Universities, *Mission Priority Examen: A Mechanism for Self-Study, Peer Review, and Assessment,* (AJCU: Washington, DC: 2010).

This document is a way to help and institution assess how well it is living out the *Characteristics* document. The *Mission Priority Examen* provides a structure for each Jesuit college and university to undertake serious discussions about how they understand their school's authentic mission, establish goals for the future, and set forth new or renewed means of realizing those goals in the years to come.

https://www.ajcunet.edu/missionexamen

(C) Catholic Health Association, Mission Statement:

The Catholic Health Association (CHA) provides numerous resources and annual in-person educational programs and webinars to help members sustain their commitment to the ideals, values and vision of Catholic health as a ministry continuing Jesus' mission of love and healing.

The mission of CHA is to advance the Catholic health ministry of the United States in caring for people and communities.

https://www.chausa.org/mission/a-shared-statement-of-identity

(D) United States Catholic Conference, *Ethical and Religious Directives for Catholic Health Care Services, Sixth Edition*, (Washington, DC: 2009/2018)

The Directives are an excellent example of addressing the questions of identity for institutionally based Catholic health care services. They are addressed directly to "sponsors, trustees, administrators, chaplains, physicians, health care personnel, and patients or residents of Catholic health care institutions."

The reader can find the Directives at:

https://www.usccb.org/issues-and-action/human-life-and-dignity/health-care/upload/Ethical-Religious-Directives-Catholic-Health-Care-Services-fifth-edition-2009.pdf

(E) Congregation for Catholic Education, "The Identity of the Catholic School for a Culture of Dialogue", (Vatican City, 2022).

This document can be found at:

https://www.vatican.va/roman_curia/congbeacuse of the regations/ccatheduc/documents/rc_con_ccatheduc_doc_20220125_istruzione-identita-scuola-cattolica_en.html

Index

K. W. Wildes, S.J., *Organizational Ethics and Moral Integrity in Secular Societies*, Philosophical Studies in Contemporary Culture 29,
https://doi.org/10.1007/978-3-031-39097-5

V

Printed in the USA
CPSIA information can be obtained
at www.ICGtesting.com
LVHW080829230224
772447LV00019B/82